KITCHEN CREAMERY

Kitchen CREAMERY

making
YOGURT, BUTTER & CHEESE
at home

Louella Hill
THE MILK MAID

PHOTOGRAPHS BY ERIN KUNKEL

CHRONICLE BOOKS
SAN FRANCISCO

Library of Congress Cataloging-in-Publication Data :
Hill, Louella.
  Kitchen creamery : making yogurt, butter, and cheese at home
  / by Louella Hill ; photographs by Erin Kunkel ; illustrations by
  Louella Hill.
    pages cm
  Includes bibliographical references and index.
  ISBN 978-1-4521-1162-9 (hardback)
  1. Cheesemaking. 2. Yogurt. 3. Butter. I. Title.
  SF271.H49 2014
  637'.3—dc23

                                         2014005140

Manufactured in China

Designed by Alice Chau
Photography by Erin Kunkel
Prop & food styling by Christine Wolheim

10 9 8 7 6 5 4 3 2 1

Chronicle Books LLC
680 Second Street
San Francisco, California 94107
www.chroniclebooks.com

To Alan, who eats the experiments.

CONTENTS

INTRODUCTION

A MEASURE OF TIME

I am lucky I don't have a rat problem. I think this every time I step into my garage and breathe in the barn-like scent that lingers there. It emanates from all the cheese projects stashed within. More than three dozen wheels sit inside my "caves" (what I like to call my converted refrigerators), ripening into flavors that maybe I—or anyone in the whole world, for that matter—have never tasted before. This transformation of milk to fragrant wheel takes place within the comfort of my own home, which sits at the end of a quiet alley in San Francisco.

Although many people assume so, I am not actually a farm girl; I just play the part well. I run a business called The Milk Maid, where I teach a range of cheese-making classes. I have also worked at enough dairies to speak knowledgeably about anything from cow breeds to ripening cultures. But the truth is, I come from the Sonoran Desert in Arizona—a place where even the cactuses look parched and not much cheese is made.

My connection to both farming and cheesemaking began when I was taking a break from college to explore "where food comes from." I was working at an *agriturismo* in Tuscany (which I'd found by word of mouth) when the neighboring farm—serendipi-tously a sheep dairy—needed an extra set of hands. The moment I walked into that milking parlor and saw the muddy backsides of those Sarda sheep, I knew it was destiny.

While me "turning farmer" may have been a tad surprising to my family, the fact that I work with my hands every day is not. I come from a family of art-ists, and I learned early on that the fun of creating is in the process. My father is an artist blacksmith, and my grandfather is a watercolor artist. My grandmother was a professional welder (not the most common job for a female in the 1960s), and *her* mother—my great-grandmother, and

namesake—was a fashion designer in the 1940s. She, like me, was a mother who needed to make a living but also felt driven to do so creatively.

To add to this genetic predisposition toward making things, I was also exposed to a multitude of environ-mental cues. I grew up not only among forges and trip hammers, but surrounded, thanks to my artist mother, by more yarn, knitting machines, fabric, patterns, and craft books than you'd find in most full-blown crafts stores. I'm not sure it would even be possible for me to have an empty garage or a blank tabletop. Acquiring tools, dreaming big, sketching ideas, making messes, and reconfiguring is what I've been doing all along. I'm so inspired by my relatives and friends who make quilts, knives, doors, sweaters, pottery, and more. They know.

I like to make the things I need instead of buying them—sometimes to a fault. My husband, Alan, will happily regale you with the story of the time I starting making toothpaste for our household. I had the bright idea to use pulverized school chalk for the calcium carbonate, and the even better idea of grinding up whole cloves to make it taste and smell good. One ridiculous family tooth-brushing later, the mirror showed us with large black chunks between every tooth.

Needless to say, I'm not making toothpaste any-more. I've matured a bit in my do-it-yourself style, letting go of the idea that I have to make *everything*, and instead focusing on making something I love to both make *and* consume.

The other day, while a vat of milk was ripening on the stove, I scattered photos for pasting into an album all over the kitchen table. I grouped them into piles: childhood, college, after college. While sorting, I thought about so many transitions, endings, and beginnings. Then I took all those eras, those layers of influence, and arranged them into one book.

I returned to my warm vat of milk. I cut the curd vertically, then horizontally. I started to stir. The curds were soft and large. I stirred and stirred.

An hour later, my whole hand softened with butterfat and my mind soaked with memories, it dawned on me how the wheel of cheese I'd just made was also an album: a collection of facts, captured clues and information about where the milk came from, how it was transformed into cheese, and finally, how the cheese would move into old age. Inside that wheel would one day be a season of thunderstorms, once-bloomed flowers, a smoky fall, and an ancient basement (or, in my case, a converted fridge tucked into an urban garage). These details combine, concentrate, and finally break down into something both concentrated and complex. Cheese is a time capsule you can taste.

BEFORE YOU BEGIN

If you're opening this book, it's very likely because you're fond of cheese—and probably also because you like to know how things are made. Excellent! These are good characteristics for a home cheesemaker to have. Although there are thousands of beautiful cheeses out there in the world already, there's still plenty of room and reasons for you to make your own.

REASONS TO MAKE CHEESE

To Keep Food Simple

By making your own cheeses and dairy products, you ensure the pureness of your food. No additives, no bleaching, and no stabilizers if you don't want them.

To Support Local Dairies

By making your own cheese, you choose where the milk comes from. This means you can actively support animals who spend time outside on grass. You can be part of preserving a stretch of open space you may drive past each day.

To Participate in the Food System

You've heard the arguments and they're true: Our current food system is oversized, centralized,

mechanized, and deeply infused with chemicals and petroleum. To have a future, we have to enter the kitchen and work the farm. Our hands have to get busy. Our aprons have to get soiled.

To Generate Zero Waste

If you haul milk home in a reusable container, turn the milk into cheese, and toss the whey to your backyard chickens, you'll have a wheel of "zero waste" cheese. No Styrofoam shipping containers. No cardboard boxes. No plastic shrink-wrap. Just landfill-free goodness.

To Save Money

Depending on your milk source and what type of cheese you make, you may find your pocketbook fattening as your cheese cave swells. Cultured dairy products (such as yogurt and kefir), which have 100 percent yield, can be made for less than a quarter of the price of store-bought versions.

To Give Unique Gifts

Who else celebrates their twentieth wedding anniversary with a twenty-month-old wheel of homemade bandage-wrapped cheddar? Who else gives moldy heart-shaped presents to friends on Valentine's Day?

To Discover New Flavors

The unique combination of your stirring arm plus milk from your friend's cow, pulverized chiles from your mom's garden, and blue mold spores generously donated from a recent gust of wind combine to create a flavor like no other. Flavor contributions from yeast and bacteria in the air and soil are what the word *terroir* (in the context of wine- and cheesemaking) is defined by. Home cheesemaking is a perfect way to capture these extra-local, extra-unique flavors.

To Make Magic

Last, and perhaps most important, the whole process of working milk from liquid to finished cheese is really, really fun. It's magical to watch living, breathing things—in this case, billions of microbes and the wheel itself—finish their journey as, say, a scrumptious, oozing tuna melt.

A LEAP OF FAITH

When I survey my students, most don't know anyone who's ever made cheese, nor have they ever milked a cow, or even been to a dairy farm. They didn't grow up with someone making quark in the kitchen or smoking mozzarella over a wood stove. For these reasons, visualizing where milk comes from and how it gets transformed into a glowing globe of provolone can be difficult, and maybe daunting. Add to this the handsome price tag many artisan cheeses carry, and you can understand why undertaking cheesemaking on one's own can seem out of reach.

But quiet any voices in your head saying cheesemaking is impossible, and remember everything seems complex from afar. This wonderful, once very common craft can, before long, be pleasantly woven into your weekend afternoons. It may soon be as old hat as kneading dough for a loaf of bread or coaxing eggs whites into a meringue.

You really *can* make cheese. You can grab a bottle of milk from the store and, in a single day, turn it into jars of beautiful fresh yogurt. Or buy a couple of bottles and make a brick of salty feta. Or, take a couple of weeks and land yourself a velvety, truffle-specked Brie. Although fine handmade cheesemaking may have, in recent history, seemed a craft of the past, it is now a revitalized art and, in many places, a roaring trend. And not just for milk-rich farm wives—for everyone. Even people in tiny city apartments. I created this book as a tool for turning your kitchen—whatever size it might be—into a thriving creamery.

Perhaps one way to demystify cheesemaking is to define it in the simplest way possible: Removing water from milk. Getting the water out means isolating the milk solids (protein, fat, sugar, vitamins, and minerals) to make a denser, safer food—a food that can be aged or easily transported. Imagine our ancestors: Seminomadic people hanging out under the noonday sun, trying to decide between hauling a sloppy pouch of milk or a nimble nugget of curd. Naturally they chose the latter.

Of course, the proposition is more than simply dehydrating milk. Making cheese involves both the science and the art of creating flavors through controlled fermentation. It's about encouraging the flavors you want and avoiding the ones you don't. Cheese *can* happen accidentally—just leave a jug of milk on your counter for a week, then strain the chunks out. But the pleasant, profound flavors you love are more likely to occur when you follow a recipe (or it follows you, as you start to tinker). And actually, your chef duties travel with your cheeses beyond the vat and for a distance—to create the flavors you want, you'll be shepherding your cheeses over the course of weeks, months, even years.

Now that you've made the leap and are willing to give cheesemaking a try, I hope this book will set you on the road to success. Like anything, successful cheesemaking is a matter of being prepared, keeping organized, and being patient—in this case, with both the cheeses and yourself. Following are some guiding principles I embrace in my own kitchen creamery.

START SIMPLY

As with any new technique you attempt in the kitchen (or workshop or studio), your best bet for learning and getting satisfying results without getting overwhelmed or frustrated is to start with some simple recipes that allow you to practice the basics. I organized *Kitchen Creamery* to match what I think is an easy and effective way to wade into cheesemaking. Adding a splash of buttermilk to heavy cream and allowing it to ferment into crème fraîche, or watching milk turn into yogurt is a perfect introduction to the role of cultures. Next, some easy or basic cheese recipes familiarize you with using rennet, cutting the curd, and draining off whey. You'll find the touch for using a thermometer while heating milk and cooking curds, and have the opportunity to test its accuracy. I also grouped the easy or beginning recipes together because they are forgiving, and because none of them need any special ingredients (such as lipase, annato or *Penicillum candidum* mold spores) or expensive equipment—for example, you don't have to invest in a cheese press until you know you are interested in making pressed, aged cheeses (and even then, you might find that a car jack or a stack of gym weights will do). Starting simply, you can add to your skills and expertise at a pace that is comfortable to you, moving through the pages of this book and your own explorations.

TAKE GOOD NOTES

Right from the start, with your beginner cheeses and absolutely as you begin making more complicated varieties, establish the habit of taking good notes. To emphasize: Write down *everything* you do as you make a cheese. To assist you, there's a standardized "make sheet" for you on page 232. Try to *over-record* instead of finding yourself with gaps in your narrative, missing details, or minimal scratchings you can't decode. Seemingly benign facts, such as which supermarket you bought the milk from or what the weather was like on the day you made the cheese, could be that tiny secret you don't want to forget when trying to re-create a success. Unlike other kitchen crafts that come to completion in just a couple of hours or a day, a cheese project can extend over many months, leaving you plenty of time to forget all the details that happened at the vat. A slight difference early on may manifest as a major characteristic months later. While you can't control many aspects of the cheesemaking process or environment (I'm assuming you don't have a home laboratory or a positive-pressure air system in your kitchen), you can do your best with what you have. Taking good notes is a must.

SECURE YOUR LABEL

Without labels, careful notes become meaningless. It is a deep, sad wail that comes from the body of a cheesemaker when she cracks into a wheel, finds it to be outstanding—and then realizes the cheese is anonymous. It has happened to me more than once. Like unlabeled baggies in the freezer, the cheesemaker may feel confident of a cheese's identity on Day One. But as time rolls forward, there's the shifting and turning of wheels, the addition of new ones, the deterioration of surfaces by fervent mites, the accidental bumping of bins, and the inexplicable vanishing of cheese labels, any of which may lead to unexpected anonymity. If this happens, a perfect cheese and impeccable notes will never be reunited.

If your notes are good and your labeling is even better, you're on track to make and possibly, hopefully, repeat a winning flavor discovery.

TRUST IN TIME

As the months pass, your cheese confidence will grow and your copy of *Kitchen Creamery* will, hopefully, become dog-eared. You'll have mastered yogurt, kefir, *queso fresco*, and more. You'll be on the road to finding the styles of cheese you are most intrigued by—your cheesemaking niche. After a long day of cheesemaking, when you have rinsed the last suds from the stockpot and the whey leaving a pressing cheese trickles in the background, you'll sit down, tired, satisfied, and ready to wait.

When you reach this point—the point when you are ready to shepherd cheeses onward to old age—listen to a lesson I've learned: Don't judge a cheese too early in the game. You have no idea what a cheese will taste like until it's in your mouth, and hopefully, it doesn't land in your mouth too soon. I offer tips later for figuring out when to open a wheel, but know it isn't a perfect science. Also know that given enough time, a cheese may mature into something very palatable, even if it wasn't so good earlier on. Sticking to fewer recipes will help you discover the perfect timetable for opening cheeses when they are ripe.

As a beginning cheesemaker, you let problems play out; that way you won't accidentally throw out something that might have been okay. Trusting in time means letting a cheese age long enough *and* it means keeping at the craft. Keep rubbing those rinds, gathering that milk, taking those notes, and repeating it all again. However, trusting in time doesn't mean every cheese you make will become incredible if you age it long enough. Some cheeses *are* destined for the compost pile. Giving bad eggs more time will make those eggs worse.

Don't judge a cheese by its cover, either. What looks like a hairy beast may be nothing more than a poorly dressed beauty. And that smooth-rinded Asiago gem you have in the back of the fridge? Heads up! It might be harder than a rock.

My hope is that your cheeses will end up close enough to what you intended to make to leave you feeling satisfied. It isn't likely you'll casually create a perfect imitation of Cowgirl Creamery's Mt. Tam or Upland's Pleasant Ridge Reserve. But with practice and patience, it is possible to craft an incredible, unique, melt-in-your mouth transformation of something that was, just months earlier, a ray of sunshine.

Enjoy this journey.

HOW TO USE THIS BOOK

In arranging the recipes of this book, I tried to start with simpler recipes before moving onto the more complex ones. The recipes in chapters one and two not only introduce you to core cheesemaking concepts (how to drain the curds or how to press a cheese), but they also are more forgiving in nature. These earlier recipes make cheeses that are eaten fresh or aged for just a short while. Because of this, some imprecision or imperfection—you heat the milk to 91°F/32°C and not 94°F/34°C when making Pot Cheese (page 88)—is fine.

The later recipes, those in chapters three through eight, are a sampling of the slightly (not breath-takingly) more complicated cheeses you can make in a kitchen creamery. These are recipes that will call for more unique ingredients or equipment or that will need to be aged for several months before they really become what they should be—there's no overnight Asiago like there is overnight yogurt.

But aside from this general grouping—simpler recipes at the beginning and more complex afterward—your journey through this book will be personal. You may find that a cheese that takes a short amount of time to make has one detail that's tricky; on the other hand, a fancy-sounding cheese with an intense rind that ages for 6 months might come together nearly without any effort. What feels easy or difficult will depend on you, your background—for example, people who make pie crusts, bread dough, or pasta

will probably have an easy time stretching mozzarella—and the specifics of your environment. One person may find cheddars to be a cinch because he or she has a good set up for pressing firm cheeses. Someone else, without a press and trying to use a stack of heavy books, may find cheddars disastrous.

Note that rather than attempting to be a conclusive text, *Kitchen Creamery* seeks to be your introduction to cheesemaking, your gateway to a marvelous craft. I've really chosen only a handful of recipes (from the hundreds of possibilities that exist) to showcase the most essential cheesemaking processes and the joys that lie therein. Many of these recipes I've personalized with a name I've made up (partly because I want to show you that home cheesemaking is about making something unique and partly because many of my recipes that started as more traditional cheeses evolved into cheeses of their own).

A NOTE ON SUBTLE DIFFERENCES

In the chapters ahead, I will guide you through various cheesemaking styles; but the truth is, all cheese styles are closely related. The difference between making a recipe for cottage cheese and one for Asiago isn't profound. Some recipes might seem like near copies of one another. You may feel as you work through the recipes that you're hearing a broken record: "Pour the milk into a heavy-bottomed stockpot and warm over medium heat to 86°F/30°C, stirring . . ."

But no two recipes in this book are identical. They are each unique, with subtle differences in things like cultures, vat temperature, and aging temperature. In many of the recipe introductions, I try to explain what exactly I feel sets the recipe apart. Thinking about the differences between recipes will increase your understanding of the cheesemaking process in general.

If you can keep at the cheese craft, subtle variance between recipes will gradually become more significant to you. When one recipe says to heat the curds to 105°F/41°C and another says to heat to 98°F/37°C, you'll soon recognize easily that that difference is A BIG DEAL!

HOW TO USE THE SIDE TABS

To gather, in a glance, details like how much time and cheesemaking know-how each recipe requires, which forms you'll need, and what types of milk will work, use the easy-to-read tabs on the edge of each recipe page. Following is the key for what each tab category means.

DIFFICULTY
MILK
SUGGESTED CULTURES
FINAL FORM
CATEGORIES
TIME TO COMPLETION

Difficulty

Each recipe is rated for level of difficulty. As you'd guess, Easy means just that—these are great cheeses to start with. Medium—this is something you can try next, or start with if you feel confident. Advanced indicates a more challenging cheese—I recommend you try these after you've run through some of the Easy and Medium recipes.

Milk

Because milk is a complicated topic, check the side tab of the recipe for which milk(s) you need or works best. Using the tab, you won't end up with a hopeless pot of unset milk by purchasing a homogenized milk for a cheese that requires unhomogenized, for example. When the tab says "All types," it means any milk, whole to skim, pasteurized or raw, homogenized or cream-line will be fine.

Suggested Cultures

Figuring out what cultures to use in a recipe can be tricky: Different culture manufacturers use different nomenclature for the same bacterial strains, then retailers repackage and retitle these cultures yet again. Plus cultures are not cheese specific—cultures you use to make a chèvre can also be used to make a cheddar. Hoping to make things slightly simpler, I've given you one specific Danisco-brand culture (or list of cultures) to start with. With time, you can do more tinkering.

Final Form

This line tells you what form the finished cheese takes; a glance will cue for you whether the cheese is a loose variety that is packed into a tub or jar, a stretched curd that is twisted into a shape, or a wheel-style cheese that emerges from a cheese form. The yield line of the recipes contains the specifics of quantity. In some cases, which form or forms you use is ultimately a personal choice. You can make three mini Havarti cheeses when the recipe tab says "large wheel," for example. Note that when making cooked, pressed cheeses, it's always easier to make one large wheel that you can press well than many small wheels that you can't press well, though this will depend on your specific equipment.

JAR OR TUB. Refers to a standard canning jar with a tight-fitting lid (either regular screw top or canning ring and lid) or plastic container; each recipe specifies the size, such as 1 qt/1 L or 1 pt/480 ml.

SMALL WHEEL. About 8 oz/225 g cheese. The cheese form should be *roughly* 3 in/7.5 cm in diameter and at least 3 in/7.5 cm in height. The form can be taller and/or slightly tapered. It can be square, round, even heart-shaped. With a 2-gal/7.5-L batch of milk, you'll produce three to four small wheels. Cheeses made in this size wheel can include anything soft-ripened, fresh, or unpressed.

MEDIUM WHEEL. About 24 oz/680 g cheese. The cheese form should be *roughly* 5 in/12 cm in diameter and roughly 5 in/12 cm in height. The form can be cylindrical, slightly tapered, open-bottomed, or any shape. With a 2-gal/7.5-L batch of milk, you'll typically produce one medium wheel of firm-pressed cheese, and more than that if making a softer cheese. Cheeses made in this size include anything from ricotta to soft-ripened cheeses such as Camembert to medium-pressed cheeses such as Havarti. If pressing a cheese, you will need a follower that fits your form.

LARGE WHEEL. About 3 lb/1.3 kg cheese. The form should be *roughly* 8 in/20 cm in diameter by 6 in/ 15 cm in height. This form, with a follower, is the most important one to have if you plan to make larger pressed and aged cheeses—small and medium unpressed or lightly pressed cheeses are more forgiving in terms of the forms that will work. To fill a large wheel form, make the recipes that use 4 gal/15 L milk. My favorite large-wheel, pressable cheese form is called a Kadova (see page 224), and it comes with a follower and an easily removable mesh liner that you use in place of cheesecloth.

FREE-FORM OR LOGS. Cheese of any quantity can be made without a true cheese form, using only cheesecloth (see page 220). When you see these terms as the Final Form side tab, it may mean cheese that drains first in a colander and is then hand-shaped (as with a mozzarella braid or a log of chèvre, for instance). Other times, with cooked and pressed cheeses, free-form refers to the method of twisting cheesecloth to form a tight pouch, then setting weights on top, forming a slightly wrinkled, asymmetrical wheel (see Baby Jack on page 152).

QUART JAR
(1 L)

COLANDER
(1.5 LB/680 G)

HAND FORMED
LOGS
(5 OZ/140G)

PYRAMIDS, HEARTS,
ROUNDS
(8 OZ/225 G)

BRAIDS, KNOTS,
BALLS
(10 OZ/280 G)

LARGER
WHEEL
(3–4LB/1.3–1.8 KG)

Categories

To give you a broader perspective on the recipe you're making, I've included categories associated with the cheese type on some of the recipes. Since how a cheese is defined depends very much on who's defining it, I've written down the main categories that apply, even if they are somewhat redundant.

Time to Completion

Some cheeses will be ready to eat in less than an hour. Others will take months. Use this estimated time frame to gauge which recipe you want to make. Note that I've listed units of time in terms of hours, days, weeks, and months.

HOW TO USE THE APPENDICES

To reduce repetition from recipe to recipe, I've gathered explanations for specific processes in the Appendices at the back of the book. In some cases (for example "Forms and Presses," page 224), I use the Appendix less to tell you how to do something and more to spell out your options for what to buy or build. Here's a preview of some things to look for in the back of the book:

Cheesemaking Processes: Get the step by step on how to cut according to flocculation point, how to flip a very soft cheese, how to apply cheese ash, and much more.

Forms and Presses: Stop here for more info on cheese forms, boards, and presses.

Cultures: When you want your head to spin, check out this section. I go over the differences between mesophillic and thermophillic, primary and secondary, mixes, and more.

Butterfat Chart: Just so you know the technical difference between half-and-half, light cream, and heavy cream, I've included a butterfat chart showing percentages.

Sanitation: Learn several simple ways to keep your cheesemaking environment in shipshape.

Sample Make Sheet for Home Cheesemaking: You can use the included make sheet or make your own but whatever you do, take good notes of your cheesemaking process.

THE REAL YIELD

Fresh cheeses, because they have more water, yield between 12 and 20 percent for cow's milk. Aged cheeses, because they have less water, yield as little as 7 percent. That means, if you have 1 gal/3.8 L milk and you make the hardest, most-aged cheese you can, you'll come up with a mere 8 oz/225 g cheese. That's roughly the size of a lemon. I get an occasional chuckle in my classes, because I know some of my students see my "enormous" vat of milk (about 6 gal/23 L) and think we are going to end up with that same volume of cheese. Not true. We get just

a fraction of that amount. Plan to make the largest batch of cheese possible when making aged varieties cheese (which is to say: go buy a large stockpot). Fresher cheeses are easily made in smaller batches.

MILK	APPROXIMATE Yield (%) CHEESE		
	FRESH	SOFT	HARD
goat	23	13	11
cow	21	13	11
sheep	45	27	19

SCALING UP, SCALING DOWN

Students often ask if they can halve cheesemaking recipes, no doubt nervous about squandering a lot of milk while practicing. The simple answer is yes—but I don't advise it for the scales used in this book. Most of the beginning recipes are based on 1- or 2-gal/3.8- or 7.5-L batches. If you cut these down too many times, you'll end up with only a thimbleful of cheese. Many of the recipes in the later chapters are based on 4-gal/15-L batches; for these, I recommend sticking to the original quantities so the finished wheels are large enough to age. In the case of the stretched-curd cheeses (2-gal/7.5-L batches), again, I recommend making the whole amount. Several hours of effort and a dime-size mozzarella ball is going to make you cry.

As for scaling up, all the power to you! Your limiting factor will likely be your vat. Though you might be tempted to make one large recipe in several pots—in hopes of having an Asiago wheel the size of a manhole cover, don't. Curds from each pot will have slightly different levels of acidity which will lead to trouble. And remember to stay within your comfort level (slinging more than one vat in your home kitchen could be hot and tiring and frustrating).

Note that for cheese recipes using cultures and rennet, the quantities should adjust proportionally, whether you are enlarging or reducing the size of a recipe—although really the quantities listed are gross measurements, possibly rounded up or down for an easy measurement that fits the yield. To determine a perfectly accurate culture amount for any batch size, see "Correct Culture Dosages" on page 228. For these perfect measurements, you will need a gram scale.

HOLDING THE HEAT

In nearly every recipe, you'll be asked to maintain the vat within a specific temperature range. If it's summertime and your kitchen is sweltering, this shouldn't be a problem. But if the surroundings are anything cooler, you may need to take action. Here are several ways to hold the heat:

- Always cover the pot when ripening or renneting the milk.
- Nest your main pot inside a larger one filled with water to form a water jacket.
- Drape a towel or sweater over the pot.
- Place the pot in a box set over a heating pad.

Remember that turning on the heat when the rennet is setting the milk is not an option. The milk is no longer fluid and will scorch near the heat source.

THINGS I JUST HAVE TO TELL YOU

- If it looks funny, cut the funny part off.
- If it doesn't smell right, give it more air and lower the aging temperature.
- Don't get hung up on making every cheese in this book. Stick to a few and make them your own.
- Find open-minded friends who are willing to taste anything.
- Host cheese parties often.
- Always send house guests home with experiments.
- Sooner than later, buy a second fridge or wine cooler.
- Don't be afraid to throw cheese away. Or feed it to the chickens.
- Keep crackers and jam on hand. You never know when the wheel is going to crack.

The BASICS

As you set up your creamery, you'll want to figure out what kind of cheeses you want to make first, the initial equipment to buy, and the type (or types) of milk to source. To help you with these decisions, I've sorted out the basic cheese styles, cheesemaking steps, milk types, and ingredients and equipment in the following section. Though this is a lot of information, don't be intimidated. Cheesemaking is incredibly *doable*, and you really don't need much to get going.

THE BASIC STEPS FOR MAKING MOST CHEESES

For the first few steps, the process of cheesemaking is identical for most cheeses—especially those made using cultures and rennet versus direct acid. That means, at the vat, 30 minutes into a recipe, it still is yet to be determined if the cheese is going to be a cheddar, a Brie, or a Stilton. Nearly all cheeses are identical, *initially*. Every cheese starts with the same first step of heating the milk—I like to think of it like the trunk of a tree. Each unique step that the cheesemaker makes thereafter is akin to a branch leading to unique end results.

Every cheese starts with heating the milk (unless you happen to be in close proximity to the milking parlor and catch the milk moments after it leaves the animal). Then, when the milk is lukewarm, cultures are added (except with direct-acid cheeses). These cultures are bacteria, which ferment, or break down, components of the milk. As they do, they create lactic acid, a component in the linking together of the milk proteins. Next, if (as we commonly are) working with pasteurized milk, we add calcium chloride ($CaCl_2$), and then rennet (the coagulant), an enzyme that causes milk proteins to link together and form a gel. The gel gets cut into pieces and cooked and stirred for a prescribed amount of

time. (With some cheeses, you don't even cut and stir, but simply scoop the gel directly into forms.) Finally, allow the cheese to drain, then press, salt, and age. Easy peasy cheesy!

At the vat, the cheesemaker defines the direction of the cheese through type of milk, type of cultures (if using cultures at all), stirring time, and temperature—but really what the cheesemaker is doing is controlling acid production and water retention in the curd. Initially, you will use time and temperature guidelines to reach ballpark goals for acid or moisture. Down the road, when you are ready, you can start reaching these benchmarks more precisely using a pH meter to read the acidity (see page 33). Don't worry about that yet, though. Now your task is to start putting mileage on your vat.

POUR WARM CULTURE

Basic STEPS of CHEESE Making

RIPEN RENNET

CHECK CUT HEAL

STIR HEAT WASH

DRAIN PRESS SALT

Browsing any cheese counter will remind you there are a near infinite number of cheeses in the world. This fact leads to the most common question I'm ever asked: "Why are cheeses different from one another?" Here's a short list of some of the reasons why.

WHAT MAKES A CHEESE DISTINCT

On the Farm

- Type of animal milk
- Breed of animal
- Phase in lactation cycle
- Diet and health of the animal
- Time of year
- Microbial ecosystem on the farm

At the Creamery

- Amount of protein and fat in the starting milk
- Type of cultures and rennet used
- Use of additives (flavorings, colorants, growth inhibitors)
- Acidity levels throughout the cheesemaking process
- Degree of cooking and heating of curds
- Length and strength of pressing
- Shape and design of cheese form
- Amount of salt

In the Cave

- Sealed (wax, vacuum bag) or breathing rind
- Temperature and humidity of cave environment
- Presence of ambient microorganisms or neighboring cheeses
- Length of time in cave
- Frequency and nature of care
- Wrapping and handling of finished cheese

As you can see, there are many, many variables that are going to affect your finished cheese. This is another reason I lobby that for a long time you stick to fewer recipes and make them repeatedly. Inevitable and subtle changes from one batch to the next will naturally lead to a diverse lineup of flavors, even if the recipe stays the same.

ABOUT MILK

Although it resonates in some contexts as the original energy drink and in others as the very definition of bland, milk is extremely complex. And its role in cheesemaking makes it more so by the multitude of factors affecting the milk on its path from teat to table.

This complexity explains why a huge factor in how your cheese turns out lies within the milk you use. Even today, scientists are still trying to perfectly understand the intricate chemistry of this first food. But we do know some things, such as milk's components; the differences in milk from different animals; and how health, stage in lactation, and environment play a role in the quantity and the quality of the milk an animal gives.

COMPONENTS of Milk

VITAMINS & MINERALS (<1%)

PROTEIN (3%)

FAT (4%)

LACTOSE (5%)

WATER (87%)

*PERCENTAGES ARE APPROXIMATE, BASED ON HOLSTEIN COW MILK

TYPE OF ANIMAL

The type of animal you collect or select milk from for cheesemaking is a huge factor in determining what cheese you'll end up with. In the United States, the "alpha" milker is, hands down, the cow. This is the same for most of Europe. (In parts of the Middle East, the Mediterranean, India, and Northern Africa, goats and sheep take the lead.) Aside from cows, goats, and sheep, other animals' milks are used for cheese and cultured dairy. In Northern Africa, the Bedouin people turn camel's milk into yogurt. Grass-fed yaks in the mountains of Nepal produce rich milk for cheesemaking. Entrepreneurs in Serbia craft cheeses from Balkan donkey's milk (called *pule*), and cheesemakers in Sweden are successfully extracting enough milk from moose to make small amounts of moose cheese.

Of course, the breed of animal is in turn equally as important as the species. For example, the floppy-eared Anglo-Nubian goat produces milk with higher butterfat than other goat breeds; the Boer goat, on the other hand, is chosen less for her milk and more for her hardiness. There are upward of seventy different goat breeds in existence and many dozens of dairy cow breeds. Nonetheless, as beginning cheesemakers, just like milk drinkers shopping for the home fridge, while you may be able to choose between animals—you can often find goat's milk in supermarkets and almost surely in natural-foods stores—you usually won't be able to choose between breeds. Unless you deliberately choose otherwise at the market or your local farm

(or raise milk-givers yourself), you'll likely be working with Holstein cow's milk.

ENVIRONMENT AND ANIMAL HEALTH

In addition to species and breed, environmental factors affect the milk and ultimately the cheese. If we took two sister Jersey cows and placed one in a field of Timothy grass in Vermont and set the other amid blue grama grass in Texas, the milk would taste different. Not only would the cows be surrounded by different soils, different plant species, and different microbes, the interaction of all of these elements would create a unique effect on the milk and the animal. Other factors such as the presence of other animals, the layout of the fields, and the animal's shelter, as well as weather conditions, create layers of effects.

There is also the animal's health and emotional state to consider. Each animal within a herd is unique, therefore producing different amounts and qualities of milk. The milk from an animal that calved three weeks earlier is different from the milk of an animal that gave birth five months ago. A healthy animal, as you would guess, produces better milk than a less-healthy one; for example, if a cow has mastitis—an infection of the udder—that will affect the way the milk turns to curd at the creamery. By a similar logic, if the herd from which you are gathering milk is small—for example, just six animals—the individuality of each cow's constitution will be far more pronounced than if the milk comes from a herd of several thousand.

STORE-BOUGHT VS. FARM FRESH

If buying milk from the supermarket, you won't need to worry about (or that is, get to embrace) most of the milk variations touched on previously. Store-bought milk, especially from major brands, comes from multiple and larger-scale dairies. Milk is comingled so much that a single carton, in theory, may contain drops of milk from thousands of different animals. While milk from larger-scale operations has the disadvantage of being more anonymous, it also will be standardized. You will know what you are working with, and this will help you create consistent cheeses.

Pasteurization. French chemist Louis Pasteur developed a process of heat-treating wine and beer to prevent it from souring, and called it, of course, pasteurization. (It was actually his graduate student, Franz Von Soxhlet, who applied the idea to milk; maybe "soxhletting" didn't roll off the tongue as easily as "pasteurization.")

CaCl₂: JUST A DROP

You will see this ingredient in many recipes in this book. It is the elemental name for calcium chloride, and we use it in cheesemaking with store-bought milk because when proteins are denatured through pasteurization they no longer form a gel as readily when you add rennet. To correct for this, add $CaCl_2$ to the milk anytime you use pasteurized milk. (See page 26 and the chart on page 23 for more on calcium chloride, and Cheesemaking Supply Companies on page 234 for where to buy it.)

Thermization. Thermization is the coolest method of heat treatment, common in Europe. The milk is heated to 145° to 150°F/63° to 65°C. The exact temperature and time vary, but do not meet the legal requirement for pasteurization. Thermized milk cheeses in the United States must be labeled as "raw" even though they are not considered raw in Europe.

Low-Temperature, Long Time (TLT). Also known as "batch pasteurization," this treatment is often used by home-scale and small-scale cheesemakers. Milk is heated to a specific temperature and held for an exact amount of time (specific to the temperature). An example: 145°F/63°C for 30 minutes. This method is accomplished vat by vat (as opposed to continuously, as we see in HTST method, following).

High-Temperature, Short-Time (HTST). Also called "continuous method," in HTST, the milk is heated to 161°F/72°C for 15 seconds. This is the most common method for medium- to large-scale cheesemaking because large amounts of milk can be processed very quickly.

Ultra-High Temperature (UTHT). The milk treated by the UTHT method is often labeled as "ultra-pasteurized." The milk is heated to 275°F/135°C for a minimum of 1 second. Milk treated by UTHT is not suitable for most cheesemaking (see chart, facing page).

Extended Shelf Life. This is the same basic process as UTHT, but the milk is heated to higher temperatures or with an additional filtration step to reduce bacteria counts. Heat treatment may also be at a higher temperature than 275°F/135°C. This is the treatment used to make those boxes of unrefrigerated milk found in many parts of Europe. Milk treated for extended shelf life is not suitable for most cheesemaking.

RAW MILK

The term "raw milk" invites extreme emotion wherever I turn—either someone is adamantly against it or zealously in favor. As a cheesemaker, I walk the middle road. I think both raw and pasteurized milk have merits in the make room and in affecting the final product.

Today, nearly any milk you reach for in a supermarket will be pasteurized. Some states allow for the sale of raw milk while others do not. In the end, I feel that, beyond what temperature the milk has been heated to (though that is meaningful), the more important questions are, "Does the milk come from healthy, well-managed animals?" and "Is this the very freshest milk I can possibly source?" If you answer yes to both, you are on the right road.

MILKING IT

I framed the recipes in this book, with a few noted exceptions, around pasteurized, store-bought cow's milk. I assume most readers will have easy access to this ingredient, whereas fewer will have access to goat's, sheep's, or even raw cow's milk. If using raw milk, complete the recipes as directed with two caveats: 1) leave out the $CaCl_2$ (if applicable) and 2) reduce the amount of cultures added (again, if applicable) by half.

HOMOGENIZATION

Almost all store-bought milk today is homogenized, a qualification that is not even necessary to label because it is so ubiquitous. Homogenization is the process of breaking down milk fat globules into smaller particles, so they stay in suspension throughout the milk instead of collecting at the top as cream. Often milk is filtered at the same time as it is homogenized, allowing producers to remove the fat and then add it back in at a specific percentage (1 percent, 2 percent, etc.).

There are benefits to homogenization: It allows the producer to sell a uniform product; it slows the breakdown of the milk because it prevents fat from rising to the surface, where it is exposed to air; and it mixes the fat evenly throughout the milk, distributing full flavor and avoiding the plug of cream at the top of the bottle or carton that flummoxes some people.

For the home cheesemaker, homogenization has both benefits and drawbacks. Generally, smaller fat particles interrupt the formation of a gel (the curd we need to make cheese), which means a weaker gel, which means a lower yield. On the plus side of homogenization, some cheese styles, including lactic-set cheeses and some styles of blue, benefit from smaller fat particles. The smaller particles allow the fat to break down quickly, leading to more flavor sooner—a great thing for a commercial enterprise. While all types of milk can work for many of the recipes in this book, for simplicity, I recommend mainly sticking to unhomogenized (also called *cream line*) milk unless noted otherwise on the side tab.

GOLDEN RULES FOR USING STORE-BOUGHT MILK

When selecting milk for cheesemaking, here are good rules of thumb:

- For rennet-set cheeses, *never* use ultra-pasteurized milk.
- If using pasteurized milk, add $CaCl_2$ before you add the rennet, and in roughly the same proportion.
- For yogurt, buttermilk, kefir, chèvre, *fromage blanc*, and cream cheese, homogenized milk is okay.

Which Milk for Which Cheese

MILK CATEGORIES BASED ON HEAT TREATMENT		
HEAT TREATMENT	USED IN CHEESEMAKING	NOTES
Raw Milk (none)	For any recipe.	You cannot legally sell nonaged raw-milk cheeses in the United States.
Pasteurized Milk	For any recipe; before renneting, add $CaCl_2$.	Pasteurized-milk cheeses require longer aging than raw-milk versions to achieve the same amount of flavor.
Ultra-Pasteurized Milk	Only okay when making yogurt, buttermilk, kefir, ricotta, or paneer.	In the same way that you heat milk to make yogurt, the heat treatment of UTHT works in your favor to create a thicker body in yogurt and lactic-set cheeses.

MILK CATEGORIES BASED ON BUTTERFAT PROCESSING		
BUTTERFAT PROCESSING	USED IN CHEESEMAKING	NOTES
Homogenized Milk	For direct-acid and lactic acid–set cheeses and all cultured dairy (yogurt, buttermilk, kefir, chèvre, *fromage blanc*, cream cheese, paneer, ricotta, mascarpone) and some blue cheese styles (Stilton, Bisbee Blue, Blue Capricorn).	Homogenized milk is also always pasteurized.
Unhomogenized Milk	For any recipe.	A "cream line" may form at the top of the vat on slower setting (i.e., lactic acid–set) cheeses. Enjoy—it's like accidental crème fraîche.

cream wax

cheese wax

Large stock pot

drying rack

aging mat

salt

CaCl₂

rennet

cultures

cake spatula or long knife

skimmer

cheese paper

ash

colorants and seasonings

pH meter or strips

citric acid

salometer

oil or fat

annatto seeds

BEYOND MILK

We have covered the most important ingredient you'll need: milk. Now let's look at everything and anything else that might go into your vat.

CULTURES

You can make cheese without adding cultures—letting whatever is naturally present in the milk play out—but I don't recommend it. Cultures, the term for microorganisms used to ferment the milk and develop flavors, are abundant all around us—in the air, on our skin, on the countertop. While some of these are the ones you want in the vat, trusting that *only* those will get in is risky to hopeless. Think about that skunky milk in the back of your fridge. It was cultured naturally and, though it likely is safe to consume, it probably doesn't taste very good. The same goes for cheesemaking—you could make cheese without adding cultures but you might not want to eat it. By purchasing selected, laboratory-grown cultures with distinct flavor outcomes, or by adding cultured buttermilk (rich with the "right" cultures), you'll more confidently guide the milk in the direction you want.

Start with Buttermilk

In the beginning, make as many cheeses as you can before purchasing equipment and fancy ingredients; the same goes for cultures. Before you get dizzy staring at the culture websites, dreaming of all the incredible cheeses you will one day make, go to the grocery store and grab a carton of buttermilk—it is alive with plenty of cultures to get you going. Buttermilk will work for any of the recipes in chapters one and two. By chapter three, it'll be time to branch out. Note: When buying buttermilk, choose a container labeled as "cultured" buttermilk. Some versions of buttermilk are made by adding acid—but not cultures—to milk, and you want to make sure not to pick up this version on accident.

Using and Storing Cultures

There are tricks to keeping your cultures as active as possible. You'll likely have to order freeze-dried cultures online (see page 234). When they arrive, immediately open the box and move the foil packets to the freezer. Keep the packets in an airtight container. Once you've opened a packet, make sure to close it tightly after each use. If possible, store the cultures in a freezer that is not self-defrosting—the less moisture these cultures come into contact with (while being stored), the more effective they'll be.

When you are ready to use your cultures, insert a clean, dry knife tip into the foil packet and remove what you need. Do not stand over the warm vat while doing this, because the steam can moisten the insides of the packet, "waking up" the cultures prematurely. Once they get wet, they tend to clump and are difficult to measure. I suggest pre-hydrating these cultures to get them up to speed before adding them to the vat (see page 101).

A MOLD BY ANY OTHER NAME

Although the words "cheese form" and "cheese mold" mean the same thing—something you use for draining your cheese—"cheese mold" can also refer to the fungi used to ripen cheese, such as *Penicillum roqueforti*. For clarity, throughout this book I use the term "form" for the containers and "mold" for the fungi.

RENNET (COAGULANT)

Rennet is a generic term for the ingredient used to coagulate milk. Traditional rennet is a mixture of enzymes that come from a mammalian stomach and include the specific enzyme rennin, also called chymosin. The story of the beginning of cheesemaking dovetails with the discovery of rennet. It is told that seminomadic people used animal stomachs to carry water and milk. Because the stomach contained these coagulating enzymes, people noticed the pleasing change in the milk carried within and started working with it to separate out the solids from the whey intentionally.

Today, because it is an animal product, adding rennet to a food makes it inappropriate to some diets. Luckily, bacterial, fungal, and plant-based coagulants also exist. Traditional cheeses used in Jewish ceremonial dinners (such as during Shabbat) used

Rennet Options

TYPE	SOURCE	BENEFITS	DRAWBACKS
Animal rennet	Stomach lining of veal calf, lamb, or goat kid	Traditional rennet, a by-product of the meat industry, has the potential for the most-authentic flavor profile	Nonvegetarian
Stomach paste	Macerated stomach	Includes other enzymes present in the stomach wall and pregastric glands, creating diverse flavor potential	Strong lipase presence, short shelf life, hard to source
Microbial rennet	Derived from the fungi *Rhizomucor miehie* and/or *Rhizomucor pusillus*	Acceptable for all dietary restrictions	Stronger potential for breaking down proteins and may lead to bitter tastes
Fermentation-produced chymosin ("vegetable rennet," or FPC)	Animal genes are inserted into bacterial host, which produces the enzyme	Highly efficient rennet-producing product with few to no flavor or dietary drawbacks	Genetically modified food additives remain controversial. FPC is used in 60 percent or more of cheeses produced in the United States
Plant extracts	Fig sap, dried capers, nettles, thistles, mallow, and ground ivy	Widespread availability, historical legacy	Less effective coagulation and flavor potential. Harder to source

sap from fig leaves to transform milk into curd, and Portuguese cheesemakers use extracts of thistle plants to make the cheese called *cardo*.

Plant-based coagulants are harder to find and considered less effective than animal rennet in causing the proteins to link up. To cheesemakers, this may mean a softer curd and a potentially lower yield. There are few commercial sources for these plant-based coagulants.

The most widespread non-animal coagulant used in the United States comes from fermentation-produced chymosin (FPC), which is sometimes labeled on the cheese package as "vegetarian" or "vegetable rennet." Arguably a misnomer, fermentation-produced chymosin (which is one of the enzymes found in the animal stomach) is 100 percent pure (meaning there are no other enzymes, such as pepsin or lipase, present). FPC is created by injecting host bacteria with DNA extracted from calf cells. The host bacteria then produce the desired chymosin. This makes the product a bacterial one and also the product of genetic modification, another controversial dietary item.

Finally, there is microbial rennet, a product extracted from the fungi *Rhizomucor miehei*. This mimic of animal rennet performs beautifully, and I've used it

personally for many years. However, because of its newness (relative to the fifteen-thousand-year-old animal rennet), there is still some uncertainty—or maybe it's a lack of familiarity—with this product.

- *Note: Rennet is available in both single and double strengths. All of the rennet amounts listed in* Kitchen Creamery *assume you are using the single-strength variety. If using a double-strength variety, use half of the amount listed.*

CALCIUM CHLORIDE

You will use calcium chloride ($CaCl_2$) whenever you make cheese with store-bought, pasteurized milk—even if it is unhomogenized (see the chart on page 23). $CaCl_2$ is a salt found in limestone. It is helpful to the cheesemaker because during pasteurization, heat damages milk proteins. Adding $CaCl_2$ helps to increase the attraction between proteins to form a stronger gel. In other words, $CaCl_2$ restores the natural calcium balance in the milk. Additionally, $CaCl_2$ is sometimes used to help goat's milk and late-lactation milk form a stronger curd.

$CaCl_2$ has many food applications beyond cheese. It firms up tofu and helps canned fruits and vegetables stay crisp. It is used in sports drinks because it has electrolytic properties. It is even used to de-ice roads. That said, when purchasing a bottle of $CaCl_2$, do so from a cheesemaking supply company to ensure you have an appropriate strength for food consumption. You will add $CaCl_2$ in the same quantity as the rennet and always before the milk is renneted. Store your bottle of $CaCl_2$ in a dark and cool place.

When to Use Calcium Chloride

USE CACL$_2$: For any rennet-set cheese (pot cheese, feta, Bel Paese, all the recipes in chapter five); any lactic acid–set cheese (chèvre, *fromage blanc*) made with pasteurized milk; and cultured mozzarella.

DO NOT USE CACL$_2$: For any cultured dairy product (yogurt, kefir, buttermilk); any direct-acid cheese (ricotta, mascarpone, paneer); quick mozzarella; anytime you are using raw milk.

VARIABLE: When using goat's milk from a small herd, you may or may not need $CaCl_2$, depending on how the milk varies over the lactation season.

LIPASE

When I taste a cheese with a distinctly picante or spicy character, I know the enzyme lipase is at work. I often associate the flavor with cheese styles that originated in Italy, such as Provolone. Lipase, like animal rennet, comes from a mammalian stomach. It breaks down fat molecules into smaller molecules and creates this signature flavor. Plan on using it when you make Provolone (page 176), Asiago (page 183), or optionally for Cultured Mozzarella (page 174).

COLORANTS AND WHITENERS

Ever wondered why some cheeses are such a bright orange? It's most likely due to annatto, a traditional colorant found in foods throughout the world. Think of the pinkish-red chicken tikka masala at your favorite Indian restaurant, or the bright red (though not spicy) mole of Oaxaca. Annatto can even be found as an ingredient in mustards, bottled spice mixes, and many processed foods.

Annatto comes from the achiote tree (*Bixa orellana*), which grows in the subtropics; I saw it once while traveling in southern Mexico. The trees reach about

15 ft/4.5 m in height. In the yard where I saw my first achiote, family members were busy gathering the tree's pompom-like seed clusters and drying them on sheets in the sun. Later, they broke the pompoms open, shook out the seeds, and pounded them into a paste using a mortar and pestle.

Modern-day annatto is chemically extracted and sold in liquid form. When using annatto for some of my cheeses, I add it after I've let the milk ripen but before I add the $CaCl_2$ and rennet. You can try making a homemade annatto paste using achiote seeds, found in most Latin grocery stores, or in many Indian markets under the name *sindoor*. It isn't as easy as buying the premade liquid extract but it might be fun anyway.

In addition to annatto, other coloring and bleaching agents are used in cheeses. Historically, carrots were grated and added to the milk, then strained out prior to adding the rennet. I've eaten a Sage Derby made with green coloring extracted from spinach. And many commercial fresh cheeses—such as *queso fresco* or fresh mozzarella—use titanium dioxide to create a brighter white. It's an area open to experimentation as you delve into cheesemaking—and also to serendipity—I once accidentally colored a cheese using saffron threads. It was a surprise, and quite pretty.

SALT

For cheesemaking, always use salt that does not contain iodine or anticaking agents. The best type to use is a flake or pickling salt. Coarser salts are better than very fine salts. Kosher salt is also generally a good bet, but check the ingredient list. Avoid very coarse rock salts, as the crystals are so large that salt uptake will be slow (with dry salting) or the crystals will be slow to dissolve (if making brine).

Salt may be applied dry to the finished wheel, by brining, or by a mixture of both methods. The salt is almost always applied after pressing and, generally, after draining. Sometimes, as with the Havarti on page 104, a small amount of salt is added to the vat before the curds are drained. This "early salt" often leaves you with a sweeter, milder cheese.

ASH

The signature black line of a Morbier (and of the kindred Marbler and Gosling cheeses on pages 118 and 134) comes from vegetable ash. These are not fireplace ashes, but a refined ash suited for cheesemaking. (It is, in fact, the same as the "activated charcoal" found at nearly any pharmacy.) You only need a small amount (less than ½ tsp for a recipe that uses 2 gal/7.5 L milk), and make sure to apply in a draft-free area. Use gloves, and tape down sheets of newspaper to the table beforehand for easier cleanup. You can also make the ash into a paste with water to brush it on the cheese.

FLAVORINGS

A world of possibility awaits you when you consider adding spices, aromatics, and other flavorful ingredients to your cheese. Maybe it's shaved truffles. Or dried cranberries. Perhaps you love caraway seeds, or have decided on a mix of ground fennel and cumin. The most important thing to remember is to start simply, making sure the recipe works for you before complicating it with spice. After you've run through a non-spiced version (perhaps a few times), try the recipe with any seasoning embellishments calling out to you.

Spices used in cheesemaking should be dried (or freeze-dried), unless you plan to consume the cheese within a couple of days. Items such as chopped fresh basil leaves or grilled peppers have too much water in them and will introduce unwanted yeasts and molds. In addition, many fresh herbs won't look appealing after exposure to a cheese's warmth, oxygen, and salt. If using fresh herbs, mix them into a spreadable cheese immediately before serving for best results.

Before adding flavorings to cheese curds, decide whether they need to be cleaned. If so, clean by simmering in boiling water for 1 to 3 minutes beforehand. A short boil will both rehydrate the ingredient (for example, sun-dried tomatoes) and, more important, help clean away molds and yeasts. Boiling is not appropriate for ground dried spices, but works for seeds and woody spices like peppercorns. Add the flavorings as you are hooping—that is, filling the cheese form(s) with the curds.

Just to share (and spare you) travails from my own cheese journeys, I've found the following flavorings mildly to completely unsuccessful: dried dill (too weak), dried cilantro (too weak), deseeded jalapeño chiles (not hot enough—I should have kept in some of the seeds), sage (too floral), and whole black peppercorns (I added too many to a cheese that was too soft, so when I cut it, the peppercorns tore the cheese). My most successful seasonings have been fenugreek or cumin seeds (a classic addition to Gouda), red pepper flakes (pulverized in the food processor beforehand), dehydrated onion or garlic flakes (excellent), dehydrated shiitake and porcini mushrooms (also chopped beforehand), and chopped sun-dried tomatoes (dry, not oil-packed).

When flavoring cultured dairy products like yogurt, buttermilk, and kefir, add the flavorings and any accompanying sweeteners just before consuming for the freshest flavor. Once I mixed peach jam into a batch of kefir, then bottled it up for the farmers' market. The next morning, before I even got to market, the bottles were swollen. The yeast in the kefir was still active, and I had fed it with the sugar in the jam. Oops!

WATER

Water is often overlooked as an ingredient in the cheesemaking process. Technically it is, oh, let's say a "processing aid," but since you are pouring it into the pot, it is worthwhile to mention. In most recipes using rennet and calcium chloride, you use water to dilute them. You'll also use it to wash curds when making cheeses in that style, such as the Gouda-style Divino (page 106) or Rising Moon (page 111), a version of Jarlsberg. Find water that is free of chlorine (which most municipal water is; you can test it easily with a home kit). If you aren't sure, prepare the water by boiling and cooling it beforehand, or purchase purified or distilled water.

CREAM

In some recipes, you will increase the amount of butterfat by adding cream to the milk. When you add cream to a cultured dairy product such as yogurt, you make it richer. When you do this in a cheese recipe, you are creating a double- or triple-cream cheese. Read the ingredients label on the cream and choose a brand that is free of stabilizers such as polysorbate 80 or carrageenan gum. Ideally, find one that is not ultra-pasteurized, a good sign that the cream comes from a more local source. Buy organic if possible.

ESSENTIAL EQUIPMENT

When it comes to equipment, special or otherwise, for beginning your cheesemaking adventure, start simply. The only two things I could not make cheese without are a proper stockpot and a good thermometer; if you don't have them, these two things are a must purchase right away. After that, try to buy as little as possible at first and then slowly acquire more as you understand the cheesemaking process and grow clearer on which styles you like to make. If you find you are fond of making bloomy-rinds, for example, a fancy press—actually, any press at all—is unnecessary.

For recommendations on the order in which to acquire things for your cheesemaking arsenal, I created the chart on page 34, with a rating for each item of one or two stars, one being "buy now" and two meaning "it can wait"—things that are not essential but make cheesemaking easier, more accurate, or more aesthetically pleasing.

Following are brief explanations of all the "buy now" items on the chart.

AGING BINS

Short (about 4-in-/10-cm-tall) plastic containers, available at any home-goods store, make great humidity controls for your aging cheese. Choose one with dimensions that suit the dimensions of your cheese. I can store one large or two medium wheels in each of my bins, if I choose my forms right. When using these familiar "snap-on lid" storage containers for ripening and aging cheeses, be sure to rest the lids on top without actually buckling them down. If the container becomes airtight, the cheese may suffocate. And if the containers emit a strong plastic odor when first purchased, air them out for several weeks before placing cheeses inside.

AGING MATS

The main function of an aging mat is to allow airflow on the underside of the cheese. The fineness of the pores in the mat should correlate to the nature of the cheese—for example, a firm-pressed cheddar can age atop a wide-weave mat, whereas a delicate double-crème bloomy-rind such as Buttercup (page 137) will need a finer weave, otherwise the cheese will seemingly melt through. There are professional cheese mats with varied pore sizes available at all cheesemaking supply companies, but I find plastic embroidery boards from the crafts store do the trick perfectly—and at a fraction of the price. Additionally, you can try resting your aging cheeses on sushi mats, plastic sink mats, or other wide washable plastic mesh. The most important feature of aging mats is that they should be easy to clean.

CHEESECLOTH

Cheesecloth, as its name suggests, is designed specifically for cheesemaking, and is an invaluable and inexpensive tool for making efficient work of separating the curds from the whey, as well as other functions. It comes in different thread counts to indicate the tightness of each weave. Choose a looser cheesecloth (#50 or less) for lining forms for pressed cheeses or if you are making a pressed cheese without a form, such as Baby Jack (page 152). Here, the cloth serves as a wick, allowing the cheese to drain more evenly, and/or helps get the cheese in and out of the form when flipping.

Choose a tight-weave, or #90, cheesecloth (a gauge identical to butter muslin, which you can always substitute) when draining cheeses with fine curds such as mascarpone or chèvre. If you use the wider weave for finer curds, the cheese will drain through the pores and be lost; likewise, if you use a super-tight weave for cooked, pressed cheeses, the whey won't be able to leave the cheese as rapidly as it should. See page 37 for a chart of cheesecloth weaves to guide you in your selection, and stock up on a few different gauges for your cheesemaking feats.

CHEESE FORMS

Perhaps surprisingly, I hesitated over adding cheese forms to the essentials list—partly because you can make many cheeses without a form and partly because you can easily repurpose a number of common household items. But expense notwithstanding, I do recommend purchasing at least one true, professional pressable cheese form sooner than later. Though many lovely shapes come from working without a professional form, cheese forms may prevent inappropriately asymmetrical cheeses and various mishaps, such as the cheese continuing to slip out of the press. I have two really nice, pressable forms (one medium, one large) and I use them all the time—for nearly any recipe—and I love them for their ease and reliability.

CREAM WAX, CHEESE WAX, AND VACUUM-SEALING BAGS

Although cream wax is not *absolutely* essential, I suggest it as an earlier purchase if you plan to make anything aged. It is very similar to cheese wax in that it coats the rind of the cheese and moderates or prevents mold growth, but different in that it is liquid at room temperature and applied using nothing more than an ordinary paint brush. It allows for some air and moisture to leave the cheese, whereas cheese wax forms a tighter seal. Although I like cheese wax, too (it's so pretty), you can't beat cream wax's ease of use. It's really a friend to the beginning cheesemaker. Note: Because it is synthetic, cream wax should be pulled or cut off the rind prior to eating the cheese.

Vacuum-sealing bags complete the list of inorganic ways to seal the cheese rind, and are an alternative to cream or cheese waxes. Eventually you should experiment with them all to see which you like working with and to understand the advantages of each. Having cream wax, cheese wax, or a vacuum sealer will make cheese aging infinitely easier, especially as you start out and, in particular, before you get your cheese cave in order.

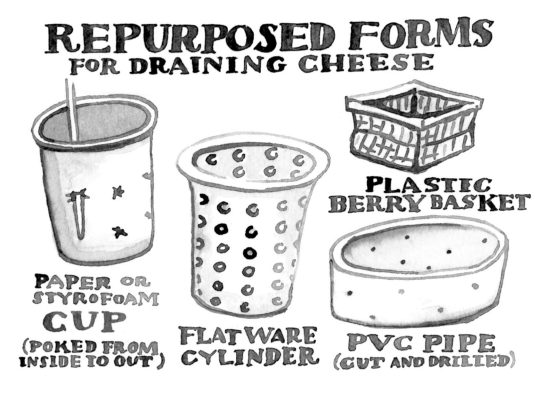

REPURPOSED FORMS FOR DRAINING CHEESE

PAPER OR STYROFOAM CUP (POKED FROM INSIDE TO OUT)

FLATWARE CYLINDER

PLASTIC BERRY BASKET

PVC PIPE (CUT AND DRILLED)

CURD KNIFE

To make the initial cuts into just-renneted milk, you can use a true curd knife, available anywhere you find cheesemaking supplies, any long knife such as a carving or cake knife, or even a sauce (flat) whisk. The sharpness of the knife is not important, but the length, of course, is. Test the knife against your pot to make sure your hand and the handle will be above the surface of the milk when it's time to cut. If the knife is too short, your hand will smash, instead of cut, the curds at the top, or you won't be cutting all the way to the bottom—leaving an unfortunate blob of uncut curd.

In a commercial creamery, cheesemakers use cheese harps, large, stainless-steel frames strung either vertically or horizontally with fine metal wires, to achieve identical cubes. If you are a tinkerer, you can fashion yourself a homemade harp to fit the size of your vat by cutting down a metal wire grid or plastic light diffuser. A professional harp is overkill for the home operation, since the home cheesemaker's vat is small (in proportion to the professional's) and he or she can cut the whole vat of set milk into curd quite quickly.

MEDICINE DROPPER

Because you're working with very small amounts of rennet and CaCl$_2$, a medicine dropper will be the best way to measure out doses. You don't want a ½ tsp rennet to casually become ¾ tsp . . . much will change. Medicine droppers are available at the drugstore. Classic teaspoons work in a pinch but give a less precise amount.

SKIMMER OR STIRRING ROD

To stir the curds, you can use a long-handled skimmer or slotted spoon. Sometimes I use a long metal spatula. My big secret for cheese I won't be selling is that my favorite "stirrer" is actually my hand—or rather, my arm! Submerging it into the vat allows me to keep a finger on things, noting if curds are starting to mat (stirring too slowly) or if they're sticking on the bottom (heat is too high). Some people like to stir with a long-handled whisk.

STOCKPOTS

The recipes in this book are designed for 1, 2, or 4 gal/3.8, 7.5, or 15 L of milk. The smaller amounts work well when making fresh and soft-ripened cheeses. Working with a larger volume makes more sense when making pressed cheeses such as Mountain Top (page 180). Since not everyone has a 4-gal/15-L stockpot on hand, this may be something to buy. To convince you of its worth, just consider the modest return on any of the pressed and aged cheeses (8 to 11 percent). After a long day of making cheese plus many long months of aging it, cracking open a 5-lb/2.3-kg wheel will be so much more encouraging than opening a 2-lb/910-g one.

Don't use aluminum or copper pots (curds and whey are acidic and may draw elements into the cheese).

THERMOMETER

A good thermometer is an essential tool—perhaps the single most important one for the home cheesemaker. I prefer digital kitchen thermometers over analog versions because they give me a quick and accurate reading. I recommend keeping a backup

CHEESE HARPS

thermometer in case that unfortunate day comes when, just after you gather 20 gal/75 L of milk, your thermometer goes kaput! Be sure your thermometer is calibrated for accuracy; a few degrees can make a difference when making cheese. To calibrate, stick your thermometer in a cup of ice water for 3 minutes. The temperature should read 32°F/0°C. If it's off, pencil in the new mark and adjust the temperatures for the recipe accordingly.

VACUUM SEALER

I'm putting a vacuum sealer on the essential equipment list because nothing else will relieve you of "affinage headaches" as well as this tool. A vacuum sealer allows you to seal any fresh, semifirm, or hard-pressed cheese, preventing the surface from growing molds or preventing further rind development on an already finished cheese. Vacuum sealers allow you to reseal pieces from a cut wheel (letting you taste test your cheese creation over time). If you aren't ready to eat through a 4-lb/1.8-kg wheel of Havarti by yourself, a vacuum sealer will save the day.

There are many more items you can buy—but none are absolutely essential. Like I said, you really need only a good thermometer and a stockpot to make cheese. The nonessential items, such as more *real* cheese forms, a press, a pH meter, a smoker, a gram scale, and so on, ramp up the fun of home cheesemaking. They make the process more efficient and help your cheeses turn out more consistently.

PH STRIPS OR PH METER

None of the recipes in this book, except (optionally) the Cultured Mozzarella (page 174), call for a specific pH or acidity level in order to make an edible cheese. You will learn to judge whether it is time to take the next step according to time, temperature, and feel. However, as you move forward in your cheese craft and want to gain better control of the cheesemaking process, you'll want first to buy some pH strips, then a pH meter.

Standard pH strips come in packs of 100 strips, which will last you quite a while, and are available from most cheesemaking supply companies. Note that these strips are safe for culinary use and are geared specifically to the pH range of cheese (4.0 to 7.0). Do not use the litmus paper made for testing swimming pools or fish tanks!

A range of pH meters are available, priced depending on quality and function. The meter needs to be maintained and calibrated with each use. Use per the manufacturer's directions; there are also helpful videos online. Once you get used to your pH meter, it will become one of your favorite tools in the creamery.

A Guide to Acquiring Your Cheesemaking Equipment (* = buy right away ** = buy eventually)

ITEM		ATTRIBUTES	POSSIBLE SUBSTITUTES
Aging bins	*	Maintains humidity around cheese while keeping contaminants out, separates varieties of cheeses	Cheese or cream wax, vacuum bags, a true cave with controlled humidity
Aging boards	**	Supports weight of cheese, imparts flavor, stabilizes moisture, allows for oxygen flow on cheese underside	Plastic boards or trays covered with aging mats, waxing or vacuum-sealing negates need for aging boards
Aging mats	*	Props up cheese to allow air to circulate underneath	Aging directly on wooden boards, or vacuum-sealing or cheese- or cream-waxing
Analog thermostat	**	Adjusts temperature of regular fridge, making it run warmer	Age in wine fridge, regular fridge (slower ripening), or true cave
Cheesecloth	*	Fine mesh fabric used to strain curds from whey	Flour-sack dish towels, lace curtain material, or other cotton fabric
Cheese press	**	Presses curds together to form a sealed rind with properly expelled moisture	Many alternatives to purchased presses though most have drawbacks; presses are only needed for milled-curd and semifirm to firm cheeses
Cheese trier	**	Allows you to monitor development of cheese wheel without halting aging process	Vegetable peeler
Cheese wax or Cream wax	*	Pliable coating that is easy to apply	Paraffin is too brittle; beeswax is brittle and expensive—note that used cheese wax can be melted, strained, and used again
Cold smoker	**	Imparts flavor, dries cheese, inhibits mold growth, and seals rind	Liquid smoke is available, but the flavor is inferior to real wood smoke
Curd knife	*	A long blade that reaches to the bottom of the pot	Cake spatula, bread knife, meat knife, or cheese harp
Form with follower for pressed cheese	*	A pressable cheese form with follower enables you to make heavily pressed cheeses such as cheddar; be sure to select a form with a capacity that corresponds to the size of your cheese vat	Cheese can be pressed using only cheesecloth (see example on page 222); this style will make an asymmetrical wheel

ITEM		ATTRIBUTES	POSSIBLE SUBSTITUTES
Forms for unpressed cheeses	**	These delicate cups and baskets allow curds to be separated from the whey and come in a variety of shapes and volumes; line with cheesecloth or select one with appropriate number and size of pores	Plastic berry basket, plastic milk jug with punctures, restaurant silverware cups, or cheesecloth and a colander
Gram scale	**	Precise measurement of powdered rennet, cultures, lipase, and acids	Consistent volume measurements using medicine dropper or teaspoons
Humidifier	**	Increases humidity in aging environment	Not necessary if using aging bins
Large stock-pot, or two large nesting stockpots	*	Holds enough milk for a nice, large, work-able cheese batch; nesting creates tem-perature buffer and prevents scorching	Bain marie, single pot with heavy bottom, or single pot set into sink of warm water
Medicine dropper	*	Precise measurement of liquid rennet and CaCl$_2$	Measuring spoons or rennet in tablet form
pH meter	**	Measures acidity as a gauge of when to move to next stage in cheesemaking process	pH strips are less expensive but less accurate; monitoring pH is not critical for beginning cheesemaking, though it will be a helpful tool eventually
Salometer	**	Measures brine strength	Follow brine recipe exactly; making a new batch for each recipe creates consistent brine strength
Skimmer or stirring rod	*	Keeps curds in motion; slots in the skimmer slow the velocity of liquid's movement, making for less curd fracturing	Metal spatula, whisk, or your own (clean) arm
Thermometer	*	Digital thermometers offer accurate measurement and are quick and easy to read	Analogue thermometer is a possible substitute
Vacuum sealer	*	Allows you to reseal cut cheeses for extended holding (up to several months)	Semifirm and firm cheese varieties may be resealed using cheese wax; fresh and soft cheeses cannot be waxed

SETUP AND SANITATION

The more careful you are about cleanliness while making cheese, the happier you'll be in the long run. There are thousands of opportunities for unwanted organisms to enter the mix. Do your best to keep them out by taking these steps.

RINSE EVERYTHING BEFORE USE.

Dust collects everywhere. Before filling the pot with milk, give it and your tools a rinse with a sanitizer or steam (see page 231). Keep a stack of white hand towels that can be routinely bleached or boiled. Use these to cover the surfaces on which you'll set out your tools; to dry off equipment; or to cover pressing cheeses in the sink.

KEEP EQUIPMENT IN A CLEAN, DESIGNATED LOCATION.

Instead of hunting for your teaspoons every time you want to make Quark, have your supplies separated and stored in a clean, ideally see-through, plastic bin. Store your largest milk pot upside down and off the floor. Make sure your supplies are in a rodent-proof, scent-free, mold-free location (which means not a damp basement).

RINSE AWAY SOAP RESIDUE.

Remember the point of cheesemaking is to grow bacteria. If you're too careful on the cleanliness front, you might end up doing more harm than good. When bleaching or soaping a surface or tool that the cheese will come into contact with, be sure to rinse extra thoroughly.

USE COMMON SENSE.

When making cheese, use common sense. You'll be spending a lot of time hovering over the pot, so tie back your hair or wear a hat. Even put away that cell phone (if you can). Try and avoid strong soaps or lotions on a cheesemaking day. Lastly, kick out the cat (or the blue jay).

READY TO ROLL

Before you get going on any recipe, follow these four steps.

1. Read through the entire recipe first. Some cheeses and cultured dairy products will need your attention for 24 hours. Others will get wrapped up in a few hours. Read through and plan ahead.

2. Gather and sanitize your tools and equipment beforehand (see page 231). After they're clean, lay everything out on a clean (I like to use white so I can see the clean) towel, near the vat.

3. Inspect the expiration dates of rennet, cultures, and ingredients.

4. Calibrate your thermometer by sticking it in a cup of ice water for 3 minutes. The temperature should read 32°F/0°C. If it's off, pencil in the new mark as 32°F/0°C and read the rest of the temperature with that adjustment accordingly.

ABOUT CHEESECLOTH

The term *cheesecloth* is a bit of a murky one. It can mean something gauzy that you would see in a Halloween display; loose-weaved stuff you might use to wrap a roast; or the exceedingly versatile and useful, tightly woven, barely transparent material, closer to a flour sack or dishcloth, that has dozens of uses in the kitchen. One reason for the sprawling definition is because cheesecloth comes in a variety of grades, or numbers of threads per square inch. The grades range from very open weave (#10) to extra-fine weave (#90). The higher grades are interchangeable with a product called "butter muslin." In general, for cheesemaking purposes (draining cheeses and lining cheese forms), use #60 to 90 gauge. The following chart shows thread counts of the different gauges and potential money-saving alternatives.

GRADE	THREAD COUNT	ALTERNATIVE
#10	20 by 12	None: Not appropriate for cheesemaking.
#40 (Loose)	24 by 20	Try a medium-weave lace-curtain material.
#60 (Medium)	32 by 28	Look in fabric stores for a loose-weave linen. Choose one that is white or lightly colored.
#90 (Tight)	44 by 36	Butter muslin, if available, or try flour-sack kitchen towels.

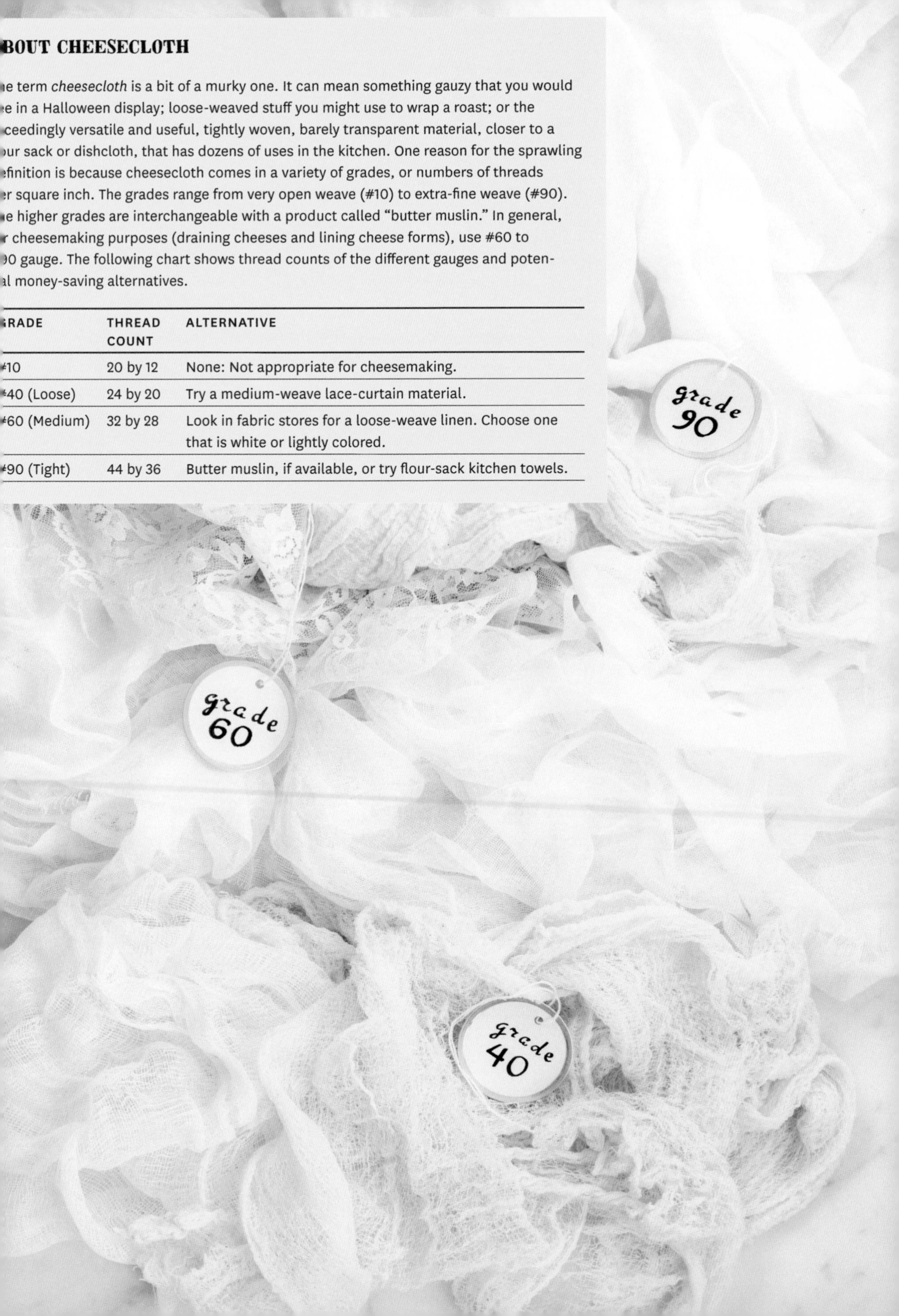

CHAPTER ONE

CULTURED MILK & CREAM

A chef once told me, "We make crème fraîche every night before we close up the restaurant. We just pour leftover buttermilk into leftover cream and leave it on the counter until morning." Making cultured dairy products—which aren't "technically" cheese because they haven't been drained—is as simple as a splash of buttermilk in a bowl of cream. You'll soon see for yourself as we turn milk and cream from a liquid into a solid.

MILK CHEMISTRY

To understand what's happening when you add cultured buttermilk to cream, let's break down what milk is made of:

- **Lactose**—The fuel for cheese cultures. Lactose is the primary sugar found in milk.

- **Protein**—The main protein in cheesemaking is called casein, which coagulates in an acid environment or under the influence of rennet. Also present in milk are whey proteins, which we'll gather when we make whey ricotta.

- **Fat**—Butterfat provides flavor, aroma, and texture.

- **Salts and Minerals**—Minerals such as calcium and phosphorus help the casein coagulate.

- **Enzymes**—Lipase and plasmin enzymes aid in the ripening of a cheese.

The elements above are, logically enough, the parts of milk that are not water. Nearly 90 percent of cow's milk is water, to give you a sense of proportions. To make yogurt, buttermilk, kefir, or crème fraîche, you'll keep that water together with those solids, but just change the way that the proteins line up. With yogurt, you have 100 percent yield. With cheese, you will have closer to 10 percent yield.

FROM LIQUID TO GEL

Once added to milk, if the temperature is right and there aren't obstacles in the way (a too-hot flame under the vat, competitor bacteria already present, some sanitizer lingering), cultures get right to work, leaving the "lag phase" and starting to produce at exponential rates, known as the "exponential growth" or "log phase." During log phase, the cultures produce enough lactic acid that milk transforms from liquid to gel (as is the case with yogurt). Under ideal conditions, this occurs within hours of inoculation.

As the cultures create acid, the milk changes from being nearly neutral (a pH of about 6.7) to being mildly acidic. In response to this acidity, the casein proteins, which normally repel each other, become attracted to one another. As milk approaches a pH level of 4.6 (known as the "isoelectric point" of casein protein), the casein proteins link together and precipitate—or fall out of solution—and the milk turns semisolid. This process can be catalyzed by either a change in the milk's acidity or the introduction of the enzyme "rennet" (which we'll talk about shortly). Water, butterfat, additional proteins, and lactose are all trapped inside this protein web.

Creating acidity in milk also, incidentally, makes milk—which is at this point yogurt or cheese—a safer food. Acidification is a process commonly used in food processing. Acidity makes foods safer but also affects texture and flavor. Think of canned

foods, salad dressings, sauces, and juices. All of these have a pH of 4.6 or lower. Pathogenic and contamination bacteria have a narrow range in which they can survive, let alone reproduce. That range is generally "sweeter" or less acidic than pH 4.6.

LEARNING TO CULTURE

You will start your journey into "the milky way" by making "milk gels." Milk gels, which you can visualize as yogurt, take only a few steps. Warm the milk or cream, add cultures, incubate, refrigerate, and then enjoy. Through these simple steps, you'll witness the transformation of milk or cream from a liquid to a solid state. This transformation occurs because of the acidity created by the cultures you've added. Once you've gotten a grip on this step, you're just one step away from making cheese.

As you make these recipes, you may notice how similar many of the recipes are to each other. Kefir is basically a variant of yogurt and yogurt is basically a variant of buttermilk. Greek-style yogurt is essentially crème fraîche, only with different amounts of protein and butterfat in the same volume. The difference is the richness of the milk or cream you start with, the cultures you use and the temperatures at which you incubate. A walk down the supermarket dairy aisle will never be the same!

When making these recipes, you may also wonder why there is such a difference in the thicknesses of the end products (if they really are so similar). This is a good question. The thickness depends on the cultures you use, the nature of the milk (is it super-rich like sheep's milk or is it thinner like cow's milk?), the temperature and length of time you incubate for, and the presence of thickeners or sweeteners. So while yogurt is essentially buttermilk, it also *isn't* buttermilk because the cultures you'll use and temperatures you'll heat the milk to are just a bit different.

TEXTURE AND MOUTHFEEL

After you've tried a few recipes, you'll probably find that the results you get are different from what you're used to in products you buy. Your buttermilk might be chunkier or entirely thickened. Your goat's-milk yogurt may be as thin as a smoothie.

Your cream cheese almost certainly will be tangier and less, how shall I say it—plastic-y—than store-bought versions. These are the "old-fashioned" textures that many of us have forgotten or never even knew.

If you really want a more store-bought-like result, you have a few options. In industrial production, fodder plant– and seaweed-based additives such as guar gum, agar, or carrageenan gum are a standard. To keep your cheese creations as simple as possible and to avoid unwanted flavors, try one of the options in the chart on the facing page if you wish to tinker with density and texture.

INCUBATION METHODS

When making the following recipes for yogurt, buttermilk, and more, you will be incubating milk for between 4 and 48 hours. Choose any of the following incubation methods—or devise your own! Set or clip a thermometer inside the incubator so you can monitor the temperature and decide if adjustments are needed.

PICNIC AND BEVERAGE COOLERS

An ordinary insulated portable cooler partially filled with hot (120°F/48°C) water is my favorite method for incubating. Choose a cooler with a tight-fitting lid and one sized proportionally to the yield of your recipe—for example, a single jar of yogurt sitting in a very large cooler will get chilly and not set properly. Bump up the temperature, if needed, by adding more hot water partway through.

YOGURT INCUBATOR

There are a number of specialty yogurt makers—electric units that produce consistent, insulated heat—to choose from. Some have single-serving cups while others are one larger container.

LIGHTBULB BOX

Just like a pet bunny, your yogurt can feel warm and cozy in a box warmed with a lightbulb. Fit a 60-watt non-LED bulb into an insulated shipping box, making sure the bulb is not touching the Styrofoam or other

Thickeners for Yogurt, Kefir, Sour Cream, and Cream Cheese

THICKENER	AMOUNT TO ADD PER 1 GAL/3.8 L MILK	METHOD
Gelatin	½ packet (⅛ oz/3.5 g)	Sprinkle the gelatin into a small bowl and add 3 tbsp warm (120°F/48°C) milk from the pot of milk in your recipe. Let stand for 3 minutes, then stir thoroughly to dissolve the gelatin before stirring it back into the pot. (The effects of the gelatin will not be noticeable until after the yogurt has set and chilled in the refrigerator.)
Powdered Milk	¼ cup/50 g	Make a slurry of the powdered milk before adding to the main pot: Put ¼ cup/50 g powdered milk in a bowl and slowly whisk in 1 cup/240 ml warm (120°F/48°C) milk from the pot you are using for your recipe. When the slurry is smooth, pour through a sieve back into the pot, catching any remaining clumps.
Rennet	1 drop	Just before incubating your yogurt or buttermilk, whisk the rennet directly into the cultured milk or cream, mixing thoroughly before proceeding. The best thing about this thickener is you might already have it on hand.

insulation, and is at least 3 in/7.5 cm away from the incubating yogurt. Also make sure the box is small enough that one bulb offers sufficient heat.

HEATING PAD

Heating pads, available at any pharmacy for medical purposes, make great incubating units. Place a towel in the bottom of a box. Put the heating pad on top, then cover with two or three more towels. Rest the yogurt container(s) on top of the towels and close the box. Set the thermostat of the heating pad to maintain the desired temperature.

PILOT LIGHT

If your oven has a pilot light, you may be in luck and have a super-convenient incubator. Before trying to make yogurt in your oven, do a test run by leaving a pot of water inside overnight. In the morning, stick a thermometer into the water. The temperature should be between 98° and 105°F/37° and 41°C. If it's outside this range, look elsewhere for your incubator.

MICROSCOPIC FRIENDS

There are two main cultures we find in yogurt: *L. delbrueckii* ssp. *bulgaricus* and *S. thermophilus*. (Many yogurts have additional strains.) Cultured buttermilk, which, as I've said elsewhere, is very similar to yogurt, often contains *L. lactis* subsp. *cremoris* and *Leuconostoc mesenteroides* subsp. *cremoris*. Icelandic yogurt will use the strain *Bifidobacterium longum*. And Bulgarian-style yogurt implies a specific ratio of *L. bulgaricus* to *S. thermophilus*.

That's a lot of Latin! But don't worry about the long names. The point is, there is an overlap in the types of cultures you'll use for different dairy products and which cultures you use is only one factor determining the end product. Differences in how the product comes out, therefore, depend in part on the type of cultures used as well as other factors. When you purchase a culture packet online, it will come with the correct strain mixes and proportions. On the websites of supply companies, you can browse various qualities of yogurt, for example, and purchase which one you want. It's a bit like shopping for the right breed of dog. (I want a thick body, very sweet, mild flavor . . .)

But before you race to the Internet to buy cultures, remember to start simple. For the first few recipes ahead, instead of using freeze-dried "DVI" cultures, you will simply need to gather some buttermilk, some Bulgarian-style yogurt, and some Icelandic-style yogurt from the local grocery store.

MAKES 4 QT/3.8 L

MILK

ALL TYPES

FINAL FORM

JAR OR TUB

This basic recipe for delicious homemade yogurt can be tinkered with to produce an array of styles. Experiment and find your favorite—see the variations listed opposite.

Note: If culturing with store-bought yogurt, choose a brand with a texture and taste you like, and ideally one without flavorings and stabilizers for the greatest chances of reproducing a similar yogurt. Do not open the container until you are ready to use it. When making future batches, use your homemade yogurt for up to four generations. After that, start with a new store-bought "mother."

INGREDIENTS

1 gal/3.8 L milk

¼ cup/60 ml store-bought or homemade plain yogurt

SPECIAL EQUIPMENT

Digital kitchen thermometer; four 1-qt/1-L jars or clear plastic tubs with lids; incubation setup (see page 40)

1. Clean all surfaces and equipment before beginning.

2. Pour the milk into a heavy-bottomed stockpot and warm over medium-high heat to 180°F/82°C. Using an up-and-down motion, stir every 2 to 3 minutes.

3. Once at temperature, remove from the heat, cover, and hold at 180°F/82°C for 5 minutes. It's okay if the temperature rises slightly (up to 195°F/91°C), but it should not dip below. For a thicker yogurt, hold at 180°F/82°C for up to 25 minutes.

4. After 5 minutes, transfer the pot to a sink filled with cold water, making sure the water doesn't spill into the hot milk. Bring the temperature of the milk down to 115°F/45°C as quickly as possible, stirring to speed it along, then remove the pot from the sink.

5. In a small bowl, stir together the yogurt and 1 cup/240 ml of the warm milk. Pour the thinned yogurt mixture back into the pot. Stir for 20 seconds.

6. Moving quickly to conserve the heat, pour the milk mixture into the jars or tubs, dividing it evenly. Screw or snap the lids on tightly. Nest the jars in your incubator.

7. Keep the incubator in a warm, vibration-free location for 8 to 10 hours, or longer if needed. The yogurt should be slightly firmed and show very subtle indentations in the side. (It will not be completely thickened until it has been refrigerated, but it should no longer be liquid.)

8. Move the jars to the refrigerator immediately and hold for 6 to 8 hours before serving.

TIME TO COMPLETION

1 DAY

VARIATIONS

EXTRA RICH: *Increase the decadence of your yogurt by adding 2 cups/480 ml heavy cream per 1 gal/4 L milk to the pot when beginning to heat the milk. The cream will sour along with the milk, leaving you with an amazingly rich yogurt that's perfect for spooning over desserts like berry cobbler.*

EXTRA THICK: *Stir together ½ cup/100 g powdered milk and 1 cup/240 ml of the just heated (180°F/82°C) milk to make a smooth slurry. Pour the slurry through a fine-mesh sieve back into the pot. Stir well and proceed as directed to cool the milk mixture to warm (115°F/45°C), then culture. Play with the amount of milk powder you use for a thicker or thinner texture.*

EXTRA TANGY: *Start with a store-bought variety that is very sour in flavor (not a mellow, pudding-like yogurt brand). Let it incubate for 10 to 20 hours longer than the suggested time. (If you are using the picnic-cooler incubator setup, add hot water water several times during the incubation time to keep tempera-ture up.) For lactose-sensitive eaters, tangier yogurt means less lactose though it is not entirely lactose-free.*

GREEK: *There are two ways to make Greek-style yogurt. The first method is the same as the Extra Thick variation: Increase the amount of milk solids relative to the amount of water before culturing to yield a denser gel. The second method is to remove water*

by straining after culturing (identical to what you'll do when you make the Fromage Blanc & Quark on page 84): Line a colander with clean fine (#90) cheesecloth. Set the colander in a sink, or over a large pot if you want to collect the whey. Scoop the freshly cultured, not yet cooled yogurt into the prepared colander. Drain for 4 to 10 hours at room temperature, or until it reaches the thickness and tanginess you like. Transfer to a bowl and mix to redis-tribute the moisture (the yogurt will be drier in the sections nearer to the cloth and wetter toward the center). You can also combine these two methods: adding powdered milk and straining afterward to make something thick enough to mortar walls.

BULGARIAN: *Bulgarian yogurt is not that different from American yogurt—the only difference being it contains only the Lac-tobacillus bulgaricus and Streptococcus thermophiles cultures, and a specific ratio of the two. American yogurts contain a handful of other cultures—some that survive in the human digestive tract (considered "probiotic") and some that cause parts of the milk to hold water molecules tightly, forming a heavy gel. Purchase a container of Bulgarian yogurt (it will say so right on the container) to use for your starter. Check to make sure that the ingredients list only Lactobacillus bulgaricus and Streptococcus thermophilus cultures.*

CONTINUED

GOAT'S-MILK: *Making goat's-milk yogurt is nearly identical to making cow's-milk yogurt, except that you'll need to add a small amount of rennet. Add 2 drops of rennet, undiluted, per 1 gal/3.8 L of goat's milk as you are stirring in the yogurt cultures. Moving quickly, pour the cultured milk into the container(s) in which your yogurt will set and then place in the incubator. (Note, for goat's-milk yogurt, it's okay to use either cow's- or goat's-milk yogurt as the inoculant.) For extra-thick goat's-milk yogurt, find powdered goat's milk and follow the directions for the Extra Thick cow's-milk variation.*

SWEET VANILLA: *At one of my creamery jobs, we rolled out a plain yogurt, which sold quite well. Then, after several more months, we rolled out a honey-vanilla version. When it hit the shelves, people went gangbusters—a testament to how a little sweetness can go a long way. Halve one (or more for stronger flavor) vanilla bean lengthwise. Scrape out the seeds, then place the seeds and pod into the milk as you are heating it initially to 180°F/82°C. While heating, also add ¾ cup/85 g honey and stir until the honey is dissolved (see Note). Remove the vanilla pod while the milk is cooling to 115°F/45°C. Proceed with the recipe as directed. The seeds from the pod will leave attractive specs in your finished yogurt.*

STIRRED-IN FLAVORINGS: *To make flavored yogurt, after the yogurt has cultured and cooled, mix in about 3 tbsp sugar or honey per 2 cups/480 ml plain yogurt along with your flavoring of choice, such as an extract or syrup. If sweetening with jam or jelly, add 3½ to 5 tbsp per 2 cups/480 ml plain yogurt. The cultures you choose and the amount of time you let the yogurt ferment will determine how sour the yogurt is, in turn affecting how much sweetener you may want to add (see Note).*

NOTE:

- *When sweetening yogurt, do not add any more honey or sugar than the recipe calls for prior to incubating the yogurt. Additional sweetener will interrupt the formation of the gel, leading to loose or unset yogurt. Instead, if you want a sweeter yogurt than the finished product you get, stir in more honey after the yogurt has set and cooled. Commerical yogurts get over this obstacle by adding thickeners and gels.*

MAKES 1 QT/0.9 L

PART SKIM OR ALL SKIM

FINAL FORM

JAR OR TUB

TIME TO COMPLETION

2 DAYS

Icelandic yogurt is similar to Greek-style yogurt, but it is tangier and has a bit more sheen to its appearance. The crucial thing for making Icelandic yogurt is to use a store-bought container of Icelandic yogurt as the starter. You can find it in well-stocked supermarkets and natural-foods stores. Also, this yogurt, unlike the previous recipe, uses rennet for thickening.

INGREDIENTS

1 gal/3.8 L part skim or all skim milk
¼ cup/60 ml store-bought Icelandic yogurt
2 drops rennet

SPECIAL EQUIPMENT

Digital kitchen thermometer; incubation setup (see page 40); 20-in/50-cm square medium or fine (#60 or #90) cheesecloth; two 1-qt/1-L jars or plastic tubs with lids

1. Clean all surfaces and equipment before beginning.

2. Pour the milk into a heavy-bottomed stockpot and warm over medium-high heat to 180°F/82°C. Using an up-and-down motion, stir every 2 to 3 minutes.

3. Once at temperature, cover and hold at 180°F/82°C for 5 minutes. It's okay if the temperature rises slightly (up to 195°F/91°C), but it should not dip below.

4. After 5 minutes, transfer the pot to a sink filled with cold water, making sure the water doesn't spill into the hot milk. Bring the temperature of the milk down to 115°F/46°C as quickly as possible, stirring to speed it along, then remove the pot from the sink.

5. In a small bowl, stir together ¼ cup/60 ml of the warm milk and the yogurt. Pour the thinned yogurt mixture back into the pot. Stir well.

6. Add the rennet to the pot, one drop at a time, then stir well.

7. Stop the motion of the milk, cover the pot, place it in an incubator, and leave for 6 to 8 hours. Be sure the pot stays warm during the incubation period; the temperature should not fall below 95°F/35°C.

8. The yogurt is ready for cutting when it has firmed into a block of curd surrounded by almost-greenish whey. Using a long knife and skimmer or a whisk, cut the curd vertically and then horizontally into 1-in/2.5-cm pieces (see page 219). Stir the curds very gently for 1 minute to release more whey.

9. Rinse the cheesecloth with hot water and wring out. Line a colander with the cheesecloth and place the colander in the sink. Ladle the curds into the colander. Allow it to drain until the level of the curds has dropped sufficiently.

10. Make a pouch by tying the corners of the cheesecloth together. Run a dowel or long-handled wooden spoon under the top knot and set over a pot so the pouch is suspended freely inside. Place the pot with the draining pouch in the refrigerator for 4 to 6 hours. During this time, you can expedite the draining by occasionally shaking the pouch gently, pushing the curds near the edges of the fabric inward and shifting the interior curds toward the outer edges of the pouch.

11. When the yogurt has reached the desired consistency (drain longer if you'd like a drier curd), transfer to a clean bowl and beat with a wooden spoon until the curds have homogenized. Alternatively, especially if the curds are very thick, use a food processor and pulse for 10 to 20 seconds.

12. Spoon the yogurt into clean jars or tubs. Cover and refrigerate.

NOTE

- *If you think you have let the curds drain for too long, you can rehydrate them by adding some of the whey collected in the pot during draining, using a whisk or a food processor. You can also whisk or pulse in 1 cup/250 ml half-and-half or heavy cream to create a richer treat.*

FARMER'S cheese

MAKES ABOUT 2 CUPS/480 ML

Your yogurt batches are going to turn out beautifully. But sometimes, by mistake or by mystery, a batch just doesn't work. Happily, there's a way to make the miss into a real hit! Here is a recipe for a simple white cheese similar to cottage cheese. Snack on it, top a lunch salad with it, or use it to stuff your next batch of pierogi or ravioli.

INGREDIENTS
1 gal/3.8 L unset yogurt milk, from any recipe
½ tsp salt, or to taste

SPECIAL EQUIPMENT
Incubation setup (see page 40); digital kitchen thermometer; 20-in/50-cm square fine (#90) cheesecloth

1. Check to see if there is any perceivable sour taste to your yogurt milk. If there is, that's good; proceed to step 2. If not, leave the culturing milk in the incubator until a sour taste develops. This should happen in less than 2 days. If not, give it more warmth and more time (you might have a very cold kitchen).

2. Move the pot of yogurt milk to the stove (or gently pour into a clean stockpot if it's in jars or tubs) and begin to heat without stirring. Around 95°F/35°C, you should start to notice the curds separating from the whey. For a softer cheese, stop heating here. For a drier cheese, continue to heat to 115°F/46°C,

with gentle and occasional stirring. Once at temperature, turn off the heat and hold for 20 minutes.

3. Rinse the cheesecloth with hot water and wring out. Line a colander with the cheesecloth and place it in the sink. Ladle the curds into the lined colander and let drain to the desired consistency, 3 to 4 hours. Transfer to a bowl and stir in the salt, then pack into an airtight container. Refrigerate until ready to enjoy.

NOTE
- *You can also make this cheese "on purpose" by making the recipe for Yogurt (page 42), but substituting buttermilk for the yogurt inoculant.*

BUTTERMILK: WHAT'S REAL? WHAT'S FAKE?

Because the word "buttermilk" seems to perennially conjure multiple meanings—which part is butter? which part is milk?—it begs some clarification.

There are three different types of buttermilk: Quick acid, traditional, and modern. The quick-acid version is really a fake, essentially we add vinegar directly to milk to make it curdle slightly and gain tanginess. You have probably done this in a pinch when your crowd was hungry for pancakes and you had no buttermilk on hand. But while it may suffice for pancakes, buttermilk created by these means (you can tell a container from the store is the quick-acid type if it doesn't advertise the words "cultures" or "cultured" but does list thickeners and emulsifiers as well as citric acid) are not good in home cheesemaking because they lack essential bacteria.

Then there's traditional buttermilk—a liquid by-product of buttermaking that's fragrant, semiopaque, and garnished with small flecks of butter. This stuff looks thinner than what you imagine buttermilk should look like (if you are accustomed to the store-bought stuff). Like it or not, you'll make this kind when you make the Cultured Butter on page 56.

Then there's a modern, store-bought version of traditional buttermilk, which is what I am referring to in the recipes calling for "cultured buttermilk." This stuff come from low-fat milk that has been fermented with active cultures (identical to the recipe on page 50), and this fermentation causes it to thicken slightly. There may be additional thickeners such as extra powdered milk or whey solids and sometimes even butterspecs (which are added so that it appears more like the traditional stuff).

For cheeemaking, either choose the modern *cultured* buttermilk from the store or gather some traditional stuff from your own buttermaking. But don't make or buy quick-acid buttermilk—there are no living cultures in it to serve your cheesemaking purposes.

MAKES 2 QT/2 L

MILK

ALL TYPES

FINAL FORM

JAR

Next up is an extra-simple cheesemaking recipe that lands you two wonderful foods: buttermilk and kefir. The buttermilk you'll make is not the traditional buttermilk (a by-product of butter making) but rather a modern buttermilk—similar to the one you can buy in the supermarket (see page 49). Kefir is similar to buttermilk but with an entirely different flavor. It's drinkable and the slightest bit effervescent (because it's partially fermented by yeasts as well as by bacteria). People love kefir and consider it very probiotic and healthful.

This recipe for "modern" buttermilk and kefir differs from the previous one for yogurt because the milk isn't heated to 180°F/82°C beforehand. Furthermore, you won't need to incubate the culturing milk to anything warmer than room temperature (as long as your house isn't too chilly!).

INGREDIENTS

2 qt/2 L milk

For Kefir: ¼ cup store-bought plain kefir

For Buttermilk: ¼ cup store-bought cultured buttermilk

SPECIAL EQUIPMENT

Digital kitchen thermometer; two 1-qt/1-L jars with lids or plastic tubs; incubation setup (page 40)

1. Clean all surfaces and equipment before beginning.

2. Pour the milk into a heavy-bottomed stockpot and warm over medium-high heat to 75°F/24°C, stirring occasionally. Remove from the heat.

3. To make the kefir: Pour the plain kefir into the warm milk.

To make the buttermilk: Pour the cultured buttermilk into the warm milk.

4. Stir the contents of the pot, using an up-and-down motion, for 20 seconds.

5. Moving quickly to conserve the heat, pour the cultured milk into the prepared jars. Screw the lids on tightly.

6. If the room temperature is cool (below 60°F/15°C), place the jars in the incubator. Otherwise, leave the jars in an undisturbed, vibration-free place for 12 to 36 hours, or until the cultured milk smells slightly tangy and coats the back of a spoon.

7. Store in the fridge, covered, until ready to enjoy or for up to 2 weeks.

MAKES ABOUT 2 CUPS/480 ML

MILK

ALL TYPES

FINAL FORM

JAR

Some people feel that kefir cultured with kefir grains—which are these strange little objects called SCOBYs—is superior to kefir made commercially from freeze-dried cultures (see page 226). To play by the kefir SCOBY rules, don't let the grains touch anything that might contaminate them, such as your hands or an unclean utensil. To buy live kefir grains, see page 234).

INGREDIENTS

2 cups/480 ml milk

½ to 1 tsp live kefir grains (or more)

SPECIAL EQUIPMENT

Digital kitchen thermometer; 1-pt/480-ml jar; wooden chopstick or wooden spoon; plastic colander

1. Clean all surfaces and equipment before beginning.

2. Pour the milk into a small pan and warm over medium heat to 75°F/24°C, stirring occasionally. Remove from the heat.

3. Transfer the milk to the jar, then add the kefir grains using the chopstick or the handle of the wooden spoon.

4. Cover the mouth of the jar with a clean cotton dishtowel or napkin and fix in place with a rubber band. (This allows the release of the fermentation gases that the kefir produces.) Leave the jar on the countertop until the milk has a sour, pleasing smell and has thickened to the consistency of thin yogurt, anywhere from 8 to 72 hours.

5. Set a plastic colander over a glass bowl. Pour the thickened milk into the colander and use the chopstick to move the grains around, helping the kefir to drain. The thickened milk you collect in the bowl below is the kefir for you to enjoy; you should have about 2 cups/480 ml. Transfer to a container, cover, and store in the fridge until ready to enjoy or for up to 1 week.

Meanwhile, the grains left in the colander are the cultures for your next batch. Transfer the grains to a clean jar and add enough milk to cover. Place the lid loosely (not airtight) on top of the jar and store in the fridge for up to 3 weeks.

6. Repeat the kefir cycle. With time, you will start to see more and more of the grains—they are growing and reproducing. The more grains used in relation to the quantity of milk, the faster the fermentation will happen; use at least ½ tsp but no more than ¼ cup/55 g grains per 2 cups/480 ml milk. At some point—perhaps six or seven generations later, when you may have too many grains—divide your stash and share the wealth with friends.

TIPS FOR MAINTAINING KEFIR GRAINS

- Do not leave the grains in the milk at room temperature for more than 4 days at a stretch. The acid being produced will start to kill away the weaker species of the microbial mix inside the SCOBY, changing the nature of the kefir.

- If the grains are not readily forming tasty, bubbly kefir, revitalize the grains by going through several recipe cycles quickly, incubating for only 8 hours and discarding the "start-up" milk until it tastes delicious and bubbly.

- The grains should eventually start to swell and duplicate. If your grains are not multiplying after six or seven generations and proper conditions, discard and start with newly purchased grains.

THE SCOBY SCOOP

Kefir grains are part of a family of compounds popularly known as SCOBYs, which stands for "symbiotic colonies of bacteria and yeast." You've seen a SCOBY before if you've tried kombucha and wondered about the particles floating around inside; or if you've purchased a bottle of natural vinegar and let it sit on the shelf for several months. In vinegars as in kombuchas, the SCOBY looks like a strange jellyfish. In kefir, I think the SCOBY looks like a mini, semitranslucent cauliflower.

MAKES ABOUT 1 QT/1 L

MILK

HALF-AND-HALF OR
LIGHT CREAM

FINAL FORM

JAR OR TUB

This easy homemade sour cream is lighter than crème fraîche but richer than Greek-style yogurt or quark. Add the powdered milk if you want a denser product.

INGREDIENTS

1 qt/1 L half-and-half or light cream

½ cup/100 g powdered milk, dissolved in ½ cup/120 ml warmed half-and-half (optional)

2 tbsp cultured buttermilk

¼ tsp salt, or to taste

SPECIAL EQUIPMENT

Digital kitchen thermometer; 1-qt/1-L jar or plastic tub; incubation setup (see page 40)

1. Clean all surfaces and equipment before beginning.

2. Pour the half-and-half into a small stockpot and warm over medium heat to 75°F/24°C, stirring occasionally. Remove from the heat.

3. Stir the powdered milk slurry (if using) into the warmed half-and-half, then add the buttermilk directly to the warm half-and-half. Stir the pot for 20 seconds, then pour the mixture into the jar. Screw on the lid tightly.

4. If the room temperature is cool (below 60°F/15°C), place the jar in the incubator. Otherwise, leave the jar in an undisturbed, vibration-free place for 15 to 24 hours, depending on the room temperature.

5. When the mixture is no longer fluid, smells aromatic, and tastes tangy, stir in the salt. Salt increases the shelf life of the sour cream as well as brings out flavor. Refrigerate for 3 hours before enjoying or store in an airtight container in the fridge for up to 3 weeks.

VARIATION

MEXICAN CREMA: *If you're familiar with the cream dolloped on top of tacos, you know crema. It's similar to sour cream but less acidic, looser, and made with more salt. Follow the recipe for sour cream, but incubate until you just start to detect the aromatic, yogurty smell (check at 6 hours and again at 10). Mix in ½ tsp salt and 2 drops of rennet, then store in the fridge for several more hours or until ready to use. Stir well before serving.*

TIME TO COMPLETION

2

DAYS

Crème FRAÎCHE

MAKES ABOUT 1 QT/1 L

This decadent soured cream is similar to the sour cream on the facing page, but denser and not salted. The beauty of crème fraîche shines when paired with bold foods such as an extra-sweet fruit tart or salty pork carnitas. If you have a source for raw cream, this is a great recipe to try it out with, because the natural milk flavors carry through well. Make sure the cream is very fresh if using raw.

INGREDIENTS

1 qt/1 L heavy cream, preferably 40% milk fat or at least 35%
2 tbsp cultured buttermilk
Pinch of salt (optional)

SPECIAL EQUIPMENT

Digital kitchen thermometer; 1-qt/1-L jar or plastic tubs; incubation setup (see page 40)

1. Clean all surfaces and equipment before beginning.

2. Pour the cream into a small stockpot and warm over medium heat to 72°F/22°C, stirring occasionally. Remove from heat.

3. Pour the buttermilk into the warm cream. Stir well for 20 seconds, then pour the mixture into the jar. Screw the lid on tightly.

4. If the room temperature is cool (below 60°F/15°C), place the jar in the incubator. Otherwise, leave the jar in an undisturbed, vibration-free place for 15 to 24 hours, depending on the room temperature. During this time, the cream will first thicken to the consistency of buttermilk, then yogurt, and finally to that of very thick Greek-style yogurt. Stir in the salt, if desired.

5. Store, tightly covered, in the refrigerator, for up to 2 weeks.

MILK

HEAVY CREAM

FINAL FORM

JAR OR TUB

TIME TO COMPLETION
2
DAYS

Cultured BUTTER

MAKES 1 LB/450 G BUTTER, PLUS
2 CUPS/480 ML BUTTERMILK

MILK

HEAVY CREAM

FINAL FORM

LOOSELY PACKED
TUB OR LOGS, OR
MOLDED

Traditionally, to make the process worth their while, farmers would accumulate cream for several days before churning it into butter. While the cream waited, yeasts and bacteria in the air and on surfaces generated a natural fermentation that produced a flavorful butter. Nowadays, nearly all butter in the supermarket comes from fermented cream, though none of it accidentally.

Whether they arrive via a gust of wind or a hermetically sealed foil packet from the culture lab, when microorganisms enter cream, they grow and multiply, creating flavor by-products in the process. The benefit of the laboratory-produced cultures we use nowadays is that we can guarantee that the ideal flavor-producing microorganisms we want are present. One of these special microscopic friends, *Leuconostoc mesenteroides* ssp *cremoris*, is actually responsible for producing what our brain thinks of as "butter flavor." *Leuconostoc mesenteroides* ssp *cremoris* turns a form of citric acid (a tiny bit of which is naturally present in milk) into a flavor compound called diacetyl. This *Leuconostoc mesenteroides* ssp *cremoris* gets into the mix when you add buttermilk to cream when making crème fraîche. This crème fraîche you'll then churn into butter—butter-flavored butter.

Cream is an emulsion of butterfat and the watery portion of milk, the whey. (If you zoomed in to a microscopic level, you'd see tiny droplets of fat suspended in a milky broth.) A special membrane called the phospholipid bilayer surrounds each droplet of fat. This membrane attracts fats on the inside and repels fats on the outside. The repulsion prevents the fats from joining together and keeps the cream emulsified. To make butter, you agitate this cream, which disrupts those membranes and causes the fat to start to stick together.

Next, you separate the sticky fat globules from the whey (which is also called buttermilk) by using a colander. You'll wash the fat globules with cold water, and knead out as much residual moisture as possible. (Understand, though, as you are developing your signature butter-making skills, that you'll never get out all the water and milk solids—commercial butters are about 80 percent butterfat, while European-style butters are closer to 85 percent. Homemade butters tend to be from 65 to 75 percent butterfat.)

Experiment with the churning methods to see which you prefer. Note that washing and drying your butter as thoroughly as possible results in better cooking qualities (you want butter that won't hiss when it hits the frying pan) and longer shelf life (water makes foods go bad more quickly). Then have fun playing with shaping and seasoning your butter—the possibilities are deliciously endless.

TIME TO COMPLETION

2
DAYS

CONTINUED

EASY

INGREDIENTS

1 recipe Crème Fraîche (page 55), prepared through step 4, prior to salting

Salt

1. After ripening, place the crème fraîche in the refrigerator for 1 hour to bring the temperature down to 50°F/10°C before proceeding. If your butter gets warmer than 60°F/16°C at any point during the following process, refrigerate to return to 50°F/10°C.

2. Once you have chilled cultured cream, proceed with churning it by one of the following methods.

FOOD PROCESSOR OR BLENDER: Pour the cultured cream into a food processor or blender, making sure the work bowl or jar is no more than halfway full. Cover and pulse or process on low speed for 5 seconds. Stop the machine and pour in 2 cups/480 ml ice water. Pulse again until you see butter particles rising to the surface of the liquid, usually 10 to 20 seconds longer. The downside of this method is it leaves you with watered-down buttermilk. The upside is that it takes very little time.

HAND-SHAKEN: If you want to make butter the *really* old-fashioned way—before the advent of even the classic wooden churn with a plunger—simply shake it by hand. (Arguably the only upside to this method: you'll burn as many calories churning the butter as you'll take in eating it.) Cut the recipe in half for your first run, because shaking is a bit of work. Pour the cultured cream into a 1-qt/1-L jar, making sure it is no more than halfway full. Screw the lid on tightly and start to shake—in any manner. (I sometimes roll the jar back and forth with my foot while I work at the computer.) Within 20 minutes, if the temperature stays in range (see step 1), the cream will separate into a grainy mush. If not, check the temperature and continue agitating. Stop agitating as

soon as the butterfat clumps are the size of rice grains.

STAND MIXER: This is my favorite method because I can see and hear the butter as it hits the perfect spot in development, before it gets over-churned. Pour the cultured cream into the bowl of a stand mixer fitted with the paddle attachment to about one-third full. (Do not overfill the work bowl; a too-full mixer will fling butter around your kitchen. Work in batches as needed.) Beat at medium speed. Watch as the cream turns fluffy, then waxy, then starts to collapse into a grainy mush. Now listen carefully for a sloshing sound. Once you hear it, turn off the mixer. Depending on the weather, the source of the cream, and the speed of the mixer, churning by mixer can take anywhere from several minutes to over half an hour! Do not raise the mixer speed to shorten the time; instead keep checking the temperature to make sure you are in the correct range (see step 1).

3. When the cream makes a sloshing sound and starts to look like grainy porridge, it is ready to be drained and washed. Pour the contents of your churner into a fine-mesh sieve or fine-holed colander placed over a bowl to catch the buttermilk. (If you use a colander, make sure the perforations are smaller than the clumps of butter, or you will lose bits of the butter into the buttermilk—which isn't the worst thing, especially if you're making biscuits afterward). Move the butter clumps around in the sieve to release more buttermilk, then transfer the buttermilk to a jar and store in the fridge for up to 1 week. Move the sieve to the sink, place under a stream of cold (50°F/10°C) water, and start to swish the butter particles around. Using your fingers, gently toss the particles until they begin to clump. Push them into a ball. If the grains are not sticking together, knead them until they get warmer,

CONTINUED

or raise the temperature of the wash water by several degrees. Continue washing and kneading until the water runs almost clear.

4. Take the butter ball and press into it to release the remaining whey. Remember, the drier the butter, the better the butter. Keep kneading until no more water is released, then fold in salt to taste, if desired. If adding salt, fold and press it in versus whipping it in. Coarser-grained salt crystals look and taste special, if you have some on hand. Finally, pack the butter into a tub, mold, or butter bell or shape into logs. Eat soon or freeze.

VARIATIONS

Here are a few ideas for making seasoned butters. The flavors will really wake up once you apply heat. These flavor mixes are scaled for 1 lb/455 g unsalted butter. Fold them in gently in when you are adding the salt.

HONEY BUTTER: *Mix in ¼ cup/85 g honey and ½ tsp salt. You might also like ¼ tsp ground cinnamon or cardamom. I use this butter on toast and roasted sweet potatoes.*

GOLDEN GARLIC: *Roast 2 heads of garlic in the oven for 1 hour at 350°F/180°C. When cooled, squeeze the garlic pulp out of the skins. Mash the garlic with a fork, then add it to the butter along with ½ tsp onion powder, ½ tsp salt, and a pinch of saffron threads.*

SNAPPY CAPER: *Mix in ¼ cup/55 g chopped capers, 2 tsp chopped fresh chives, ½ tsp salt, ½ tsp red pepper flakes, and the zest of 1 lemon. Try this flavor with grilled fish.*

FRENCH HERB: *Mix in 1 tsp each of dried savory, thyme, marjoram, crushed fennel seed, and lavender, plus ½ tsp salt. Melt a pat of this butter in the pan when making scrambled eggs for something surprisingly fragrant.*

TIPS FOR BETTER BUTTER

- *Use the highest-quality cream possible, such as an organic product from a small farm, and select the carton furthest from expiration.*

- *Choose brands that contain only cream and no stabilizers.*

- *Keep the cream between 50° and 60°F/ 10° and 16°C throughout the process.*

- *Do not churn butter beyond the "porridge" consistency or your butter will be greasy.*

- *For fun, try specialty salts such as smoked sea salt or Himalayan pink salt, in addition to the variations.*

BETTER BUTTER STORAGE

To preserve the angelic flavor of home-made butter, you have two options: 1) eat promptly, or 2) wrap well and freeze immediately. If neither of these work for you, a third option for storing butter at room temperature is a device called a French butter bell (or butter dish). This ceramic cup is packed full of butter, then inverted and set over a pool of water to form an air lock, which limits the butter's exposure to air. Adding salt to your butter will also help preserve its flavor and extend its shelf life. Finally, I advise placing butter far away from stinky neighbors such as onions, curry, smoked ham, blue cheese, and so on when in the fridge.

BUTTER MOLD PATTERNS

Butter GADGETS

BUTTER PADDLES

GROOVED PADDLE CURLER

BALLER

BUTTER STAMP

BUTTER PRESS WITH TONGS

BUTTER CHURN

Butter

H2O

BUTTER BELL

BUTTER WORKER

BUTTER MOLDS

SHAPING BUTTER

If you think of butter as sunlight that was transformed into grass, then into milk, then into cream, *then* into butter, you'll remember what a precious food you're working with. It's the fat of the land, the toast of the town. It's metamorphosed sunlight! Honor this magical food by molding it into something even more beautiful.

WOODEN MOLDS AND STAMPS: Antique butter molds, if in decent shape, can still be used to mold butter per their original intention. Find them in flea markets, antique stores, and through online auction sites. (I admit, though they are charming, I find antique butter equipment can often carry the flavor of old basements. Be careful.) Alternatively, you can purchase new wooden molds (see Hoegger's, page 234). You can even carve your own.

To prepare a wooden mold, place it in cool water for 30 minutes prior to packing in the butter. When the butter is washed and dry but still malleable, take the mold from the water and pack it with the butter. Place the mold in the refrigerator for 1 hour. After an hour, remove from the fridge and unmold by gently tapping the mold upside down on a clean surface. (It may take a few runs to get your mold working properly.)

CANDY MOLDS: Silicone candy molds make easy butter molds. Pack the butter into the molds while malleable. Chill for 30 minutes before unmolding.

BUTTER CURLER: Butter curlers are tools with toothed or ribbed metal tips. To use, shape the butter into a bar about the size of an index card. Refrigerate until thoroughly firm, at least 1 hour. When you're ready to curl the butter, dip the butter curler into hot water, then draw it across the surface of the bar. The resulting flake will curl up and around, forming a beautiful spiral. Carefully place the butter flake on a parchment paper–lined baking sheet. Chill until ready to serve. Do not store butter curls for more than 1 day, as they lose their butter flavor.

Ghee

MAKES 1½ CUPS/360 ML

Ghee looks like liquid gold and keeps for months without refrigeration, unlike butter, which goes rancid or changes flavors because moisture trapped inside allows the butter to continue to ferment. Because of this quality, places in warm parts of the globe, including India, the Middle East, and northern Africa, make much use of ghee in their cuisines.

The process for making ghee is nearly identical to making clarified butter, except it gets cooked longer and so gathers a wonderful toasted flavor. I love drizzling ghee over warm basmati rice or using it on the frying pan when I'm making crepes. Because it doesn't have the milk solids, which are what burn, it can be heated hotter than butter.

MILK

BUTTER

FINAL FORM

JAR OR TUB

INGREDIENTS
1 lb/455 g unsalted butter

SPECIAL EQUIPMENT
Fine (#90) cheesecloth

1. Put the butter in a saucepan over low heat. Let the butter melt without stirring. The melted butter should never come to a boil. If it starts to, lower the heat.

2. Cook for 1 to 3 hours, depending on the intensity of your burner. Keep it very low and still do not stir. You will notice foam gathering on top; then, with more time, most of the foam will sink and the liquid will appear perfectly clear. You will also notice a distinct aroma—that of butter browning—rising from the pan.

3. To test the ghee's doneness, use a teaspoon to carefully scoop a small amount of sediment up from the bottom of the pan. The sediment should be light brown—the color of milky coffee. These are the toasted milk solids that flavor the ghee. Take care that you don't overcook them; if they are dark brown or black, the ghee will have the wrong flavor.

4. When the ghee is done, remove it from the heat. Line a colander with the cheesecloth and set the colander over a bowl. Pour the ghee carefully into the colander to strain it. Discard the toasted milk solids left behind. Transfer the strained ghee to an airtight container—I like to keep mine in half-pint jars.

5. Store, tightly covered, at room temperature for up to 2 months, or in the fridge for up to 4 months.

TIME TO COMPLETION
1 TO 3 HOURS

CHAPTER TWO

BEGINNING

cheeses

To me, cheesemaking means standing in the kitchen, next to the stove, stirring. I've stood in one spot in my kitchen for so many hours, I'm surprised the floorboards haven't worn away. I don't detest the stationary nature of the work. Standing and stirring is the only moment during the day when I'm not in fierce motion. The cheese vat, like a polenta pot, calligraphy, or a garden, requires me to slow down and to watch, to commit to a place.

Vat time is neither lonely nor boring. I have stirred the vat and rocked the baby to sleep (he lay in a rocker on the floor and I used my foot). I've stirred and read a magazine or made soup on the next burner. I've stirred and hung out with neighbors, posed for a picture, even caught a robber in the midst of a break-in! While stirring, I've waited for plumbers, scratched "history" off the stovetop, even stirred and hosted a dinner party (bad timing). In this chapter, we move from making cultured dairy products to true cheeses, which means starting to remove water. To do this, for most of the recipes ahead, you are going to start to stir!

Before we really stir things up, though, I'd like to talk about the three main ways milk turns into cheese. Cheese, in all its complexity and variety, can be imagined as milk with a portion of the water removed. To get the water out, we tinker with the chemistry of the milk to cause it to form a gel, which we then break into curds and whey. We can form that gel—or cause milk to coagulate—through three main methods:

1. Direct Acid Coagulation

2. Lactic-Acid Coagulation

3. Rennet Coagulation

I'll outline these three methods now then run-through the basic steps of cheesemaking. You'll soon see that, while every cheese does start with a coagulation (be it direct acid, lactic acid, or rennet), not every cheese passes through each of the basic steps (some cheeses don't get stirred, others don't get heated, many don't get washed). My goal is to give you the big picture of cheese-making so you can start to put cheesemaking processes into chronological order.

DIRECT-ACID CHEESES

Of the paths to get from milk to cheese, this is by far the simplest. Direct-acid coagulation, which produces cheeses such as Paneer (page 74), Whole Milk Ricotta (page 80), and Mascarpone (page 81), is really an outlier process. This is because you won't even use cultures (so in turn, the cheese is not actually fermented). Instead, you'll combine heat with a splash of acid to cause the milk to "break" into curds and whey. If you can imagine a cream sauce you've accidentally "broken" through heating and adding lemon juice, you can imagine how direct-acid cheeses come about. These cheese recipes are a great place to start if you don't have rennet on hand (and want to start making cheese right away) or if you want a cheese that is ready almost instantly. Direct-acid cheeses are always eaten fresh and always taste of simple milky goodness. They are never stinky.

LACTIC-ACID CHEESES

If you've played around with any of the recipes in chapter one, you've practically already made lactic-acid cheeses. This path from milk to cheese is the next simplest one after direct acid. The process entails making a gel (basically a yogurt), moving slivers of this gel into a cheese form, then allowing the cheese to drain with gravity and time. The finished product is a cheese with tangy flavor and often a creamy, crumbly, brittle, smooth texture. Think of Chèvre (page 82). While versions of lactic-acid cheeses can be aged, the ones you'll make in this chapter are best when fresh. Later, you'll make more ageable versions when you make the semi-lactic-acid-set Gosling (page 134) and Stilton (page 140).

BASIC RENNETED CHEESES

And now, the final and main road cheesemakers take to get from milk to cheese: using cultures and rennet to get the milk to coagulate. This method is the most common and likely because it leads to the greatest variety in flavors, textures, and shapes.

While you do use a few drops of rennet to make goat's-milk and Icelandic yogurts, chèvre, fromage blanc, and cream cheese, these are not considered

4 hours later

6 hours later

"rennet-coagulated" cheeses because their long ripening period (often a couple of hours to as long as a day) allows the cultures lots of time to create lots of lactic acid. It is this acid, more than that drop of rennet, that causes the coagulation and subsequent transformation into curd.

Just to recap: You can take any of these paths to move from milk to cheese. While I've broken the coagulation process out into three distinct paths or methods, it isn't quite that simple. Many cheeses really fall somewhere in between lactic-acid and rennet coagulation (I'll categorize them as "semi-lactic"). As you move through the recipes of this book and grow more familiar with the processes of cheesemaking, you'll be able to see what it means to use a little more rennet or a little more time to form a little more lactic acid. Or vice versa.

CHEESEMAKING BASICS

Here's an outline of the basic steps of cheesemaking. Remember that we're thinking about lactic-acid and rennet-coagulated cheeses here, and not so much the direct-acid cheeses.

COAGULATE THE MILK

The first step of cheesemaking is to cause the milk to turn from a liquid to a solid state—to form that milk gel. If you are making yogurt, you stop here. But if you're making cheese, you take further steps to draw some of the water out. After coagulating the milk, the next step is to draw the water out by scooping, slicing, or cutting the curd.

CUT THE CURD

Coagulation transforms milk into a solid yogurt-like or panna cota–like gel. In some recipes, you will scoop this gel directly into forms to drain—the cuts formed by the scooping spoon being parallel to what you will do with a curd knife in other recipes. You'll practice this direct scooping when you make Quark, chèvre, and fromage blanc.

Often, when the gel is scooped directly into forms (that is, not cut first into cubes and stirred and cooked), it is because the curd was made by lactic-acid coagulation, or more a lactic-acid than a rennet coagulation. Curds (and so cheeses) resulting from mainly lactic-acid coagulation are more brittle—they couldn't stand up to the aggressive cooking and stirring action used when making, say, a Havarti.

Ways to Turn Milk into Cheese

CHEESEMAKING STYLE	METHOD	EXAMPLES
Direct-Acid Coagulation	Add acid directly to hot milk to create dense curds that separate from the whey.	ricotta, paneer
Lactic-Acid Coagulation	Add cultures to milk to make a yogurt-like gel, then drain slowly over many hours. Binding of proteins happens because of the effects of the lactic acid and less the effects of the rennet.	chèvre, traditional cottage cheese
Cultured-Rennet (also called Standard-Rennet) Coagulation	Add rennet and cultures to milk to form a gel, then cut and stir to release whey. Binding of the proteins is due to the combined effects of both the lactic acid generated by the cultures and the rennet.	most cheeses, including semifirm, firm, molded, and rinded styles like cheddar, Jack, Brie, Gouda, and blues

Alternatively, if you take a cheese knife or harp and cut the gel into cubes or chunks, you are probably working with a more rennet-driven coagulation. Renneted milk creates a curd that is firmer, more malleable, and shinier than a lactic-acid curd, and, at times, nearly rubbery, depending on the type of milk, the amount of rennet, and how long the rennet has set.

Curds formed from rennet have a wider range of ways in which they are manipulated, which is why the majority of cheeses we eat are made through the rennet-coagulation method. While direct- and lactic-acid curds are scooped and drained, rennet-coagulated curds can be cut, stirred, cooked, washed, stretched, cheddared, and pressed. As assortment of these additional steps is partially what leads to the great variety of cheeses found throughout the world. Using a rennet coagulation lets us drive out moisture in more thorough and complex ways.

START TO STIR

For many recipes (and specifically those using a rennet coagulation), after cutting the curd, you will stir. Stirring the curds reminds me of putting wet clothes on the spin cycle in the washing machine. As the machine spins, water droplets are flung out. The same happens as you stir the vat: Motion tosses out whey. As the curds lose moisture, they shrink and tighten.

ADD HEAT

With many cheese styles, you will use heat to shrink the curds further and to create cheeses that can be aged longer. Think of a Swiss or an Asiago, cheesemakers cook these styles at heats as high as 120°F/49°C—and that's hot, for cheesemaking. Other cheeses are cooked but more minimally—maybe to 95°F/35°C. When cooking curds, know that heating more slowly at first (for example creeping up 10°F/5°C over 45 minutes) will flush more of the water out than heating quickly (for example, jumping 10 degrees in 10 minutes).

Sometimes a cheesemaker adds heat not by putting the pot over a flame but through a washing step (you'll get to practice when you make the Divino on page 106). Here, you'll remove a portion of the whey from the vat and replace it with warmer water to increase overall vat temperature.

DRAIN THE WHEY

Finally, separating the curds from the whey, or draining the cheese, feels, in most recipes, like draining a pot of pasta. When the curds are "done," remove the pot from the heat and dump its contents through a colander. Initially, you will rely on the guidance the recipe offers for determining the right moment to drain; but eventually, you'll become familiar with how your vat is progressing, and you will start to drain based on how the curd is feeling in your hand—a rough estimation of moisture content and acidity development.

In some recipes—and especially if you are working with a very large volume of milk—you'll want to wait a moment between realizing the curd is "done" and actually dumping the vat. This brief pause of a minute or two is known as "pitching." It allows the curds to sink to the bottom where they start to knit together into larger clumps. At this point, in recipes such as Mountain Top (page 180), you will "pre-press" the curds while they are still in the whey, settling at the bottom of the vat. Pre-pressing tightens the curds into large, dense chunks. These you can move out of the whey and right into the forms.

Separating the curds from the whey is the final major step of the vat phase of cheesemaking. It is significant because after the curds pack together into one wheel (or many smaller wheels or even just a draining pouch of cheesecloth), you can no longer wring more moisture out of the curds through heat and stirring. The moisture and chemistry trapped inside each tiny curd is set and will only be moderately affected by the upcoming processes of pressing, salting, even aging. Because of this, in spite of all that transpires in the brine or on the rinds or in the caves, many cheesemakers say, "The cheese is made in the vat."

APPLY PRESSURE

Once the curds are out of the pot and collected in a lined cheese form, you can begin to press (if the recipe calls for it). Not all cheeses are meant to be pressed, but those that are pressed turn out drier and firmer (the pressing pushes out more whey and compacts the curds into a tighter arrangement. Pressed cheeses are almost always aged for a length of time. The purpose of pressing is to push the curds together into one complete shape, usually a wheel, with a nicely sealed rind.

The shape and style of your cheese form determines how your cheese will drain and how effectively you can press it. If you put curds in a form with large and numerous pores, the cheese will drain more quickly and be drier. If you put the cheese in a form with very few holes, it will have more moisture. Cheeses that are meant to be pressed must be "dried" sufficiently in the vat and then coupled with the right cheese form. You could never press a cheese that has the texture of soft yogurt—the curds would simply squirt out the pores of the form! Luckily, matching up a recipe with the right form is a more forgiving task than you think. I make Brie all the time in my ricotta basket, and just about everything else in my Kadova (Gouda-shaped) form. (See page 224 for more information on cheese forms.)

When you press, apply weight by degrees, depending on the cheese you are making. For the lightest pressing, start with just your fingertips or a small book. Progress until you are pressing moderately or heavily, as you'll do with cheeses in chapter eight. When you get to heavy pressing, you will need a form that has a follower as well as a way to apply up to 50 lb/25 kg of weight. Milled cheeses, such as a Traditional Cheddar (page 156), can use even more weight than that! During pressing, be sure to take the cheese out of the press to flip regularly, making sure the cheese is pressing symmetrically and that folds of cheesecloth are not getting lost inside the wheel.

And remember, some cheeses are not pressed at all. These are the ones you should start with if you feel uncertain about having the right form, follower, or weights on hand. (See page 224 for ideas on how to press.)

ADD SALT

Finally, you'll drive more of that water out through salting. Salting is accomplished either by dry salting or by brining. The salting phase can start either after the cheese has been pressed or before, in the vat, after draining (as you'll practice when you make the Queso Fresco, page 91). Salting can take anywhere from a few seconds (throwing 1 tsp of salt into a pot of ricotta) to half an hour (think small, high-moisture cheeses such as Camembert) to even months (this is the extreme and takes place with very large format, professionally made cheeses). You will brine or dry-salt most of the cooked and pressed cheeses in this book for about half a day.

From this point forward, the only way that more moisture leaves the cheese is through aging. Initially, during the drying period, a cheese loses moisture to the atmosphere through ordinary evaporation. The drying period, Days 0 through 3, is when the cheese forms its rind. Interestingly, once this rind forms, your focus will start to shift from thinking about "getting the water out" to "keeping the water in." This is not something that you'll have to worry about with the upcoming recipes for fresh cheese, but something that will become very interesting later, in chapter eight, as you make aging cheeses and struggle to keep the humidity high in your aging cave.

GRAPE HAZELNUT PINTO LENTIL

CURD SIZES

CLARIFYING SOME CHEESE SLANG

The following three recipes are excellent beginner cheeses. They are delicious almost right out of the vat—or aged for a few weeks. As you work your way through them, you'll see several procedures that may have come up in earlier recipes but here are used regularly.

Stir in an up-and-down motion.

Though it may seem like cheesemaker lore, stirring your vat in one particular fashion has scientific reasoning behind it. Instead of stirring in a circular or whisking motion, move your skimmer up and down as though it is riding a Ferris wheel. In this way, you slow down the velocity of the moving liquid (which prevents tender curds from breaking) and you also lift curds up from the bottom where the heat is most intense (preventing them from sticking or scorching).

Stop the motion of the milk.

After adding the rennet and mixing it in, it is critical to stop the movement of the milk. If the milk is slowly swirling as the rennet starts to set, it will not form a solid gel but a broken, feathered gel that is marked by the pattern of the turning fluid. I add the rennet, stir for 20 seconds, counter-stir for 5 seconds, then remove the skimmer from the vat and cover the pot.

Allow the milk to ripen.

Allowing milk (or curds) to "ripen" is an easy step; it simply means leaving the vat alone. Mainly you'll ripen the milk once the cultures have been added but you'll also practice ripening on the stretched-curd recipes of chapter seven. If the temperature is correct, the microorganisms go to work, producing lactic acid and getting you just where you want to be.

Check for a clean break.

Using the "clean break" test is one way to determine when to cut the curd. Insert your clean fingers or a spoon at a 45-degree angle into the milk. Pull gently upward and note how the curd splits. If it breaks open into a clean fissure, it is ready to cut. (See page 218 for more on the Clean Break Method.)

Cut the curds into hazelnut-size cubes.

The goal when cutting the curd is to form same-size pieces. The size of these pieces helps determine how much moisture will be in the finished cheese. The smaller the cut, the drier the cheese. I will use common household foods such as lentils and hazelnuts for size reference.

Allow the curds to heal.

Once you've made the initial cuts in the curd, pause for 2 minutes for what is known as the "healing period." Before your very eyes, you will see the vat change as yellow whey weeps out from the places where your knife made cuts. Within the course of this brief period, a once flat white surface will become a sea of white squares floating in whey.

Pitch the curds.

When your curds have reached a target texture and pH (which you'll estimate initially using just time and temperature), it is time to pitch them. This funny term refers to the last leg of the (vat) journey when you stop stirring and allow the curds to settle to the bottom. At this point, you may be pressing them into tighter blocks under the whey (pre-pressing), or you may start pouring the whey off the top and transfer the curds to form(s) immediately.

PANEER

MAKES ABOUT ¾ LB/340 G

MILK

ALL TYPES

FINAL FORM

SMALL WHEEL

CATEGORIES

DIRECT-ACID

This direct-acid cheese from India is the most basic cheese you can make. It is bland, firm, and waiting to absorb delicious flavors from the dish it gets cooked into, such as the very popular *saag paneer*.

INGREDIENTS

1 gal/3.8 L milk

½ cup/120 ml fresh lemon juice, strained, plus 2 tbsp or 2½ tsp citric acid powder dissolved in 1¼ cups/300 ml warm water

SPECIAL EQUIPMENT

Cheesecloth; digital kitchen thermometer

1. Clean all surfaces and equipment before beginning. Rinse the cheesecloth in hot water and wring out. Line a colander with the cheesecloth and place in the sink.

2. Pour the milk into a heavy-bottomed stockpot and warm over medium-high heat to 195°F/91°C, while stirring. The milk will become frothy on top and look like it is getting close to boiling when it is near the correct temperature.

3. Once at temperature, remove the pot from the heat and add the ½ cup/120 ml lemon juice or 1 cup/240 ml of the citric-acid solution all at once. Stir very slowly for 1 minute. White chunks of cheese should appear immediately in the milk. These are the curds separating from the whey.

4. If the milk does not start separating into white clumps and greenish whey right away, add the remaining 2 tbsp lemon juice or ¼ cup/60 ml citric-acid solution.

5. Now bring the pot to the sink. Add cold tap water to the curds and whey, being careful to not lose curds if the liquid in the pot spills over. The goal is to bring the temperature of the pot down to 115°F/45°C. (If the cheese is placed in the cheesecloth while still very warm, it will stick.)

6. Pour the curds and whey into the colander and drain for 1 minute, then gather the corners of the cloth and knot them together to form a pouch (see page 220).

7. Twist the pouch to wring out more whey, then open up the cheesecloth, flip the cheese so the top becomes the bottom, and close to make a pouch again (this ensures that the cheese is gathered into one ball instead of an obscure shape with lots of folds).

8. Slide the pouch onto the faucet neck of the sink, or run a dowel or long-handled spoon under the knots and set over a pot so the pouch is suspended freely inside. Let drain for 1 hour. (For a firmer cheese, after draining, place the cheese pouch between two dinner plates. Place a 10-lb/4.5-kg weight on top of the upper plate; see page 220. Press for 2 hours more.)

9. Remove the cheese from the cloth and place in a bowl of cool water for 2 hours. This washing period draws out additional lemon juice and will give the cheese a sweeter taste. It is best to use paneer the day you make it, but it will keep, tightly wrapped, in the freezer for up to 1 month.

NOTE

- *Paneer will not melt because it doesn't have the right level of acidity. Don't plan to use it in a quesadilla or grilled cheese. Also, because this cheese doesn't use rennet, it is vegetarian friendly and a source of protein for vegetarians in the Indian subcontinent.*

- *Because paneer contains neither salt nor cultures, it will go bad quickly if left in the fridge.*

ACID SUBSTITUTION IN DIRECT-ACID CHEESES

Students often ask me about substituting acids—vinegar can have gluten; someone has a lemon tree they'd love to utilize; tartaric acid seems foreign. Substituting one form of acid for another is possible, but it will take some fiddling. Acids come in different strengths and forms (dry crystals versus liquid), and the amount of casein protein—what's absorbing that acid—in a given milk will vary, meaning the amount of acid you'll need will also vary. The following chart gives you a ballpark sense of how acids compare to one another. If you plan on substituting, I suggest first making the recipe with the acid called for in the recipe then altering.

Lemon Juice	6 to 8 tbsp/ 90 to 120 ml
Citric-Acid Powder	1 tsp
Tartaric-Acid Powder	1¼ tsp
White Vinegar (5%)	8 to 10 tbsp/ 120 to 150 ml

MAKES ABOUT ¾ LB/340 G

MILK

NONE—FRESH
WHEY

FINAL FORM

MEDIUM WHEEL

CATEGORIES

DIRECT-ACID

As the title suggests, rather than starting with milk, this ricotta is made with just the whey leftover from another cheese recipe. In addition to providing a delicious use for something that would otherwise go to waste, it has a special delicate texture and taste.

Two important things to note: This recipe will work best with whey from any of the cheeses in Chapters 3, 4, 6, 7, and 8. It will *not* work with whey from a lactic acid–set cheese such as chèvre or Quark. Also, no more than 3 hours can pass between the draining of the cheese recipe and the start of the ricotta recipe. The whey is active, and the longer it sits the more the cultures within break it down. After a certain point, the whey proteins will no longer link up to form clusters of cheese.

Because the yield on whey ricotta is low (sometimes less than 5 percent), you'll want to start this recipe with as much whey as you possibly can. This is the recipe to go to after you make a 4-gal/15-L batch of Asiago (page 183) or Traditional Cheddar (page 156), for example; if you have more than 2 gal/7.5 L of whey, bump up the amounts below accordingly and use it all!

INGREDIENTS

2 gal/7.5 L fresh whey

1 cup/240 ml milk (any type)

2 tbsp salt

¼ tsp citric-acid powder dissolved in
  1 cup/240 ml water (see Note)

SPECIAL EQUIPMENT

Fine (#90) cheesecloth, medium cheese form, or ricotta basket; digital kitchen thermometer

1. Clean all surfaces and equipment before beginning. Line a colander with the cheesecloth and place in the sink.

2. Pour the whey into a heavy-bottomed stockpot, cover, and warm over high heat to 160°F/71°C, stirring occasionally.

3. At 160°F/71°C, add the milk and salt. Continue stirring and heating. As foam gathers, skim it from the top of the vat. Important: Do not add the milk until the whey reaches 160°F/71°C, or it will react with residual rennet.

4. Heat to 190°F/88°C, then quickly mix in the citric-acid solution. Stir rapidly for 5 seconds, then stop stirring while continuing to heat. Look for tiny white grains or clumps forming in the liquid. These clumps should come together quickly and form a cover over the top of the vat.

CONTINUED

TIME TO COMPLETION

1

HOUR

5. When the cheese layer that has formed at the top of the vat looks thick and dense and then suddenly the surface of it breaks open from built-up steam underneath, turn off the heat.

6. Let the curds rest in the pot for 10 minutes, then ladle into the prepared colander or cheese form. Drain for at least 15 minutes and up to 1 hour, depending on the desired dryness.

7. Transfer to a well-sealed container and store in the fridge for up to 1 week. Ricotta goes bad quickly, so enjoy it sooner than later.

NOTE:

- *When making whey ricotta, the amount of acid you need varies more than when making Whole Milk Ricotta (page 80). If you think your whey is more acidic (because of the nature of the cheese it came from, for example, or because it sat for a long time before you started the ricotta recipe), start with less citric acid and then slowly add more until you see the protein clumps forming. When you have hit the correct amount of acid, the whey left behind should look semiclear, not overly milky but not translucent either. The resulting cheese ideally is tender and sweet and not tough and tangy.*

TWO TYPES OF RICOTTA

Whey ricotta, also called *ricatone*, is perhaps the truest form of ricotta because, per its name, it is "re-cooked"—an ingenious way to get two cheeses out of one batch of milk. The first cooking happens when a batch of cheese is made; the second when the resulting whey is made into ricotta. The magic works because the average cheese recipe, while it does gather a percentage of the solids from the milk used, also leaves a lot of solids behind. The frugal farmer or thrifty cheesemaker wouldn't dump these extras away—especially when the milk has been hard-earned, as most farmstead milk was and is. Whey ricotta has a caramelized flavor (because it's cooked twice), a delicate texture, and is leaner, because much of the fat gets caught in the first round of cheese.

But there are more types of ricotta than just whey ricotta and whole milk ricotta. There is also true whole milk ricotta—ricotta made only with milk and not with whey. You might find it sold in old-fashioned tins at Italian delis. Or it might have to be something you have to make for yourself (using the recipe on page 80) as it isn't always easy to find. True whole milk ricotta is a fuller, richer cheese that reminds me of soft mozzarella almost as much as it makes me think of ricotta. It is made through a method similar to paneer; mixing acid directly into hot milk.

Interestingly, if you increase the amount of milk fat in your whole milk ricotta recipe, you nearly end up with mascarpone. This cheese, best known as an ingredient in tiramisu, is essentially whole milk ricotta made entirely from cream. Hopefully you are starting to see how the direct-acid cheeses are all quite similar: paneer is nearly whole milk ricotta but with different temperatures and different amounts of acid. Whole milk ricotta is nearly mascarpone but with different milk fats. Whey ricotta is the same process as whole milk ricotta but with a different base ingredient.

MAKES ABOUT 1¼ LB/570 G

MILK

ALL TYPES

FINAL FORM

MEDIUM WHEEL

CATEGORIES

DIRECT-ACID

TIME TO COMPLETION

1

HOUR

Whole milk ricotta is a great standby recipe, one to "take on the road" as a little bit of citric acid is easy to pack and the recipe works with any milk you can find (whole, skim, ultra-pasteurized, raw, etc.). Whole milk ricotta is more curd-like and milky than whey ricotta but equally delicious.

INGREDIENTS

1 tsp citric-acid powder, dissolved in ⅓ cup/75 ml warm water
1 gal/3.8 L whole milk
3 tsp salt

SPECIAL EQUIPMENT

Fine (#90) cheesecloth; digital kitchen thermometer

1. Clean all surfaces and equipment before beginning. Rinse the cheesecloth in hot water and wring out. Line a large colander with the cheesecloth and place in the sink.

2. Divide the citric-acid solution between two bowls. Set aside.

3. Pour the milk and 1½ tsp of the salt into a heavy-bottomed stockpot or the top pan of a double boiler and warm over medium heat to 190°F/88°C, stirring gently and constantly. It is very important to use a heavy pot for this recipe. Do not walk away from the pot; if you stop stirring the milk, it will easily start to stick and burn and the damage is irreparable. If the milk starts to scorch on the bottom of the pot, your only option is to immediately transfer the milk into a new pot and then continue heating.

4. At 190°F/88°C, pour one bowl of citric-acid solution into the center of the pot. Stir for 5 seconds, then remove from the heat. Cover and let rest for 20 minutes. During this period, curds will form and rise to top of the liquid. Do not stir or agitate. Make sure the heat is off.

5. Using a perforated ladle or skimmer, transfer the curds to the prepared colander. Drain for at least 15 minutes and up to 30 minutes, depending on the desired dryness.

6. After removing the curds, return the pot to medium heat. Stir in the remaining 1½ tsp salt, proceeding from step 4 forward; let rest and then drain the curds as before. The second yield of ricotta will be larger than the first. After draining, transfer to a well-sealed container and store in the fridge for up to 1 week. Ricotta goes bad quickly, so enjoy it sooner than later.

MAKES ABOUT 4 OZ/115 G

While making mascarpone is very similar to making ricotta, it is also more subtle. When the curds break out of the liquid, you have to get your nose right down next to the vat and squint your eyes. The curd particles are so fine (unlike the larger, more obvious chunks you see when making ricotta), you'll need to use a double layer of fine (#90) cheesecloth when draining. Otherwise, your decadent cheese will slip through the weave and down the drain.

MILK

HEAVY CREAM

FINAL FORM

JAR OR TUB

CATEGORIES
DIRECT-ACID

INGREDIENTS

4 cups/960 ml heavy cream, preferably 40% milk fat and at least 35%

¼ tsp tartaric-acid powder or ¾ tsp citric-acid powder, dissolved in ¼ cup/60 ml warm water

SPECIAL EQUIPMENT

Fine (#90) cheesecloth; digital kitchen thermometer

1. Clean all surfaces and equipment before beginning. Rinse three 20-in/50-cm squares of cheesecloth in hot water and wring out. Line a colander with the cheesecloth, making a triple layer. Nest the colander over a bowl.

2. Pour the cream into the top pan of a double boiler and warm over simmering water to 195°F/91°C, stirring occasionally.

3. When the cream reaches 195°F/91°C, remove from the heat and remove the top pan from the bottom pan of the double boiler to make sure the temperature of the cream stops rising.

4. Add the acid solution to the cream and slowly stir for 3 minutes, or until you see it begin to break or curdle very slightly. It should have the consistency of Cream of Wheat. Stop stirring.

5. Carefully ladle the cream into the prepared colander. Wrap the whole draining setup inside a plastic bag and transfer to the refrigerator. Let drain for 10 to 12 hours, depending on the desired thickness of the mascarpone. (Covering the whole contraption with the plastic bag will prevent unwanted flavors from getting into the cheese while it drains.)

6. Spoon the mascarpone into an airtight container, cover tightly, and store in the fridge for up to 3 days. This cheese is very, very perishable, so plan to use it quickly.

TIME TO COMPLETION
1
DAY

MAKES ABOUT 1 LB/455 G

GOAT'S MILK

FINAL FORM

LOOSE-PACKED
TUBS OR LOGS, OR
SMALL WHEELS

CATEGORIES

LACTIC-ACID

TIME TO COMPLETION

2

DAYS

Although the word *chèvre* ("goat" in French) is about as specific a term as *queso fresco* ("fresh cheese" in Spanish), it has come to mean the spreadable or crumbly fresh white cheese made from goat's milk we all know so well. I adore this cheese and remember eating it every morning for breakfast on toast with olive oil and ripe tomatoes when I lived on a goat farm.

INGREDIENTS

1 gal/3.8 L goat's milk

2 tbsp cultured buttermilk

1 drop CaCl₂

1 drop rennet

Salt

SPECIAL EQUIPMENT

Digital kitchen thermometer; medium or fine (#60 or #90) cheesecloth or 3 small cheese forms, about 3 in/7.5 cm in diameter and 4 in/10 cm in height

1. Clean all surfaces and equipment before beginning.

2. Pour the milk into a heavy-bottomed stockpot and warm over medium heat to 76°F/24°C, stirring occasionally (it should only take a minute or so to reach temperature). Remove from the heat.

3. Pour the buttermilk directly into the warm milk. Stir gently for 1 minute, using an up-and-down motion.

4. While stirring, add the CaCl₂, then the rennet. Stir for 30 seconds, then stop the motion of the liquid. Cover the pot and set in a warm, agitation-free place for 12 to 18 hours.

5. When the curd is set, you should see yellowish whey collecting at the sides of the pot. Also look for an aromatic smell when you lift the lid. When pressed softly with a fingertip, the curd should be a tiny bit springy but break under slightly more pressure. Proceed with draining according to whether you'd like shapes or loosely packed tubs of cheese.

FOR LOOSE-PACKED TUBS OR LOGS: Rinse the cheesecloth in hot water and place over a colander set over a bowl or in the sink. Scoop the curds from the pot into the cloth. When all curds are in the colander, make a pouch by tying the corners of the cheesecloth together. Run a dowel or a long-handled wooden spoon under the knots and set over a pot so the pouch is suspended freely inside. Allow to drain at room temperature for 10 to 12 hours. For more rapid draining, gently shake the pouch to open up new channels for the whey to drain out about halfway through the draining time. Next, transfer the curds to a large bowl. Using your hands or a potato masher, mix the cheese to redistribute the moisture and homogenize the curd. Add salt slowly to taste, stirring well as you do. Finally, pack the finished cheese into tubs or handroll into logs. Cover tightly and store in the fridge for up to 2 weeks.

FOR FORMED CHEESES: Instead of scooping the curds into a cheesecloth pouch, set cleaned cheese forms on a draining rack set in the sink. (Remember that the volume of the form must accommodate the bulkiness of the initial curd. Your final cheese will be smaller as whey drains off.) Scoop the curds into the forms, making sure to fill each up to the top before starting to fill the next. When all the forms have been filled, let drain for about 1 hour. Gently flip so the top becomes the bottom, then continue draining. Drain at room temperature for 10 to 12 hours.

After draining, sprinkle the top of each cheese with ¼ tsp salt. Let the salt soak in for 2 hours, then flip the cheeses and salt the other side, again about ¼ tsp each. If desired, roll in herbs or apply vegetable ash for an interesting rind aesthetic.

MAKES ABOUT 1 LB/455 G

MILK

ALL TYPES
(NOT ULTRA-
PASTEURIZED)

FINAL FORM

TUBS OR LOGS

CATEGORIES

LACTIC-ACID

TIME TO COMPLETION
2
DAYS

This recipe will lead you to either *fromage blanc* or Quark. The cheeses are very similar, differing only in the type of cultures you might use, as well as the fat content of the starting milk. If you don't love the goatiness of chèvre, these are great alternatives for you to make (and eat). Quark, in particular, also works nicely as a lower-fat substitute for cream cheese.

INGREDIENTS

1 gal/3.8 L milk (Quark tends to be made from lower-fat milks; fromage blanc can be made with full-fat milk or a partially skimmed one)
2 tbsp cultured buttermilk
2 drops CaCl$_2$
2 drops rennet
Salt

SPECIAL EQUIPMENT

Fine (#90) cheesecloth; digital kitchen thermometer

1. Clean all surfaces and equipment before beginning. Rinse the cheesecloth in hot water and wring out. Line a colander with the cheesecloth and place it in the sink.

2. Pour the milk into a heavy-bottomed stockpot and warm over medium-high heat to 86°F/30°C, stirring occasionally. Remove from the heat.

3. Pour the buttermilk directly into the warm milk. Stir gently for 20 seconds.

4. While stirring, add the CaCl$_2$, then the rennet. Stir thoroughly for several seconds longer, then stop the motion of the liquid. Cover the pot and set in a warm, agitation-free place for 10 to 12 hours.

5. When the curd is set, you should start to see it pulling away from the sides of the pot. You may notice whey gathering a bit on the top and sides.

6. Gently scoop the curds from the pot into the prepared colander. When the colander is full, make a pouch by tying the corners of the cloth together. Run a dowel or a long-handled wooden spoon under the knots and set over a pot so the pouch is suspended freely inside.

7. Let the cheese drain at room temperature for 8 to 10 hours. For a less acidic cheese, you can drain in the fridge instead. For best draining results, shake the pouch to open up new channels for the whey to drain out about halfway through the draining time. (You'll notice when you empty the pouch that the curds closer to the cloth are much drier than the curds in the middle.)

8. When the curds have drained sufficiently (longer if you want a drier cheese and for less time if you want it more moist), transfer to a large bowl. Using your hands or a potato masher, work the cheese to redistribute the moisture and homogenize the curd. Add the salt slowly to taste. Store in airtight containers in the fridge for up to 2 weeks.

MAKES ½ LB/225 G
(MORE CHEESE IF LIGHTLY
DRAINED, LESS CHEESE IF
WELL-DRAINED)

MILK

HALF-AND-HALF

**SUGGESTED
CULTURE**

AROMA B OR
BUTTERMILK

FINAL FORM

LOOSE-PACKED TUB

CATEGORIES

LACTIC-ACID

TIME TO COMPLETION
2
DAYS

Store-bought cream cheese is very different from this rendition—because the store-bought one is stabilized with gums. The gum gives it a super-smooth, almost chewy texture. This cheese will be grainier, but wonderful. It is slightly richer than fromage blanc (see page 84).

INGREDIENTS

2 qt/4 L half-and-half
**⅛ tsp prehydrated mesophilic cultures
    or 2 tbsp buttermilk**
2 drops CaCl₂
2 drops rennet
Salt
¼ cup/60 ml heavy cream (optional)

SPECIAL EQUIPMENT

**Medium or fine (#60 or #90) cheesecloth;
digital kitchen thermometer**

1. Clean all surfaces and equipment before beginning. Rinse the cheesecloth in hot water and wring it out. Line a large colander with the cheesecloth and place it in the sink.

2. Pour the half-and-half into a heavy-bottomed stockpot and warm over medium heat to 82°F/28°C, stirring occasionally. Remove from the heat.

3. Pour the prehydrated cultures directly into the warm half-and-half. Stir gently for 20 seconds.

4. Still stirring, add the CaCl₂, then the rennet. Stir for 10 seconds longer, then stop the motion of the liquid. Remove from the heat. Cover the pot and set in a warm, agitation-free place for 12 to 14 hours. When the cream has set, it will look like solid cream cheese.

5. In a saucepan, heat 1 qt/1 L water to 170°F/77°C. Meanwhile, with a long, clean knife, roughly chop the curd into 1-in/2.5-cm pieces.

6. When the water is hot, while gently stirring, pour it over the curd pieces. Stir very gently for 1 minute, then check that the final temperature of the mixture is at least 130°F/54°C. Remove from the heat. This washing step removes some of the acid and stops the bacteria from further acid production.

7. Gently scoop the curds from the pot into the prepared colander. If needed, form a pouch (see page 220) and suspend it over a pot or bowl. Drain at room temperature for 8 to 12 hours, depending on the desired thickness (more time makes drier curds). You can expedite the draining process by shaking the bag to move the curds around slightly midway through the draining time.

8. Unwrap the cheese from the cheesecloth and place in a bowl. Using a whisk or wooden spoon, whip the curds to smooth the texture, then beat in the salt to taste. If desired, you can also beat in the heavy cream for an even smoother, richer texture.

9. Store in an airtight container in the fridge for up to 10 days.

BAKER'S VS. COTTAGE VS. FARMER'S VS. POT

From a cheesemaker's perspective, baker's, cottage, farmer's, and pot cheeses are nearly identical; they just use varying amounts of acid, moisture, butterfat, and pressure. Moreover, these titles refer, really, to a broad range of styles, many of which overlap. I've done my best to sort out what each cheese is best known for as well as to give ideas for how to vary the pot cheese recipe (page 88) to make each.

BAKER'S CHEESE. Arguably identical to finely milled pot cheese, baker's cheese is very fine grained and used to make cheesecakes. Your best bet for a baker's cheese mimic is Cream Cheese (facing page).

COTTAGE CHEESE. Freshly made cheese curds that, after being rinsed with cold water to maintain distinction between curds, can be mixed with cream or a thickened low-fat milk base.

CALIFORNIA-STYLE COTTAGE CHEESE. After draining and cooling the curds, transfer to a large bowl. Add 2 cups/480 ml light cream. Use a whisk or an electric mixer to beat together the curds and cream at low speed until light and fluffy, 1 to 2 minutes. Season with salt. Using less cream will make a drier cheese.

FLAVORED COTTAGE CHEESE: Try mixing the master recipe for pot cheese with fresh fruit such as strawberries or pineapple chunks. Mix in lemon juice, lemon zest, powdered sugar, and vanilla for something even more delicious. After flavoring your cheese, serve immediately.

FARMER'S CHEESE. Nearly identical to pot or cottage cheese, but made using more of a lactic-acid than a rennet set. When made entirely from a lactic-acid set (little to no rennet), farmer's cheese becomes Neufchatel. Farmer's cheese can mean very different things depending on what part of the country you're in. Midwesterners have a firm farmer's cheese, more like a Jack (see page 152). Easterners know farmer's cheese as something closer to cottage cheese.

POT CHEESE. A cheese midway between cottage cheese and farmer's cheese, with curds that are often less distinct than cottage cheese curds. You can achieve this by hand-milling some of the curds when adding the salt. Pot cheese isn't remixed with cream, so it stays drier.

MAKES 1½ TO 2 LB/680 TO 910 G

MILK

UNHOMOGENIZED

FINAL FORM

LOOSE-PACKED TUB
OR LOGS

When I think of pot cheese, I think of Borough Park in Brooklyn where Gita, my best friend's ancient Jewish grandmother, lived. Gita always had fresh pot cheese in her fridge, which she ate on toast with raspberry jam. Sometimes she put it on her mashed potatoes. Traditionally, before the advent of non-animal rennet, pot cheese and other traditional Jewish cheeses were made using only cultures (a purely lactic-acid coagulation). Today, pot cheese and other kosher cheeses are usually made using non-animal rennets.

INGREDIENTS
2 gal/7.5 L unhomogenized milk
4 tbsp cultured buttermilk
½ tsp CaCl₂ diluted in ¼ cup/60 ml water
½ tsp rennet diluted in ¼ cup/60 ml water
3 to 4 tsp salt

SPECIAL EQUIPMENT
Medium or fine (#60 or #90) cheesecloth; digital kitchen thermometer

1. Clean all surfaces and equipment before beginning. Rinse the cheesecloth in hot water. Line a large colander with the cheesecloth and place it in the sink.

2. Pour the milk into a heavy-bottomed stockpot and warm over medium heat to 94°F/34°C, stirring occasionally. Remove from the heat.

3. Pour the buttermilk directly into the warm milk. Stir in gently.

4. Cover the pot and let the milk ripen for 1 hour.

5. Uncover the pot and stir in the CaCl₂ solution and then the rennet solution, stirring for about 20 seconds each. When both have been added, stop the motion of the milk.

6. Cover the pot and let rest for 40 minutes. After 40 minutes, check for a clean break (see page 218). If there isn't one, let the milk sit for 10 to 15 minutes more.

7. Cut the curd into hazelnut-size pieces, about ¾ in/2 cm (see page 219). Let the curds heal (or rest) for 2 minutes, then begin stirring gently. Start at the top of the pot and move downward. When all curds are in motion, turn on the heat to low.

8. Stir and cook the curds for 30 minutes as you bring the temperature of the pot up to 110°F/43°C. Do not let the temperature rise too quickly. The curds will shrink significantly during this time. When the pot reaches temperature and time, remove from the heat. Pitch the curds (see page 73) for 5 minutes.

TIME TO COMPLETION

1

DAY

9. Pour the contents of the pot into the prepared colander, then quickly run cold tap water over all the curds, tossing so the cold water reaches everywhere (like running cold water over hot pasta to stop it from sticking together). Continue to cool with running water until the curds are cool to the touch, 1 to 2 minutes. Let drain for about 20 minutes longer, stirring midway through the draining time.

10. Gather the ends of the cheesecloth together to form a pouch (see page 220). Twist to squeeze out a bit more whey, then transfer the curds to a large bowl.

11. Add salt to the curds ½ tsp at a time, until you reach the saltiness you like. (The more salt you add, the longer the cheese will last.)

12. Pack the curds loosely into containers or continue to mash the curds until you can press them into loose logs. Store in the fridge for up to 5 days.

MAKES 1½ TO 2 LB/680 TO 910 G

There are hundreds of versions of *queso fresco* made throughout Latin America. This one, which I learned from my Guatemalan friend Arturo, is sweet and crumbly. Arturo is a quiet cheesemaker, and he explained his recipe to me while leaning over at the waist into a large vat of curds, his hands gripping and fiercely milling all of them into delicate paste. I always felt that the care with which Arturo milled the curds was why the cheese tasted so good.

This cheese, though in many ways a version of Pot Cheese (page 88), is sweeter due to a short ripening time (just 10 minutes) and less cultures. In villages where this cheese is made, often no cultures are added because the milk is raw and therefore already cultured from native bacteria from the air, the milk room, and other local surfaces.

MILK

UNHOMOGENIZED

FINAL FORM

FREE-FORM WHEEL

CATEGORIES
LACTIC-ACID

INGREDIENTS

2 gal/7.5 L unhomogenized milk
2 tbsp buttermilk
½ tsp CaCl₂ diluted in ¼ cup/60 ml water
½ tsp rennet diluted in ¼ cup/60 ml water
2 to 3 tbsp salt

SPECIAL EQUIPMENT

Medium or fine (#60 or #90) cheesecloth or medium cheese form; digital kitchen thermometer

1. Clean all surfaces and equipment before beginning. Rinse the cheesecloth with hot water and wring it out. Line a large colander with the cheesecloth and place it in the sink.

2. Pour the milk into a heavy-bottomed stockpot and warm over medium heat to 90°F/32°C, stirring occasionally with an up-and-down motion. Remove from the heat.

3. Stir in the buttermilk. Cover and let the milk ripen for 10 minutes.

4. Now stir in the CaCl₂ solution and then the rennet solution, stirring for 20 seconds after each.

5. Cover the pot and let the rennet set for 30 minutes. After 30 minutes, check for a clean break (see page 218). If there isn't one, let the milk sit for 10 to 15 minutes more.

6. Cut the curd into hazelnut-size pieces, about ¾ in/2 cm (see page 219). Let the curds heal for 2 minutes, then begin stirring gently. Start at the top of the pot and move downward. When all the curds are in motion, turn on the heat to low. Stir and cook the curds for 20 minutes as you bring the temperature of the pot up to 95°F/35°C.

CONTINUED

TIME TO COMPLETION

1 DAY

7. Once at 95°F/35°C, remove from the heat. Pitch the curds (see page 73). Pour off the whey from the top of the pot, then pour the curds into the prepared colander (save the whey to make Whey Ricotta, page 76, if desired). Let curds drain in the colander for 1 minute, then return the curds to the pot.

8. Add the salt to the curds, 1 tbsp at a time. After each addition, with clean hands, toss the curds in the pot to mix in the salt and also squeeze the curds through tightened fists—"hand-milling." Continue adding salt and hand-milling until the curds are salted to your taste and perfectly fluffy.

9. Cover the pot to try and maintain the heat for 20 minutes more. This ripening period lets the salt soak in and allows more whey to be released.

10. Finally, transfer the curds back to the colander lined with cheesecloth (or a cheese form with a follower). Gather the ends of the cloth and twist to wring out more whey. Knot the ends of the cloth to form a pouch (see page 220) or pack into prepared cheese forms. If using a cheese form, use your fingertips to pack into place. Flip the cheese within the first 5 minutes, then return to the form. Wrap the wheel tightly and store in the fridge for up to 1 week.

FIRMER CHEESE: For a slightly firmer cheese, press the pouch lightly (about 10 lb/4.5 kg of weight) for 10 minutes, then open up the cheesecloth and flip the cheese over so the top becomes the bottom. Return the cheese to the cheesecloth and press for an additional 30 minutes at medium pressure (about 20 lb/9 kg). The longer you press, the drier and firmer the cheese becomes. Pressing is not necessary, however.

MAKES 1½ TO 2 LB/680 TO 910 G

MILK

UNHOMOGENIZED

SUGGESTED CULTURE

BUTTERMILK OR TA60

FINAL FORM

MEDIUM WHEEL

CATEGORIES

LACTIC-ACID

TIME TO COMPLETION

2 WEEKS

Bel Paese, meaning "beautiful country" in Italian, is similar to a soft "pizza mozzarella" (meaning the Cultured Mozzarella on page 174, not the Quick Mozz on page 168). When you cut it, a sticky, creamy residue remains on the knife. It is best enjoyed at 2 to 3 weeks, although you can age it for up to a month, if you'd like.

If you'd like to age it, the best way to do so, especially if you add jalapeño flakes, is to seal it in a vacuum bag and store it in the fridge. You can also let the cheese dry for a day at room temperature, then dip it in cheese wax. If you don't have the equipment for these two options, be adamant about keeping the rind rubbed down and clean. Store the cheese on an aging mat in an aging bin. Turn daily and wash, regularly, with a light brine. Scrape away spots of undesired molds as needed.

This recipe is different from Pot Cheese (page 88) and Queso Fresco (page 91), because you add the rennet when the milk is particularly warm. You also salt the cheese in a brine *after* it has been pressed instead of before, in the vat. Though this is a fresh cheese, it is best if ripened for a week or two. That said, it is right on the border between a fresh cheese and a ripened one. It is wonderful and highly likely to jog a memory for someone who eats it.

INGREDIENTS

2 gal/7.5 L unhomogenized milk

2 tbsp buttermilk or ¼ tsp prehydrated thermophilic culture

½ tsp CaCl₂ diluted in ¼ cup/60 ml water

½ tsp rennet diluted in ¼ cup/60 ml water

¼ cup/35 g jalapeño chile flakes (optional)

Saturated brine (see page 221)

SPECIAL EQUIPMENT

Medium cheese form, with follower; loose or medium (#40 or #60) cheesecloth to fit the form; digital kitchen thermometer; aging mat and bin

1. Clean all surfaces and equipment before beginning. Set up a draining station by lining a clean form with cheesecloth and placing it on a draining rack in the sink. Place a colander in the sink as well.

2. Pour the milk into a heavy-bottomed stockpot and warm over medium heat to 106°F/41°C, while stirring. Remove from the heat.

3. Add the buttermilk and stir in gently. Cover the pot and let the milk ripen for 10 minutes.

4. Add the CaCl₂ solution and stir in. Add the rennet solution, stirring for 20 seconds.

5. Cover the pot and let the rennet set for 30 minutes. After 30 minutes, check for a clean break (see page 218). If there isn't one, let the milk sit for 10 minutes more.

6. Cut the curd into grape-size pieces, about 1 in/2.5 cm (see page 219). Let the curds heal for 2 minutes, then begin stirring gently, gradually gaining speed and cutting large pieces as they rise to the top. Stir the pot for 30 minutes. The curds will shrink significantly during this time, even though the temperature will stay the same.

7. Pitch the curds (see page 73) for 5 minutes.

8. Drain off the whey from the top of the pot (save it for the Whey Ricotta on page 76, if desired), then pour the curds into the colander. Let drain for 1 minute, then transfer to the prepared cheese form. If using the chile flakes, sprinkle these in while filling the form with curds. Distribute the flakes as evenly as possible.

9. When all the curds are in the form, cover with the cheesecloth, then the follower. Using your hands and body weight, press down on the cheese for 2 minutes, then open up the form and flip the cheese so the top becomes the bottom.

10. Redress the cheese (see page 220) and press with very light weight (about 5 lb/2.3 kg) for 5 hours. Flip and redress the cheese at least once during this time period.

11. Remove the cheese from its form and place in the brine for 3 hours. Make sure the temperature of the brine is near 65°F/18°C, and cover any exposed part of the cheese—the part floating above the brine surface—with salt.

12. Afterward, remove the cheese from the brine and let it dry at room temperature on the aging mat for 1 to 2 days, covered with cheesecloth. Flip regularly to encourage even drying. Later, vacuum-seal (see page 33) or wax dip (see pages 222 to 223). Age for 2 to 3 weeks, ideally at 55°F/13°C or at regular fridge temperature for longer. Enjoy the cheese by 6 weeks of age.

VARIATION

BEER-RIPENED BEL PAESE: *To create a different version of Bel Paese, omit the jalapeño flakes. After brining and drying the cheese, move it to a clean aging bin with an aging mat inside. Place the aging bin in a 55°F/13°C cave or aging area. Wash the cheese daily for the first week using a clean cloth dipped in pale ale–style beer, blotting up any built-up moisture from beneath the aging mat and from around the corners of the bin each day.*

After 1 week, start to wash every third day. Prevent the cheese from becoming too wet by removing built-up moisture from the bin and by washing only the top and side parts of the cheese (not the bottom where the moisture will be trapped). If the cheese seems too dry, wash more often. After 2 weeks, the rind should begin to have a fragrant yeasty smell and feel sticky when touched—this is what you are looking for. Age for up to 2 weeks longer. Then enjoy!

MAKES 1½ TO 2 LB/680 TO 910 G

MILK

UNHOMOGENIZED

SUGGESTED CULTURE

FETA MIX MT1

FINAL FORM

SQUARES, STORED IN BRINE

CATEGORIES

BRINED, SEMI-LACTIC ACID SET

This cheese is a good one to make early in your cheesemaking adventures. It requires little time at the vat, doesn't need an aging cave, doesn't need a press, doesn't need a special cheese form, and is ready to eat after several weeks, although you can continue aging it for months, even years more, if you want.

This cheese is the only one in *Kitchen Creamery* that ripens in a brine (all the others are dry-ripened). The secret to a successful feta brining is making sure the acidity of the brine and the amount of calcium ions is balanced. You do this simply by adding white vinegar to the brine solution for the former and $CaCl_2$ for the latter. In this way, a feta brine is different then the brine used to salt cheeses later in this book.

INGREDIENTS

2 gal/7.5 L unhomogenized milk (goat's or sheep's milk, or a combination, is ideal but not required)

¼ cup/60 ml cultured buttermilk or ⅛ tsp prehydrated mesophilic culture

Pinch of lipase powder (optional; see Note)

½ tsp $CaCl_2$ diluted in ¼ cup/60 ml water

½ tsp rennet diluted in ¼ cup/60 ml water

½ cup/115 g salt

Feta Brine (page 99), chilled

SPECIAL EQUIPMENT

Medium or large cheese form (preferably square, no follower); digital kitchen thermometer; medium (#60) cheesecloth; large jar with lid or other airtight container

1. Clean all surfaces and equipment before beginning. Set up a draining station by placing the clean form on a draining rack in the sink. (It is not necessary to line the cheese form with cheesecloth.)

2. Pour the milk into a heavy-bottomed stockpot over medium heat and warm to 84°F/29°C, stirring occasionally. Remove from the heat.

3. Add the buttermilk and stir using an up-and-down motion. If you want a more pungent flavor to your feta, sprinkle in the lipase. Cover the pot and let the milk ripen for 30 minutes.

4. Stir in the $CaCl_2$ solution and then the rennet solution, stirring for 20 seconds after each.

5. Cover the pot and let the rennet set for 40 minutes. Check for a clean break (see page 218). If there isn't one, let the milk sit for 10 minutes more.

6. Cut the curd into grape-size pieces, about 1 in/2.5 cm (see page 219). Let the curds heal for 2 minutes, then begin stirring gently, starting near the top of the vat and moving downward.

CONTINUED

7. Stir for 5 minutes, then place the pot over medium-low heat and bring the temperature up to 88°F/31°C over the course of 20 minutes, while stirring constantly. Remove from the heat.

8. Pitch the curds (see page 73) for 5 minutes.

9. Drain off the whey from the top of the pot and pour the curds into the prepared form or a colander. After the first 5 minutes of draining, flip the cheese block so that the top becomes the bottom. Cover the cheese with a piece of cheesecloth, then let the cheese rest, in the sink, draining freely, for the next 10 to 15 hours (more time if the ambient temperature is cool, less time if it is warm). You do not need to flip or refrigerate the cheese during this period. By the end of this ripening period, the cheese should smell cheesy (especially if you added the lipase) and be semifirm to the touch.

10. Take the cheese out of its form and cut into 2-in/5-cm chunks (this is why a square draining form works best). Set the chunks back in the form or colander and sprinkle heavily with the salt. Cover again with the cheesecloth and allow to drain, at room temperature, for another 24 hours. In total, your cheese will drain at room temperature for nearly 40 hours.

11. Finally, arrange the feta cubes neatly in the large jar with a tight-fitting lid. Add enough of the chilled brine to cover thoroughly. Push down on the cheese to make sure it is submerged below the surface of

the brine, using a weight if needed. If the cheese pokes above the surface of the brine, it will become moldy and off-flavored.

12. Place the jar in a 60°F/15°C or cooler location for up to 5 months. You can also store the jar in the fridge for up to 1 year. Keep checking to confirm that the cheese stays submerged. Remove any molds that develop on the brine surface.

NOTE

- *Lipase is often used to get cow's-milk cheese to taste closer to the flavor of goat's or sheep's milks. Lipase is always an animal product, something to note if you are vegetarian.*

FETA BRINE

MAKES 1 GAL/3.8 L

This simple brine has a couple of secret ingredients to make it the perfect bath for your feta. I reuse my brine over the course of months and many batches of feta, filtering the brine between each use. You can also boil it before setting up a new cheese, if you want to be certain not to cross-contaminate. I store my brine, when it's not in use, in a closed jar in the fridge. When I'm ready to make a fresh brine batch, I'll finish off the old stuff by using it to brine a chicken.

INGREDIENTS

1 gal/3.8 L water
1 lb/455 g kosher or pickling salt
1 tbsp CaCl$_2$
1 tsp white vinegar

1. In a saucepan over high heat, bring the water to a boil. Remove from the heat and let cool to 100°F/38°C.

2. Pour the salt into a clean container with about a 1-gal/3.8-L capacity. (I use an old glass pickle jar.)

3. Add the boiled water to the container and stir for several minutes to dissolve the salt. Stir in the CaCl$_2$ and vinegar. Chill the brine in the refrigerator for at least 1 hour (ideally to 60°F/15°C) before using as directed.

NOTES

- *If you are planning on aging your feta for more than a month, use pH strips (see page 33) to confirm the brine acidity. The pH should be between 4.8 and 5.2. If it isn't, you will need to lower the pH by adding more vinegar or raise the pH with baking soda.*

- *If you intend to age your cheese for a longer period, a safe bet is to use a saturated brine (see page 221), which is stronger than this brine recipe. The saturated brine will make the cheese saltier than is pleasant to eat. When you are ready to eat the feta, draw some of the salt out of it by placing the cheese in cool water for 1 to 2 hours beforehand. Change the water during this time as much as you can to encourage the extraction. Pat the cheese dry before serving.*

CHAPTER THREE

WASHED-CURD

Cheeses

By "washing the curds" in the vat—or rather removing a portion of the whey and replacing it with water—you produce a softer cheese with an often glistening, elastic paste. Think of young Gouda and its chewy texture. Sometimes the replacement water is the same temperature as the whey you removed. Other times, it is warmer; in which case you'll be cooking as well as washing the cheese. The cooler the wash water, the more moisture retained in the final curd. The more moisture in the final curd, the softer the cheese will be.

On a microscopic level, washing lowers the amount of lactose, or milk sugar, in the vat. Lactose becomes more concentrated inside the curd and less in the surrounding whey once you add the water. This creates a concentration gradient. As you stir, the lactose moves out of the curd and into the whey, equalizing the concentration difference. Since the cultures in the vat feed on the lactose, and because they are trapped in the curds, they now have less to eat and so will produce less acid. This process produces a sweeter, less tangy or sharp cheese.

WITH AND WITHOUT EYES

The washed-curd cheese style includes a number of cheeses, some with classic "Swiss eyes" and some with eyes that aren't considered Swiss. Those cheeses that use *Propionic* bacteria, a specific gas-producing bacteria, will have the signature large, round eyeholes and classic "Swissy" taste. Other openings or eyes in the Dutch-style cheeses that aren't accompanied by that distinct Swiss flavor are small, more irregularly shaped, and caused by other bacteria or the mechanics of how the curds settled into their final form. You can have several different types of eyes or openings in one cheese.

In this chapter, you'll be using *Propionic* bacteria to make the Rising Moon (page 111). You'll use *Propionic* bacteria, later, when making the Gruyere-style cheese, Mountain Top (page 180). With both of these recipes, the initial aging temperature is a key to success. For the first three weeks, age at 50°F/10°C or cooler. Next, move the cheese to a warmer location of at least 70°F/21°C for three weeks more. Finally, finish ripening at 55°F/13°C for another two to five months. Giving the cheese a cool period followed by a warm period allows the *Propionic* bacteria to prosper. If you leave the cheese in an area too warm initially, there'll be an overproduction of gas. If you leave the cheese in an area too cold for too long, you'll have no eyes at all.

PREHYDRATING FREEZE-DRIED CULTURES

Prehydrating your freeze-dried cultures is identical to waking up bread yeast—with some heat, some food, and some moisture, the organisms come alive. It is extremely helpful to prehydrate any DVI ("Direct Vat Inoculant")—also known as freeze-dried—cultures. Two hours before beginning your batch of cheese, take 1 cup/240 ml of warm (about 86°F/30°) milk (just grab it from the milk you'll be using) and sprinkle the freeze-dried cultures over the surface. Wait 2 minutes for them to hydrate, then stir in. Hold this cup in a warm location for up to 2 hours, and ideally no less than 1 hour before adding it to the vat when called for in the recipe. When using store-bought or homemade kefir, buttermilk, or yogurt as the inoculant, no prehydration is necessary.

MAKES ONE 1-LB/455-G WHEEL

MILK

UNHOMOGENIZED

SUGGESTED CULTURES

MA11 OR MM 100

FINAL FORM

MEDIUM WHEEL

CATEGORIES

WASHED-CURD

TIME TO COMPLETION **6** WEEKS

This Havarti is a pleasant, easy cheese. What's special about the recipe is you'll be adding a small amount of salt right to the vat, before draining off any whey—something you'll do only in this recipe. This early salt makes the cheese mild. To spice things up, you can wash the rind of your Havarti to turn it into a Tilsiter (see page 122). This is also the first recipe where you'll start to determine when to cut the curd based on a flocculation point.

INGREDIENTS

2 gal/7.5 L unhomogenized milk
¼ tsp prehydrated mesophilic cultures
½ tsp CaCl₂ diluted in ¼ cup/60 ml water
½ tsp rennet diluted in ¼ cup/60 ml water
½ cup/115 g salt
Heavy brine (see page 221)

SPECIAL EQUIPMENT

Medium cheese form, with follower; loose or medium (#40 or #60) cheesecloth; digital kitchen thermometer

1. Clean all surfaces and equipment before beginning. Set up a draining station by lining the cheese form with wet cheesecloth and placing it on a draining rack in the sink.

2. Pour the milk into a heavy-bottomed stockpot and warm over medium heat to 91°F/33°C. Remove from the heat.

3. Pour the prehydrated cultures into the milk and stir gently. Cover the pot and let the milk ripen for 40 minutes.

4. Add the CaCl₂ solution and stir. Add the rennet solution. Stir for 20 seconds. As you add the rennet, start a timer and watch for the flocculation point (see page 218). When reached, stop the timer. Multiply the number of minutes elapsed by 3.5. This is how long you need to wait before you cut the curd. Goal time is 35 to 40 minutes.

5. At the timed moment, cut the curd into hazelnut-size pieces, about ¾ in/2 cm (see page 219). After cutting, let the curds heal for 2 minutes.

6. Begin to stir slowly, starting at the top of the pot and gradually working the curds into motion. Cut up any large chunks that float up from below using the side of the skimmer or spoon. Gradually increasing in speed, stir the curds for 10 minutes, then stop stirring and let the curds settle.

7. To begin the washing process, remove 2 qt/2 L whey from the pot and replace it gradually (2 to 3 minutes) with an equal amount of 165°F/74°C water, stirring constantly to avoid scorching. The final temperature in the pot should be 100°F/38°C and the

end volume should be the same as the amount you started with. (The temperature of the pot is more important than the exact volume of liquid, though both affect the final product.)

8. Stir constantly for 5 minutes, then add the salt directly to the pot. Stir to dissolve the salt, and then stir every 3 minutes or so over the next 30 minutes. The curds should feel spongy and springy to the touch.

9. Pitch the curds (see page 73) briefly, then drain off the whey, collecting the curds in a warmed colander. Quickly transfer the warm curds to the prepared form and cover with the cheesecloth and follower.

10. Press the cheese with your fingertips for 5 minutes. Unwrap the cheese, flip, redress, and then press under medium weight (10 to 15 lb/4.5 to 6.8 kg) for 30 minutes. Flip the cheese one last time, then leave in the press under medium weight for 4 to 5 hours.

11. Remove the cheese from the form and place in the brine to cover for 2 hours. (Brine for less time if using smaller forms.)

12. Remove the cheese from the brine and air-dry on a clean aging mat at room temperature for 2 days, turning regularly to encourage even drying. While drying, cover with the cheesecloth to protect the surface from dust and airborne contaminants.

13. When the cheese has dried, proceed with cheese- or cream-waxing, or choose another rind treatment (see pages 222 to 223). Store on an aging mat in an aging bin at 55°F/13°C for 6 to 8 weeks.

INTRODUCING THE FLOCCULATION POINT

One big difference between the beginning recipes and the advanced ones is that in the advanced ones, you will be cutting the curd based on a flocculation point—a measure of how long it takes for the milk to turn from a liquid to a solid—instead of cutting based on a prescribed number of minutes or a "clean break" test. The Flocculation Method is a more accurate way of determining when to cut because it accommodates the variables of milk, cultures, and the environment better than a simple timetable. A few of the following recipes still gauge when to cut by a distinct number of minutes but most use the Flocculation Method. For how to judge the Flocculation point, see page 218.

(GOUDA STYLE)

MAKES ONE 3- TO 4-LB/1.4- TO
1.8-KG WHEEL

MILK

UNHOMOGENIZED

**SUGGESTED
CULTURES**

FLORA DANICA
PLUS LM57

FINAL FORM

LARGE WHEEL

CATEGORIES

WASHED-CURD,
WAXED

TIME TO COMPLETION

4

MONTHS

I named this cheese after the cheese Divine Providence made by Narragansett Creamery, a family-run creamery that I helped to establish in 2007. For the launch party, we invited everyone we knew to a small wine shop in the city's downtown. It was December and brutally cold. Wind whipped through the street, but inside, people were warm, standing shoulder to shoulder. Wine flowed and lights twinkled. Finally, after a few speeches, the mayor took the podium with a double-handled cheese knife. On a cutting board in front of him sat a wheel of what was to be the state's first cheese (since all earlier creameries had become extinct).

There was perfect silence as the mayor held the knife and began to cut. The wheel opened and inside several eyeholes garnished a creamy, dense paste—stars in the night sky. He took one bite, smiled widely, and the crowd burst into applause.

INGREDIENTS

4 gal/15 L unhomogenized milk
½ tsp prehydrated mesophilic cultures
⅛ tsp prehydrated LM 57 cultures
¾ tsp CaCl₂ diluted in ¼ cup/60 ml water
¾ tsp rennet diluted in ¼ cup/60 ml water
Saturated brine (see page 221)
Salt

SPECIAL EQUIPMENT

Large cheese form, with follower; loose or medium (#40 or #60) cheesecloth to fit the form; digital kitchen thermometer; cheese press or other pressing setup; cheese wax

1. Clean all surfaces and equipment before beginning. Set up a draining station by lining the cheese form with wet cheesecloth and placing it on a draining rack in the sink.

2. Pour the milk into a heavy-bottomed stockpot and warm over medium heat to 86°F/29°C, stirring occasionally.

3. When at temperature, pour the prehydrated cultures into the milk and stir, using an up-and-down motion. Cover the pot and let the milk ripen for 20 minutes.

4. Add the CaCl₂ solution and stir. Add the rennet solution. Stir for 20 seconds, then stop the motion of the milk. As you add the rennet, start a timer and watch for the flocculation point (see page 218). When reached, stop the timer. Multiply the number of minutes elapsed by 3. This is how long you need to wait before you cut the curd.

5. At the timed moment, cut the curd into hazelnut-size pieces, about ¾ in/2 cm (see page 219). After cutting, let the curds heal for 2 minutes.

CONTINUED

6. Begin to stir slowly, starting at the top of the pot and gradually working the curds into motion. Cut up any large chunks that float up from below (especially important when working with a larger volume of milk). Stir for about 20 minutes; during this time, you'll notice the curds shrinking significantly. After 20 minutes, stop stirring and allow the curds to settle.

7. To begin the washing process, remove about 20 percent of the total volume of whey in the pot, taking care to not remove any curds (and making sure you don't remove *more* than 20 percent). Replace the whey with an equal amount of 140°F/60°C water, adding it slowly and stirring the entire time to give each curd a similar exposure to the heat. The goal is to raise the temperature of the pot to 100°F/38°C. If you get to this temperature before you've finished adding water to replace the whey, finish off with 100°F/38°C water. If you've added all the water and the temperature is below 100°F/38°C, place over low heat and bring up the temperature while stirring.

8. When the vat is at the right volume and temperature, stir for another 40 minutes. When finished, check to see if the curds are ready by grabbing a fistful. They should clump into one mass but fall back apart easily if you try and crumble them with your fingertips. If they aren't crumbling appropriately, stir for another 15 minutes and try again.

9. Pitch the curds (see page 73) for 5 minutes. With clean hands, reach into the vat and press downward into the curd mass. Press well with your hands for 3 to 5 minutes, helping the curds to start to fuse together. Afterward, pour off the whey from the vat (save it to make Whey Ricotta, page 76, if desired) until you see the curd block at the bottom.

10. Grab chunks of the curd block with both hands and move them to the prepared cheese form set up in the sink. Fill the form with all the curds, then tug on the cheesecloth to tighten. Fold the loose ends over the top and apply the follower.

11. Immediately apply medium weight (15 lb/ 7 kg) for 10 minutes, then remove the weight. Take the cheese out of its form, unwrap, and flip the cheese so the top becomes the bottom. Rewrap and continue pressing at medium weight.

12. After 1 hour, increase the pressure to heavy weight (25 to 30 lb/11 to 14 kg). Leave the cheese under the heavy weight for 2 to 3 hours if making a young cheese (up to 3 months), or 8 to 10 hours if making an aged cheese (up to 10 months). While pressing, make sure the cheese doesn't slide out of place. Also make sure folds of cheesecloth are not lost inside the pressing wheel.

13. After pressing, unwrap the cheese, transfer to a pot, and add the brine to cover. Brine for 6 to 8 hours, sprinkling dry salt over parts that float above the surface. Flip the wheel once midway through.

14. Afterward, air-dry the cheese on a drying rack, covered with a piece of cheesecloth, at room temperature for 2 days. Flip regularly. Make sure the drying temperature stays near 65°F/18°C.

15. When the rind feels dry but still barely moist, the cheese is ready to be coated with cheese wax or cream wax, or vacuum sealed.

16. Age at 55°F/13°C for at least 3 months and up to 1 year.

VARIATION

CUMIN GOUDA: *Follow the recipe through step 8. Before you start to drain the whey, in a small saucepan combine ¼ cup/35 g cumin seeds and water to cover and bring to a boil. Cook for 2 minutes. Strain, discarding the boiling water, and set the seeds aside. Pour the whey out of the pot until only the curd block remains. Using your hands, crumble the curds into walnut-size chunks, then quickly mix in the cumin seeds. Transfer to the prepared form and proceed as directed.*

CLASSIC YELLOW-COLORED GOUDA: *Add ⅛ tsp liquid annatto to the milk prior to adding the rennet (step 4). The curds will be a light yellow while in the vat but become a progressively deeper yellow as the wheel ages.*

RISING MOON
(JARLSBERG STYLE)

MAKES ONE 3- TO 4-LB/1.4- TO
1.8-KG WHEEL

This cheese contains eyes that form from the gas-producing bacteria *Propionibacterium freudenreichii* subsp. *shermanii*. These special microorganisms also create that distinct flavor I think of as "Swissy." I love to cut open a wheel of Rising Moon because the inside always surprises me (even though I know what's going to be there). It's also a good cheese to make with lower-fat milk, if desired. Exchange 1 gal/3.8 L skim milk for an equal amount of the whole milk. Make this cheese in the largest batch size possible (4 gal/15 L being the minimum). For a successful eye formation, your wheel should be a minumim of 4 in/10 cm tall (and no more than 7 in/18 cm) with a minimim diameter of 6 to 8 in/ 15 to 20 cm. With this style of cheese in particular; the bigger the batch, the better. Don't halve this recipe.

INGREDIENTS

4 gal/15 L unhomogenized whole or part-skim milk

½ tsp prehydrated thermophilic cultures

⅛ tsp prehydrated *Propionic* bacteria powder

¾ tsp $CaCl_2$ diluted in ¼ cup/60 ml water

¾ tsp rennet diluted in ¼ cup/60 ml water

Saturated brine (see page 221)

Salt

SPECIAL EQUIPMENT

Medium cheese form, with follower; loose or medium (#40 or #60) cheesecloth to fit the form; digital kitchen thermometer; cheese press or other pressing setup

1. Clean all surfaces and equipment before beginning. Set up a draining station by lining the cheese form with wet cheesecloth and placing it on a draining rack in the sink.

2. Pour the milk into a heavy-bottomed stockpot and warm over medium heat to 91°F/33°C, stirring occasionally.

3. When at temperature, turn off the heat and add the prehydrated thermophilic and propionic cultures to the milk. Stir in, then cover the pot and ripen for 45 hours.

4. Add the $CaCl_2$ solution to the milk and stir. Add the rennet solution. Stir for 20 seconds, then stop the motion of the milk. As you add the rennet, start a timer and watch for the flocculation point (see page 218). When reached, stop the timer. Multiply the number of minutes elapsed by 3. This is how long you need to wait before you cut the curd. Goal time is 25 to 30 minutes.

5. At the timed moment, cut the curd into lentil-size pieces, about ¼ in/6 mm. After cutting, let the curds heal for 2 minutes.

CONTINUED

UNHOMOGENIZED;
WHOLE MILK OR
PART SKIM

SUGGESTED CULTURES

TA60 OR 61 PLUS
PROPIONIC
BACTERIA

FINAL FORM

LARGE WHEEL

CATEGORIES

WASHED-CURD
WITH EYES,
SWISS-STYLE

TIME TO COMPLETION
4 MONTHS

6. Starting gently but slowly increasing in speed, stir the curds for 20 minutes, cutting up large chunks that float up from below. After 20 minutes, let the curds settle for 5 minutes.

7. To begin the washing process, remove 1 gal/15 L whey from the top of the pot and replace it gradually (over the course of 2 to 3 minutes), with an equal amount of 145°F/63°C water, stirring continuously to give all curds equal exposure. The final temperature in the pot should be 100°F/38°C and the end volume should be the same amount you started with. (The temperature of the pot is more important than the exact volume of liquid, though both affect the final product.)

8. Turn the heat to low and raise the temperature to 108°F/42°C over the course of 30 minutes, stirring gently and continuously. Do not heat too quickly. Stir briskly enough that the curds don't mat on the bottom of the vat. After 30 minutes and when at temperature, turn off the heat and pitch the curds (see page 73) for 5 minutes.

9. With clean hands, reach into the vat and gently move the curds together into a block. Press on the block for 2 to 3 minutes, then pour off the whey until you see the surface of the curds. With both hands, transfer the curds quickly to the prepared cheese form. Pull the ends of the cheesecloth to tighten, then cover the cheese with the follower.

10. Press at medium weight (15 lb/7 kg) for 30 minutes, flipping once after 5 minutes to make sure the cheese is pressing symmetrically.

11. After 30 minutes, take the cheese out of the press, remove the cheesecloth, flip, rewrap, and press again but now more heavily (25 to 30 lb/11 to 14 kg) for 10 to 12 hours.

12. Remove the cheese from the press. Place in the brine for 6 to 8 hours. Sprinkle dry salt on exposed surfaces. Flip half way through the brining.

13. Remove the cheese from the brine and dry on an aging mat at room temperature, covered with cheesecloth, for 2 to 3 days, turning regularly. When the rind feels dry but still the slightest bit moist, coat with cheese wax or cream wax or vacuum-seal.

Alternatively, after the cheese has air-dried, rub with oil (vegetable or olive) and place on an aging mat inside an aging bin. Flip and oil daily for the first 2 weeks, then biweekly for the next 3 to 4 months. Remove molds using a piece of coarse cheesecloth dipped in salt brine or a stiff bristled brush. Make sure there is plenty of air and that the cheese does not get too moist.

14. Regardless of the rind treatment, for the first 3 weeks, age at 50°F/10°C or cooler. Next, move the cheese to a warmer location of at least 70°F/21°C for 3 weeks more. Finally, finish ripening at 55°F/13°C for 2 to 5 months more.

REGULAR EYES

WHEN WE PRESS THE CURDS WELL
THEN AGE AT CORRECT TEMPERATURES
WE GET ROUND, REGULAR EYES

IRREGULAR EYES

WHEN AIR ENTERS THE CURDS
DURING **HOOPING** THEN WE PRESS
ONLY LIGHTLY, WE FORM A MORE
OPEN TEXTURE WITH SMALLER,
IRREGULAR EYES.

Read THE Eyes

BLIND CHEESE

WHEN EYES FAIL TO FORM
IN A CHEESE WHERE WE
INTENDED FOR THEM, WE CALL
THE CHEESE "BLIND".

SLITS

SLITS OR FISSURES MAY
MEAN THE ACIDITY WAS
LOW OR THE CHEESE WENT
THROUGH TEMP FLUXUATIONS

EDGE HOLES

EYES VERY CLOSE
TO THE RIND MAY
MEAN THE CHEESE
WASN'T PRESSED
PROPERLY.

OVERDEVELOPED

EXTREMELY LARGE EYE HOLES
CAN HAPPEN RANDOMLY OR BE
A SIGN OF CONTAMINATION.

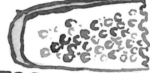

TOO MANY

TOO MANY EYES CAN BE
PREVENTED BY LOWERING
THE AGING TEMPERATURE.

TOO SMALL

VERY SMALL EYES MAY
MEAN THE BACTERIAL
CULTURES WERE
WEAK OR THE AGING
TEMPERATURES
WERE TOO COLD.

TOO FEW

TOO FEW EYES MAY
SIGNIFY OVERSALTING
OR SLOW CULTURES.

EARLY BLOWING

IF CHEESE PUFFS OR EXPLODES
IN THE FIRST 48 HOURS, IT'S LIKELY
CONTAMINED WITH E. COLI BACTERIA.
DISCARD THE CHEESE.

LATE BLOWING

IF CHEESE PUFFS OR EXPLODES AFTER
3 WEEKS OF AGING, IT MAT MEAN
CONTAMINATION BY **PROPIONIC** OR
CLOSTRIDIUM BACTERIA.

HOLES IN CHEESE, CALLED EYES, TELL US ABOUT A CHEESE'S
RECIPE, FLAVOR AND SAFETY. THE EYES FORM WHEN
STARTER CULTURES FERMENT PARTS OF THE MILK TO PRODUCE
CO_2 GAS. THE GAS DISSOLVES INTO THE CURD FIRST THEN STARTS
TO COLLECT AT TINY OPENINGS CALLED NUCLEI SITES. BUILDING
PRESSURE PUSHES THE SITES OPEN INTO LARGER EYES.
CULTURES, TEMPERATURES AND SALT AFFECT NUMBER, SHAPE AND DISTRIBUTION.

CHAPTER FOUR

WASHED-RIND

Cheeses

Washed-rind cheeses—what I'm thinking of when I say "stinky"—are cheeses with red to pinkish rinds resulting from a mixture of surface-ripening bacteria, molds, and yeasts. These cheeses, due in large part to what's on their rinds, mature into soft to semifirm cheeses. The inner paste will range from firm and grainy (younger) to smooth and chewy (middle-aged) to gooey and silky (well-aged) depending both on the recipe and the length of the aging. In the chapter ahead, I'll be covering washed rinds with a semisoft inner paste. Think of a Taleggio or a traditional Muenster.

THE STINKY CHEESES

The lead characters helping to create these stinky cheeses are a type of bacteria called *Coryneform*. Specifically, it's the genuses *Brevibacterium* and *Arthrobacter* that are at work along with many others. Interestingly, similar strains to these bacteria are found on our skin, which is why a washed-rind cheese's "bouquet" sometimes reminds people of stinky feet. For simplicity, I'll refer to these red-rind cultures as *Coryneform* from this point forward.

In addition to *Coryneform* bacteria, another fungal microbe called *Geotrichum candidum* also likes to colonize washed rinds. It's a group you'll meet later when you make a wheel of Camembert. Like *Coryneform*, *Geotrichum candidum* is abundant in the natural environment and can come in numerous different wild and cultivated strains. One reason why one washed-rind cheese may look and taste so different from the next is that we may be sensing the effects of different *Geotrichum candidum* or other microbial strains, even though, broadly speaking, washed-rind cheeses are colonized by roughly the same types of microorganisms.

Finally, in addition to the category of washed-rind cheeses, there are also smear-rinded cheeses. The two categories overlap and should more appropriately be thought of as a spectrum. By some people's categorizations, smear rinds have firmer pastes and are aged longer, such as Mountain Top

on page 180 or a 12-month-old Beaufort. Washed rinds, on the other hand, have softer pastes (because the cheesemaker let the rennet set longer, cut the curd into larger pieces, then cooked and stirred less to create a more moist paste) and are aged for shorter periods. The amount of moisture inside of any cheese and on the rind dictates the nature of the microbial communities—and the successions of microbial communities—that will prosper there. Again, it's that blurry world of cheese categorization—but you get the idea.

MAKE UP YOUR RIND

There are several ways to "catch" a cocktail of flavor-making microorganisms:

Into the Milk

You'll use this method in the recipe for making Marbler (page 118) by adding a pinch of freeze-dried *Coryneform* cultures to the warm milk. It's the same method used to inoculate the bloomy-rinds and blues in chapter five, just different microorganisms. Adding cultures directly to the vat ensures that the organisms have plenty of time to "wake up"—that is, rehydrate—as well as plenty of time to disperse.

Red-Rind Wash

Another way to grow a red rind is to make a tea using the appropriate freeze-dried cultures, then use the tea to wash the cheese. My recipe for Red-Rind Wash is on page 121. Use this solution to regularly rub the rind; it's similar to adding the cultures to the milk in that you have a reasonable idea of what will be growing.

Instead of making up a specific wash, you can also wash the rind with beer, which is thick with sugars and yeasts. I've had a lot of success with this method. It's what you may have practiced when you made the Beer-Ripened Bel Paese variation on page 95. Here's how to do it: At the end of a long day, open a bottle of beer. Pour a bit onto your cheese and while you lovingly tend the rind, wash down the rest of the bottle yourself.

From a Friend

It happens to me sometimes that I "catch a red rind" without intending to. This tells you that you don't even need to purchase *Coryneform* cultures in order to have a red stinker. Sometimes, the cultures that live in the air and naturally land on the cheese are a strain of *Coryneform*. Other times, it may be mixtures of airborne yeasts or other molds that also may form a delicious, stinky rind. Whatever the case, given the correct growing conditions, micro-organisms will go to town.

SUCCESS WITH SUCCESSIONS

Observing the successions of molds, yeasts, and bacteria growing on a washed-rind, bloomy-rind, or natural-rind cheese reminds me of forest succession and how one rapidly growing tree species is inevitably overtaken by another, often slower-growing one. Initial species often prep the environment for the later species by changing the pH or nutrient availability or even just by holding the space and keeping back other populations from crowding in.

Remember this as you work on your washed rind. Your cheese will not turn the color of a peachy sunset the day you make it. Plan to see changes in the rind over the first several weeks. There will be molds and yeasts that stop in, uninvited. They come from the air around you. Keep moving these temporary visitors along by continuing to gently wash or brush the rind. It's okay if other microorganisms pop up— just don't let them move in permanently.

Tending your rind through rubbing and washing (making sure you don't leave the rind too wet) as well as rotating the cheese regularly (flipping top to bottom and checking under the mats for accumulated moisture) allows your cheeses to breathe. It will also keep other populations in check. With patience and diligence, a balance of organisms, including, hopefully, what you've inoculated for, will settle in and call your cheese "home."

AGING ADVICE

Pay the most attention to your washed-rind cheese during the first several weeks of aging. Check on it daily. After you notice the colors and textures of the rind stabilizing—which should be within 3 to 4 weeks—start to flip and wash the cheese just once per week. Here are some other tips.

- Flip your cheese once per day (but not more) to ensure the cheese gets air on all sides. Air will allow the right molds and bacteria to grow. Lack of air will cause the cheese to rot or develop off-flavors.

- Remove accumulated moisture from the aging bin with a clean rag or paper towel.

- Don't open the lid of the aging bin too often (no more than once a day) or all the ambient moisture collected inside the box will be lost and the cheese will dry out.

- Set the lid of the aging bin on lightly, do not snap it down. This allows for moderate airflow. Your cheese will neither suffocate nor dry out if you do this.

- Choose an aging bin that is five times the volume of the cheese. Too small a bin means too little air, and the obvious corollary—too big means too much air.

- Set up ripening cheeses so that they do not touch one another in an aging bin.

- Keep your hands very clean while handling aging cheeses. Think about which surfaces you touch between the sink and the cheese itself. For ease, I keep a box of disposable gloves near "the caves."

- As a general rule, factors that increase the rate of ripening also increase the risk of off-flavor development. This means if you are thinking about speeding up the aging process by increasing the aging temperature, beware. Slow and steady wins the race!

JUDGING RIPENESS

After the proper aging period passes, it is time to decide when to cut your washed-rind wheel. Remember that if you've held your cheese in the fridge or an area colder than the suggested aging temperature, it will need more time. When ripe, this style of cheese should look evenly coated, colorful, and bright. There may be small nicks and spots where other molds tried to grow but on the whole, the rind should be relatively uniform in color. There may be a light white frosting on top of the reddish rind.

You can also get a sense of ripeness by smelling the cheese. If the cheese is *too stinky* and you're not sure it's okay, find that cheesemonger friend and let him or her take a whiff to make sure things are on track.

(MORBIER STYLE)

MAKES ONE 3- TO 4-LB/
1.4- TO 1.8-KG WHEEL

MILK

UNHOMOGENIZED

SUGGESTED CULTURES

MM100,
CORYNEFORM,
AND GEO 13

FINAL FORM

LARGE WHEEL

CATEGORIES

WASHED-CURD,
WASHED-RIND,
ASHED

TIME TO COMPLETION

2

MONTHS

This cheese has a moist, chewy paste with a gorgeous thin black line through the middle. This line of ash makes me think of veins in marble. Marbler was the first of my homemade cheeses that stopped me in my tracks. It looks *that* fancy.

INGREDIENTS

4 gal/15 L unhomogenized milk
½ tsp prehydrated mesophilic cultures
¹⁄₁₆ tsp prehydrated *Coryneform* cultures
¹⁄₁₆ tsp prehydrated *Geotrichum* mold spores
¾ tsp CaCl₂ diluted in ¼ cup/60 ml water
¾ tsp rennet diluted in ¼ cup/60 ml water
½ tsp vegetable ash (see page 28)
Saturated brine (see page 221)
Red-Rind Wash (page 121; you can substitute beer or mead)

SPECIAL EQUIPMENT

Large cheese form, with follower; medium or fine (#60 or #90) cheesecloth to fit the form; digital kitchen thermometer; cheese press or other pressing setup

1. Clean all surfaces and equipment before beginning. Set up a draining station by lining the cheese form with wet cheesecloth and placing it on a draining rack in the sink. Rinse a colander and place in the sink as well.

2. Pour the milk into a heavy-bottomed stockpot and warm over medium heat to 86°F/30°C, stirring occasionally. When at temperature, turn off the heat and pour in the prehydrated cultures. Stir gently, then cover the pot and let the milk ripen for 50 minutes.

3. Add the CaCl₂ solution and stir. Add the rennet solution. Stir for 20 seconds, then stop the motion of the milk. As you add the rennet, start a timer and watch for the flocculation point (see page 218). When reached, stop the timer. Multiply the number of minutes elapsed by 3.5. This is how long you need to wait before you cut the curd. Goal time is 35 to 40 minutes.

4. At the timed moment, cut the curd into pinto bean–size pieces, about ½ in/12 mm (see page 219). After cutting, let the curds heal for 2 minutes, then begin to stir, starting at the top of the pot and moving downward, gently bringing all of the curds into motion.

5. Place the pot over low heat and slowly raise the temperature to 100°F/38°C over the course of 25 minutes. Stir constantly and gently the entire time, making sure the temperature doesn't rise too quickly. If it is rising too quickly, turn off the heat intermittently. At 100°F/38°C, remove from the heat and let the curds rest for 5 minutes.

CONTINUED

6. To begin the washing process, remove 2 qt/2 L of whey from the pot and replace it gradually (2 to 3 minutes) with an equal amount of 100°F/38°C water, stirring gently. When the volume has returned to where you started, stir the curds gently for 5 minutes more, then pitch the curds (see page 73).

7. Reach into the vat and gently move the curds together into a block. Press on the block with your fingertips for 2 to 3 minutes, then pour off the whey until you see the surface of the curds. Drain off the rest of the whey and dump the curds into the colander in the sink. Let drain for 5 minutes.

8. For this next step, work quickly to get the wheel assembled while the curds are still warm. Move half of the drained curds from the colander into the prepared cheese form. Press them down gently with your fingertips. Sprinkle the vegetable ash over the curds, doing your best to distribute the ash evenly. Cover the ash layer with the second half of the curds.

9. Tug on the ends of the cheesecloth to tighten, then cover the cheese with the follower and press immediately with your hands for 2 minutes. After 2 minutes, remove the wheel from the cheese form, flip, redress, and return the cheese to its form. Apply light pressure (10 lb/4.5 kg) to the top of the cheese for the next 12 to 14 hours, making sure the whey continues to drain freely away. Flip every 2 to 3 hours during pressing.

10. Remove the cheese from the press, place in a pot with enough of the brine to cover, and brine in a cool place for 5 hours, flipping the cheese once halfway through. The temperature of the brine should be near 55°F/13°C.

11. Remove the cheese from the brine and let air-dry, covered with a piece of cheesecloth, on an aging mat at room temperature for 2 days or until the rind feels only faintly moist. Flip regularly.

12. Finally, set the cheese on the aging mat inside an aging bin. Place the bin at 55°F/13°C. Let ripen for 8 to 10 weeks, turning the cheese daily for the first week, then twice per week for the ensuing time.

13. Each time you flip the cheese, rub the sides and top with the wash. Do not rub the bottom side; the freshly washed side should always be on top. Make sure the cheese has air on all sides and that the bin is not too moist. Remove unwanted molds by rubbing them away.

14. After 3 to 4 weeks, you should notice a reddish coat establishing on the surface. If not, make a fresh batch of wash or confirm that the cheese has enough humidity and that the temperature is not too cold. After 8 weeks, the cheese will be ready to enjoy, though it can be aged for another 4 to 10 weeks for even more flavor and an even softer inner paste.

RED-RIND WASH

MAKES 1 CUP/240 ML, OR ENOUGH FOR 3 TO 4 RIND WASHINGS

The effects of this wash are similar to what happens when you follow the steps for making a Tilsiter (page 122).

1 cup/240 ml water
1 tsp salt
Pinch of freeze-dried *Coryneform* cultures

1. In a saucepan over high heat, bring the water to a boil. Pour into a clean glass jar. Let cool to room temperature, then add the salt and the cultures. Cover and shake gently to mix. Let stand on the countertop overnight.

2. When flipping and cleaning any cheese when using the wash, create a barrier of cheesecloth between the cheese and the jar. Pour the wash through the cheesecloth and onto the cheese. Do not let the cheesecloth touch the mouth of the jar or the cloth will contaminate the jar's contents with unwanted molds and bacteria. Store unused wash in a labeled jar in the refrigerator for up to 3 weeks.

TILSITER

MAKES ONE 1-LB/455-G WHEEL

SUGGESTED CULTURE

CORYNEFORM BACTERIA CAPTURED FROM STORE-BOUGHT CHEESE

FINAL FORM

MEDIUM WHEEL

CATEGORIES

WASHED-CURD, WASHED-RIND

To make this cheese, you start with a batch of Havarti. Once the cheese has brined and dried, it is ready to grab some character from any delicious and stinky washed-rind cheese you can get ahold of. I offer some suggestions, but it will be best to find something made locally.

INGREDIENTS

1 recipe Havarti (page 104)

4 oz/115 g store-bought red-rinded cheese such as Cowgirl Creamery's Red Hawk, Meadow Creek Dairy's Grayson, or Consider Bardwell's Dorset

SPECIAL EQUIPMENT

Aging mat; cheesecloth; aging bin

1. Remove the cheese from the brine and allow it to air dry on an aging mat at room temperature for 2 days, covered with a piece of cheesecloth.

2. Smear the rind of the purchased washed-rind cheese, as best as possible, evenly over the Havarti's surface. Sprinkle on a bit of water to help with the smearing if the surface is too dry. Alternatively, use a blender to make a paste of the store-bought rind and water. Smear this paste over the cheese surface.

3. Store the cheese on an aging mat inside an aging bin at 55°F/13°C, turning and smearing or washing every 2 to 3 days, for 6 to 8 weeks. As molds grow on the cheese's surface, rub or brush them down. Re-smear with the rind of an established, stinky red-rinded cheese, if needed. Age for 6 to 8 weeks.

TIME TO COMPLETION
6
WEEKS

(APPENZELLER STYLE)

MAKES ONE 3- TO 4-LB/1.4- TO 1.8-KG WHEEL

Zeller is my version of an Appenzeller, a cooked, pressed cheese from Switzerland. I love this recipe because it takes little time—just 3 hours from pot to press. If you have lots of milk but little time, make this recipe.

What makes Zeller unique is personalizing the wash you use to develop the rind. Try and gather herbs that grow near you to give the cheese a special *terroir*. Also unique to this recipe is how you'll cut the curds using a long-handled whisk to get extra-small (lentil-size) curd pieces. The finished cheese has a smooth, dense but creamy paste and few to no "eyes."

INGREDIENTS

4 gal/15 L unhomogenized milk
½ tsp prehydrated thermophilic cultures
¾ tsp CaCl$_2$ diluted in ¼ cup/60 ml water
¾ tsp rennet diluted in ¼ cup/60 ml water
Saturated brine (see page 221)
Herb Wash (page 125)

SPECIAL EQUIPMENT

Large cheese form with follower; cheese-cloth to fit the form; digital kitchen thermometer; cheese press or other pressing setup

1. Clean all surfaces and equipment before beginning. Set up a draining station by lining the cheese form with wet cheesecloth and placing it on a draining rack in the sink. Rinse a colander, line with cheesecloth, and place it in the sink as well.

2. Pour the milk into a heavy-bottomed stockpot and warm over medium heat to 90°F/32°C. Remove from the heat.

3. Add the prehydrated cultures to the milk and stir in gently. Cover the pot and allow the milk to ripen for 1 hour.

4. Add the CaCl$_2$ solution and stir. Add the rennet solution. Stir for 20 seconds, then stop the motion of the milk. As you add the rennet, start a timer and watch for the flocculation point (see page 218). When reached, stop the timer. Multiply the number of minutes elapsed by 2.5. This is how long you need to wait before you cut the curd. Goal time is 20 to 25 minutes.

5. At the timed moment, using a long-handled whisk or curd knife, cut the curd into lentil-size pieces, about ¼ in/6 mm (see page 219). After cutting, let the curds heal for 2 minutes.

6. Starting gently and slowly increasing in speed, stir the curds for 5 minutes, then place the pot over low heat. Begin to raise the temperature to 115°F/46°C; adjust so it takes about 25 minutes to get there.

CONTINUED

SUGGESTED CULTURES

TA 60 OR 61, CORYNEFORM BACTERIA FOR WASH

FINAL FORM

LARGE WHEEL

CATEGORIES

WASHED-CURD, WASHED-RIND

TIME TO COMPLETION
3 MONTHS

7. Once at temperature, remove from the heat. Let the curds settle to the bottom of the pot for 3 minutes, then ladle off about 10 percent of the whey. (This should be about 1½ qt/1.5 L.)

8. Replace the removed whey with an equal amount of 115°F/45°C water. Stir for 10 minutes more, then let the curds settle again to the bottom of the pot.

9. Ladle the whey off the top of the vat, pouring through the prepared colander. Remove the whey until you see the top of the curd block.

10. Press down onto the curd block using your fingertips, encouraging all the curds to gather into one mass. Press with your fingertips for 2 minutes, then quickly move chunks of curd into a prepared cheese form. Cover with the follower.

11. Press with medium weight (15 lb/7 kg) for 25 minutes, then open, flip, and redress.

12. Next, increase the weight to heavy (25 to 30 lb/11 to 13 kg) and press for 8 hours.

13. Afterward, remove the cheese from the press. Unwrap and place in a large pot and cover with the brine. Brine for 6 to 8 hours. The temperature of the brine should be near 55°F/13°C.

14. Afterward, air-dry the cheese on a drying rack, covered with cheesecloth, at room temperature for 2 days. Flip daily.

15. When the skin feels almost dry, set the cheese on top of an aging mat, inside an aging box. Place the aging box in a 55°F/13°C location. Check and turn the cheese daily for the first week, removing built-up moisture and wiping the skin lightly with a dry piece of cheesecloth.

16. After 1 week, start to rub the cheese every other day with cheesecloth dipped in the Herb Wash.

17. Continue turning and rubbing the cheese. If too much moisture builds up in the box, place several paper towels underneath the aging mat, underneath the cheese. Leave the lid slightly ajar for several hours each day until the rind feels damp but not dry.

18. Age at 55°F/13°C for at least 3 and up to 6 months.

HERB WASH

MAKES 1 CUP/240 ML, OR ENOUGH FOR 3 TO 4 RIND WASHINGS.

This wash is a variation of Red-Rind Wash (page 121).

1 cup/240 ml water

1 tsp *each* dried marjoram, thyme, chamomile flowers, and rosemary, or any combination of your choice

½ cup/120 ml dry white wine

1 tsp salt

Pinch of *Coryneform* cultures

1. In a saucepan over high heat, bring the water to a boil. Remove from the heat, add the herbs, and let steep for 10 minutes.

2. Strain out the herbs. Cool to room temperature, then add the wine, salt, and *coryneform* cultures. Cover and let stand on the countertop overnight.

3. Store the wash in the fridge. Each time you wash a cheese, wet a clean towel with the wash then rub onto cheese rind.

CHAPTER FIVE

MOLD-RIPENED
Cheeses

Most of the cheesemaking process is quite subtle. You can't see what's happening so you just trust that it is. Except with mold-ripened cheeses. Here, you can confidently see that change is taking place. Beautiful change. When the surface of a bloomy-rind bursts into a blanket of white or you wake one morning to find a wheel covered in fresh, baby-blue velvet, you will feel confident about what's going on. You will see that magic is at your fingertips.

Mold-ripened cheeses come in two varieties: interior ripened and exterior mold ripened. While bloomy-rinds have a telltale white coat, blues reveal themselves once cut. The insides of both can range from crumbly and creamy to shiny and gooey. The paste of both is a consequence of how long the cheese has aged and the amount of milk fat within as well as how the milk was worked in the vat.

BLOOMY-RIND CHEESES: CAMEMBERT, GOSLING, BUTTERCUP

SURFACE RIPENED: FROM THE OUTSIDE IN

The molds at work on the surface of a bloomy-rind are primarily *Pencilium candidum* and *Geotrichum candidum*. On some bloomy-rinded cheeses, the rinds are composed entirely of *Geotrichum candidum* without any *Pencilium candidum*, such as the Redwood Hill's Crottin or Vermont Creamery's Cremont. In this book, you'll make the Buttercup on page 137 using only *Geotrichum candidum*.

You can add mold spores directly to the vat (as you will do in the recipes ahead) or spray them onto the cheese during the ripening period (which is more often done in a commercial setting). The molds will then form a velvety covering, which can range from white to pale grey to light pink. Commercial cheeses are available only in the white variety— another reason to make your own.

What the skin of a bloomy-rind is doing is digesting the cheese from the outside inward, the way mushrooms in the forest break down a tree stump. In order to flourish, the rind of the cheese needs just

three essential elements: food (the fats and proteins in the cheese), moisture (in the cheese and surrounding air), and oxygen (in the surrounding air). Given these, the cheese will ripen rapidly, far more quickly than a vacuum-sealed cheddar for instance.

SURFACE AREA TO VOLUME

Though it might have been an accident originally, there is a reason why bloomy-rind cheeses are small in size and especially short in height. It's the surface area to volume ratio! This means that from any point inside the cheese, the distance to the exterior is no greater than 2 to 3 in/5 to 8 cm. This guarantees that as nutrients travel from inside the cheese to feed the surface mold, they don't have to travel far. The molds grow evenly and their enzymes penetrate the cheese, digesting the insides all the way to the cheese's center.

Here is a good place to comment on the close relationship between Camembert and Brie cheeses, well-known members of the bloomy-rind category. Their relationship is so close that sometimes I use the titles interchangeably. The only true difference between the two cheeses is the size of the draining form: A Camembert is roughly 5 in/13 cm in diameter whereas the Brie is closer to 10 in/25 cm. This difference, though subtle, means a different surface to volume ratio that translates into how much oxygen is available to the surface molds, busy digesting the cheese.

AGING ADVICE

Pay attention to your bloomy-rind during the first two weeks while it establishes an initial coat. After that, check on the cheeses every several days. Additionally, some more tips for successful bloomy-rinds.

- Flip regularly to ensure the cheese gets oxygen on all sides for the molds to grow. Also, by touching and flipping the cheeses regularly, you keep the mold coat from growing too big. You can also wrap your bloomy-rind in cheese paper to help keep those surface molds in check.

- Remove accumulated moisture from the aging box regularly using a clean rag or paper towel.

Day Two

Day Eight

- Don't open the lid of the aging box too often (as in multiple times a day, depending on your climate) or all ambient moisture inside the box will be lost.

- Set the lid of the aging box on lightly, do not snap it down. This allows for the right amount of oxygen flow without suffocating your cheese project.

- Choose an aging box that is five to ten times the volume of your cheese. Too small of a box means not enough oxygen. Too big of a box means too much air in relation to the cheese, which causes the cheese to dry out.

- Position ripening cheeses so that they do not touch each other in the aging box. If cheeses are too close, the mold of their coats will grow together. When you try to separate or flip them, the skins will tear open and the cheeses can no longer be aged.

- Keep your hands clean when handling the aging box or the cheeses. Think about which surfaces you might touch between the sink and the cheese itself. For ease, keep a box of disposable gloves nearby and put on a fresh pair right before flipping.

JUDGING RIPENESS

To tell if the cheese is ready, look for a change in shape or a "relaxing" of the edges. Sniff the cheese and see if you sense a light ammoniac odor. Finally, with your finger, press down on the center of the wheel and see if you sense a softening (check early on when the cheese is young so you have something to compare it to). The center should feel more like a soft peach than a firm eraser.

Bloomy-rinds are fun to make because they are ready to eat after a relatively short amount of time— perhaps as little as 3 weeks. But don't jump the gun! If a cheese is eaten too soon, your microscopic friends won't have had enough time to transform the curd. On the other hand, these cheeses can become overripe easily as well. Whereas you can stockpile wheels of Gouda or bricks of cheddar, you cannot stockpile bloomy-rinds. The whole fleet will ripen at once, like a box of avocados. Having friends in position, ready to eat as the ripening date nears is always a good idea.

An interesting side note: The rapid ripening of bloomy-rinds makes them a nearly impossible cheese to make commercially with raw milk. Because a traditional Camembert—a raw-milk bloomy-rind—ripens quickly, and because the USDA mandates a 60-day aging period for all raw-milk cheeses, Camembert and other raw-milk bloomy-rinds would ripen before the cheesemaker is allowed to sell them. This, to me, is one more reason to make your own cheese. You can make "illegal cheeses"—raw-milk cheeses aged for less than 60 days—to enjoy whenever you want.

BLUE CHEESES: STILTON, BISBEE BLUE, BLUE CAPRICORN

Now that we've thought about cheeses that ripen with surface molds, let's explore those with interior molds.

GROWING BLUE

Blue, or bleu, cheese means any cheese ripened internally with the help of blue mold spores (mainly *Penicillium roquerforti* but also *Pencillium glaucum*). I had a cheddar once accidentally get some blue mold invasions. When I brought it to the farmers' market, I overheard customers referring to "that blue cheese." For this reason, the descriptor "blue" must trump whatever else the cheese might be. If it looks blue, it's blue. If it tastes blue, it's blue.

Characteristically, many blues have a shorter-grained paste (as opposed to a longer, more elastic texture you'll find in a Gouda, for example). This is because blues are made using a lactic-acid set or slow rennet set. Think of lactic-set cheeses as spaghetti strands that have been chopped up—a fork can't twist these short strands the same as if they were longer. Similarly, a piece of blue cheese

THE CHEESE THAT RAN AWAY FROM THE SPOON

It was the Fourth of July and we were on our way to a potluck. We didn't know the hosts well but were excited to get to know them better. I luckily had two medium-size Camembert cheeses that I knew needed to be eaten. They were soft when pressed gently in the middle, and when I opened the aging box to flip them, the scent of ammonia was getting stronger and stronger. This party would be a perfect occasion to open them up.

I set the two cheeses up on a wooden board, nested nectarines and toasted almonds around them, then garnished everything with edible flowers. As we arrived at the party, I proudly watched as the eyes followed me—or rather my cheese—in through the door. The cheese *was* eye-catching. I rested the board on the food table and, feeling a titch modest, backed away as the crowd tightened in. I was tickled to bring such an impressive food to a party.

A half hour later, hungry for food myself, I returned to the table, grabbed a plate, and surveyed the offerings. Suddenly, I spied a problem. My wooden board and the wheels of cheese were there, but so was a strange line reaching all the way down to the floor. A glistening puddle appeared near my foot.

Then I noticed the cheeses were in fact empty white shells, like vacant amphitheaters. I blinked in disbelief as I put together what had happened. The insides of the cheese had been so ripe that the poor partygoer who opened them must have found him- or herself in the path of a sudden cheese torrent. The insides of the cheese had run off the board, over the table, and onto the floor. I paused in disbelief for only a second longer, then hurriedly scraped the mess off the floor and left the area as quickly as those guts had probably left the cheese.

will not bend the same as a piece of Swiss-style cheese, where the protein chains are longer and, therefore, more pliable.

As far as aging, blues need at least 6 weeks but usually not more than 6 months to ripen. The amount of time needed depends on the size of the wheel, the aging conditions, the strains of cultures used, and the moisture level in the cheese. Personally, I'm careful to not overage my blue cheeses because I don't like them when they get spicey and pungent. I prefer my blues on the sweeter side. Blues also tend to be salty cheeses (the blue mold spores thrive in a saltier environment). Don't skimp on the salt. A decent amount of flavor can also come from our old friends—those who form stinky red rinds—*coryneform* bacteria.

I find blues to be both easy and tricky. The aging environment as well as the acidity of the rind plays a huge role, and though I do my best to manage these factors, I can't ever perfectly control them. I'm embarrassed to admit that the number of times I've accidentally made a great blue almost outnumber the times I've intended to make one and failed. That's okay. The more cheese I make, the more I learn.

NUTRIENT FLOW

The color in blue cheese is the fruiting body of a fungus. This fungus is larger than just the colorful parts you can see as there are also the mycelia, or rootlike structures, which are invisible to the naked eye. The mycelia penetrate the cheese around the fruiting body and digest it. So while exterior mold-ripened cheeses (e.g., Brie) break down at the rind, blues cheeses break down on the inside.

To digest the cheese, the fungus transforms fats and proteins—complex molecules in the milk—into simpler ones (amino acids, monosaccharides, fatty acids). We perceive these smaller molecules as flavor. That's why an older, more broken-down cheese is more interesting in many ways than a *queso fresco*, for instance. In addition to creating flavor, the fungus also changes the cheese's texture, usually turning it from firm and brittle to soft and creamy.

I love to think about how this flavor-creating fungal process is also a mandatory turn in the wheel of life. When a fungus breaks down organic matter, it frees the nutrients within. Eventually this allows the nutrients to cycle into other life forms. Think of all the decomposers working on a fallen log in the forest. As they feed, they release nutrients (and perhaps flavor too, though I've never eaten a fallen log). Our goal as blue-cheese makers is to hold the reins on that decomposition, to keep things precise enough that unwanted invaders don't join in, and then, to catch the transformation at just the right moment.

GATHER YOUR OWN BLUE

Purchasing freeze-dried *Pencillium roqueforti* cultures can be expensive. You could pay as much as $20 for spores for culturing only 8 gal/30.2 L of milk. If you are purchasing milk from the store and spending at least half a day converting that milk into cheese, this extra expense might bump blues to the realm of unrealistic.

So let's dash to the past. Before there were culture companies, such as the ones listed on page 234, there were ways to perpetuate desired microorganisms for fermentation processes. The most common method was simply using a porous (wooden) instrument each day or aging the cheeses in a distinctly colonized environment, such as the caves at Roquefort.

More recently and more locally, I know of a cheese-maker who simply mixes one well-veined chunk of inexpensive store-bought blue cheese with milk until the chunks have dissolved. Next, she adds this to her vat in place of *Pencillium roqueforti* spores. Likely, she spent time finding a brand of cheese that worked. One way to tell if the spores in a store-bought blue are active is by opening and cutting the store-bought cheese, then rewrapping it and storing it in the fridge for several weeks longer. Afterward, reopen the cheese and look to see if new mold has grown where the cut was made.

A BLUE INVASION

Keep your blue cheeses isolated or else the mold spores they contain will contaminate other cheese projects in the house. Isolating these cheeses should start at the vat. Don't make a blue on the same day as a non-blue. Use separate aging bins or even fridges if possible. Never tend to an aging blue cheese then a non-blue cheese without first changing gloves or washing hands (and maybe even changing clothes). Blue molds are fierce and love to jump into things.

Even if you do everything within your power to separate the blue cheeses from the non-blues, you might still get invasions. That's because blue mold spores are naturally present everywhere. Even if you've never made blue cheese in your kitchen, you may see blue molds popping up at some point. By propagating purchased spores in your kitchen creamery, you increase the likelihood of a blue invasion. If you are having trouble controlling your blues, decide to either specialize in this style or avoid it all together.

MAKES TWO 12-OZ/340-G WHEELS

TIME TO COMPLETION

5

WEEKS

Camembert may become your favorite cheese to make for several reasons: 1) You don't need any special forms or presses; 2) the size of the cheese is small and manageable, allowing you to easily gather enough milk; 3) the ripening time is short so even impatient cheesemakers are soon satisfied; 4) you get to see a tangible change in the cheese when the coat blooms; and 5) the result tastes so good.

INGREDIENTS

2 gal/7.5 L unhomogenized milk

1 cup/240 ml heavy cream

1/8 tsp prehydrated mesophilic cultures

Pinch of prehydrated *Penicillium candidum* mold powder

Pinch of prehydrated *Geotrichum candidium* mold powder

1/4 tsp CaCl$_2$ diluted in 1/4 cup/60 ml water

1/4 tsp rennet diluted in 1/4 cup/60 ml water

2 to 3 tsp salt

SPECIAL EQUIPMENT

2 medium-size cheese forms (may be Camembert or similar forms, approximately 4 in/10 cm round base by 4 in/10 cm height, open bottom, untapered); digital kitchen thermometer; cheese paper

1. Clean all surfaces and equipment before beginning. Set up a draining station by placing the cheese forms on a draining rack in the sink.

2. Pour the milk and cream into a heavy-bottomed stockpot and warm over medium heat to 86°F/30°C, stirring gently. Remove from the heat.

3. Add the prehydrated cultures and mold powders to the milk, then stir using an up-and-down motion.

4. Add the CaCl$_2$ solution and stir. Add the rennet solution. Stir for 20 seconds, then stop the motion of the milk. As you add the rennet, start a timer and watch for the flocculation point (see page 218). When reached, stop the timer. Multiply the number of minutes elapsed by 5. This is how long you need to wait before you cut the curd. Goal time is 60 to 90 minutes.

5. At the timed moment, cut the curd into 1½-in/4-cm pieces. Then, without stirring, let the curd sit for 45 minutes. During this time, the curd will sink below the surface of the whey.

6. Remove the whey from the top of the pot until you see the surface of the curd again, then begin to stir (working from the top of the pot and moving downward) for 3 minutes. This action is more one of lifting and moving the curds than actually stirring. Allow the curds to rest in the pot for another 5 minutes.

7. Finally, scoop the curds out of the pot and fill each form. Fill the forms all the way to the top before moving on to the next form. Depending on the height of your form, you may need to fill it, then wait 10 to 20 minutes for the curd level to drop sufficiently, then fill again. If you are absolutely certain you can't fit all your curds into the prepared forms, add another.

8. Let the curds drain for 8 to 12 hours, flipping regularly, covered at room temperature.

9. Sprinkle ¼ to ½ tsp salt on the top of each cheese while it is still in the form. Let the salt soak in for half an hour, then flip the cheese and repeat the salting on the opposite side. Let the salt soak in for 10 hours more at room temperature. During this time, make sure the whey can flow freely away, so that the cheese does not sit in a puddle.

10. Remove the cheeses from their forms and set on a clean aging mat, cover with cheesecloth, and allow the cheese to air-dry at room temperature for 1 day more. Finally, blot the cheese extra-dry with a clean paper towel. Place the cheese on the aging mat in the aging bin and place in a 45°F/7°C location. If unavailable, store in the refrigerator.

11. For the first 2 weeks, with clean hands or wearing gloves, flip the cheeses every day, and remove any accumulated moisture with a clean cloth or paper towel. You should start to see *Geotrichum candidium* mold growing on the rind after about 1 week. It looks like shimmery velvet. Next, you should see a heavier white mold grow in—the *Penicillium candidum*.

12. When the cheeses are fully covered in mold, wrap in cheese paper (see page 203) to prevent the mold coat from growing too thick, or skip the paper and simply continue to flip and pat down the cheese rind on a weekly basis.

13. After 4 weeks, check the cheese for ripeness by looking for a softness at the center (see page 128). When ripe, enjoy. Store, uncut, in the fridge for up to 2 weeks more, and no longer.

VARIATION

TRUFFLE BRIE: *Make a Camembert into a Brie by changing the shape of the form you drain the curds in and raising the vat temperature slightly (from 86°F/30°C to 92°F/ 33°C). For the form, instead of two rounds, drain everything in one large round. If you have an open-bottomed cylinder, it will make the first flip easier.*

To add a special touch to your wheel of Brie, add ½ cup/15 g chopped dried truffle pieces (or any dried mushrooms). Add the truffle as you are hooping the cheese into its form. Age the Brie 2 to 3 weeks longer than you would a Camembert.

Gosling

(VALENÇAY STYLE)

MAKES FOUR 8-OZ/240-G
PYRAMID-SHAPED CHEESES

MILK

GOAT OR COW

SUGGESTED CULTURES

BUTTERMILK;
PENICILLIUM
CANDIDUM AND
GEOTRICHUM
CANDIDIUM MOLD
POWDERS

FINAL FORM

PYRAMIDS

CATEGORIES

LACTIC-ACID,
BLOOMY-RIND,
SOFT-RIPENED,
ASHED

These pyramid-shaped cheeses are pure entertainment. At first, they're firm, geometric, and black with ash: brand new. A week later, they're fuzzy and gray: adolescent. With time, they become white with softened edges: middle-aged. Finally, they slump as the insides become soft: mature. This recipe can be made with cow's milk if goat's milk is not available and, traditionally, Valençay is an raw-milk cheese.

INGREDIENTS

2 gal/7.5 L goat's milk or cow's milk

2 tbsp buttermilk

Pinch of prehydrated *Penicillium candidum* mold powder

Pinch of prehydrated *Geotrichum candidum* mold powder

4 drops CaCl₂

4 drops rennet

Salt

2 tsp vegetable ash (see page 28)

SPECIAL EQUIPMENT

4 pyramid-shaped 8-oz/240-g cheese forms, or other shape of your choice; digital kitchen thermometer

1. Clean all surfaces and equipment before beginning. Set up a draining station by placing the cheese forms on a draining rack in the sink.

2. Pour the milk into a heavy-bottomed stockpot and warm over medium heat to 72°F/22°C. Remove from the heat.

3. Add buttermilk and mold powders to the milk, then stir using an up-and-down motion.

4. Add the CaCl₂, stirring with an up-and-down motion. Repeat this process with the rennet. Cover the pot and place in a warm, undisturbed, vibration-free place for 15 to 17 hours. (If needed, incubate the pot to keep the temperature from fluctuating.) When the curd has firmed up, you will notice a small amount of clearish (almost greenish-yellow) whey collecting on the top and sides of the curd block.

5. Using a skimmer, gently scoop the curds into the prepared forms. It will seem that there is too much curd for too few forms. Wait 10 to 15 minutes for the level of the curds to drop, and then fill them to the top again. Continue doing this until all of the curd has been used. If it is clear that the curd amount is disproportionate, add another form.

CONTINUED

TIME TO COMPLETION

3 WEEKS

6. Set the filled pyramids inside a tall, clean aging bin, with an aging mat on the bottom. Place the lid on the tub and allow the pyramids to drain for 4 hours, removing the whey as frequently as needed. Alternatively, let the pyramids drain in the sink over a rack, making sure they are supported and won't tip over. After 4 hours, invert the pyramids onto the aging mat (the cheese will have firmed enough to allow you to do so).

7. After another 8 hours of draining at room temperature (12 hours in total), remove the forms so the cheeses stand independently. Carefully dry the inside of the tub using a clean cloth, then sprinkle each pyramid with ½ to ¾ tsp salt over all surfaces as evenly as possible.

8. Allow the salt to soak in while the pyramids continue draining in the covered bin at room temperature. (Remove built-up whey as needed). Drain for 25 to 30 hours more.

9. Once the cheeses have stopped releasing whey, cover them with the vegetable ash.

10. Place the salted, ashed cheeses in a clean bin on top of clean aging mats. Cover with the lid and place in a 48°F/9°C location. Rotate the cheeses two times each week for the next 3 to 4 weeks. If aging the cheeses in the refrigerator, age for 3 to 4 weeks longer. When the cheeses have a softness when gently squeezed and when the sharp lines of the pyramids start to bulge and curve, the cheeses are done.

11. Wrap in breathable cheese paper and store in the fridge for up to 2 weeks.

NOTES

- *If you're thinking this recipe is similar to the Chèvre on page 82, you are right! By taking a base recipe and adding a few more steps, you build your knowledge of cheesemaking. All recipes overlap. Small variations—in this case, the form the cheese drains in as well as the use of secondary ripening cultures—change a fresh, unripened cheese into a soft ripened variety.*

- *The pyramid shape is unlike the wheel form that nearly all cheeses come in. When flipping, you can't flip between just two surfaces. Instead, rotate the cheese 90 degrees each time you turn it.*

BUTTERCUP

(COULOMMIERS STYLE)

MAKES TWO
12-OZ/340-G WHEELS

This recipe for a double-crème, Coulommiers-style (a cousin of Brie) cheese is a special one. Why? Because it is quick to make and, in only a handful of weeks, the cheese is done. When ripened, the added butterfat makes the inner paste so rich that when people eat it, they make soft, happy sounds. This recipe is different from the other bloomy-rinds because it contains the greatest percentage of butterfat and uses only *Geotrichum* molds, no *Penicillum candidum*. The rind will be less thick and spongy and more wrinkly and matte.

INGREDIENTS

2 gal/7.5 L unhomogenized milk

2¼ cups/540 ml heavy cream

¼ tsp prehydrated mesophilic cultures

Pinch of prehydrated *Geotrichum candidum* mold powder

¼ tsp CaCl₂ diluted in ¼ cup/60 ml water

¼ tsp rennet diluted in ¼ cup/60 ml water

1 tsp salt

SPECIAL EQUIPMENT

2 medium cheese forms; digital kitchen thermometer

1. Clean all surfaces and equipment before beginning. Set up a draining station by placing the cheese forms on a draining rack in the sink.

2. Pour the milk and cream into a heavy-bottomed stockpot and warm over medium heat to 90°F/32°C. Remove from the heat.

3. Add the prehydrated cultures and mold powder to the milk. Stir in gently.

4. Add the CaCl₂ solution while stirring. Add the rennet solution and stir in. As you add the rennet, start a timer and watch for the flocculation point (see page 218).

Once reached, stop the timer. Multiply the number of minutes elapsed by 6. This is how long you need to wait before you cut the curd. Goal time is 90 minutes.

5. Cut the curd into 1-in/2.5-cm squares. After cutting, let the curds heal for 2 minutes. They will feel particularly soft.

6. Gently scoop the curds from the edge of the pot and slide them toward the center. This is not really stirring, but rather shifting the curds around to flush out more whey. Move the curds in this manner for 15 minutes.

7. Finally, after removing any whey collected at the top of the vat, scoop the curds into the prepared forms. Fill each form to the very top, and then set in the prepared draining area. Allow the cheeses to drain for 45 minutes, covered.

CONTINUED

MILK

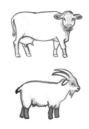

UNHOMOGENIZED MILK, HEAVY CREAM

SUGGESTED CULTURES

AROMA B OR FLORA DANICA; GEOTRICHUM CANDIDUM MOLD POWDER

FINAL FORM

MEDIUM WHEELS

CATEGORIES

BLOOMY RIND, SOFT RIPENED, DOUBLE CRÈME

TIME TO COMPLETION

4 WEEKS

8. Next, refill each form to the top, then cover and allow to drain at room temperature for 12 to 14 hours. If necessary, add additional cheese forms in order to use up the curds. During this period, the level of the curds should fall by nearly half or more but will stay extremely soft, almost the texture of pudding.

9. As soon as the curd has drained enough to be firm, gently flip the cheese, so the top becomes the bottom, then set back onto the aging mat. If using a bottomless form, simply invert the form. If the cheese is still too soft, wait another 4 to 5 hours. If you flip the cheese and it goes back in its form cockeyed, don't worry, you will continue to flip the cheese and the cockeyedness will straighten out.

10. After 15 to 20 hours and when there is a strong yogurty smell, sprinkle ¼ tsp of the salt on top of each form. Let the salt soak in for 1 hour, then flip. Salt the other side with another ¼ tsp.

11. Keep the cheeses at room temperature for 1 day more, making sure they are covered and also actively draining, not sitting in whey.

12. Finally, once the cheeses have stopped releasing whey and feel firmer, remove them from their forms and set on top of dry, clean aging mats, inside of aging bins. Place the bins in a 48°F/9°C area. For the first 2 weeks, carefully monitor the cheeses to make sure they are not too moist. Flip daily and remove built-up moisture.

13. After 10 days, you should see a shimmery white coat covering the cheeses. I enjoy eating one of the wheels at this point. It is still very simple in flavor and crumbly in texture but pleasant, and it's nice to taste how much the cheeses have already changed by then.

14. Age for another 3 to 5 weeks, or until when you press on the cheese it has a softness similar to when you squeeze the flesh between your pointer finger and your thumb. Do not overripen.

15. Enjoy right away, warmed to room temperature, or wrap in cheese paper and store in the fridge for up to 1 week.

NOTES

- *This cheese drains especially slowly because of the butterfat. Plan for the draining to take twice as long as the other bloomy-rind recipes. If you'd like a more traditional Brie-like rind but this same luxurious butter-like paste, add a pinch of* Penicillium candidum *when you add the cultures at step 3.*

- *I also tried this recipe being purposefully less strict about keeping the rind unexposed, thinking I might catch more "native" flavor. It worked, and I ended up with a primarily white rind but with spots of blues (*Penicillium roqueforti*) and reds (*Coryneform*). It reminds me of a wilder looking version of the cheese Pouligny-Saint-Pierre.*

MAKES ONE 1½-LB/680-G WHEEL

Start your journey through the blues here, with this forgiving and delicious cheese. If you use smaller forms, the cheese will be ready around six weeks. If you make one slightly taller cheese, it may need a few weeks more. Once, after a class in which I'd taught this recipe, a student returned to tell me about the success of his take-home project (and his first attempt at making cheese). He said (in an English accent), "That was about the best Stilton I've ever had, and I know Stilton!" I had to blush.

MILK

ALL TYPES
(NOT ULTRA-
PASTEURIZED)

SUGGESTED CULTURES
BUTTERMILK OR MM100; PENICILLIUM ROQUEFORTI MOLD SPORES

FINAL FORM
EXTRA-TALL MEDIUM WHEEL

CATEGORIES
MOLD-RIPENED, SEMI-LACTIC, MILLED-CURD

TIME TO COMPLETION
6 WEEKS

INGREDIENTS
2 gal/7.5 L milk
¼ tsp prehydrated mesophilic cultures
⅛ tsp prehydrated *Penicillium roqueforti* mold spores
¼ tsp CaCl₂ diluted in ¼ cup/60 ml water
¼ tsp rennet diluted in ¼ cup/60 ml water
4 to 5 tsp salt

SPECIAL EQUIPMENT
Medium (60#) cheesecloth; digital kitchen thermometer; medium cheese form, ideally extra-tall and open-bottomed (a 32-oz/950-ml can with both the top and bottom taken off to form a hoop works perfectly); #6 knitting needle or equivalent for piercing

1. Clean all surfaces and equipment before beginning. Set up a draining station by placing a clean colander lined with the cheesecloth in the sink.

2. Pour the milk into a heavy-bottomed stockpot and warm over medium heat to 86°F/30°C, stirring gently. Remove from the heat.

3. Add the cultures and mold to the milk. Allow them to hydrate for 2 minutes, then stir in, using an up-and-down motion.

4. Add the CaCl₂ solution and stir briefly. Add the rennet solution. Stir in for 20 seconds, then stop the motion of the milk. As you add the rennet, start a timer and watch for the flocculation point (see page 218). When reached, stop the timer. Multiply the number of minutes elapsed by 5.5. This is how long you need to wait before you cut the curd. Goal time is 90 minutes.

5. At the timed moment, cut the curd into ½-in/12-mm pieces. Stir gently for 10 minutes, then let the curds settle to the bottom of the pot for another 10 minutes.

6. Pour off the whey that has collected at the top of the pot, then gently pour the curds into the prepared colander. Cover the colander with additional cheesecloth or knot the corners of the cloth to form a pouch (see page 220). Drain for 12 hours at room temperature.

7. Afterward, open up the cheesecloth and move the drained curds to a bowl. With clean hands, break the curd into walnut-size chunks. Add half the salt to the curd chunks, toss to incorporate, then wait 2 minutes. Add the remaining salt and repeat the mixing process. The curds will taste very salty.

8. After salting, fill your prepared cheese form with the curds, packing them in, using your fingertips to *very gently* press down on the cheese. Do not press too hard (or you will compact all the spaces where the blue mold is going to grow) but use enough pressure that the cheese starts to knit together slightly. An underpressed cheese will fall apart when flipped. Place the curd-filled form on a draining rack.

9. Keep the cheese in its form, at room temperature, for 8 to 10 hours more, flipping after 2 hours and again after 6 hours. Flipping is especially easy if you are using an open-bottomed form.

10. Finally, remove the cheese from its form by gently pushing it out and onto an aging mat. With a knife or spatula, gently smear the sides of the cheese—as though you were frosting a cake—to help fill in gaps and to form a more closed rind. Move slowly; I know it's difficult to do because the cheese is crumbly. Move the cheese into a clean aging bin. Cover with the lid. Place

the bin in a 65°F/24°C location for 2 to 3 days. This warmer period is important for acid development that activates the blue mold spores. Remove built-up moisture from the bin as needed.

11. After 2 to 3 days, take the knitting needle and pierce the cheese a half dozen times horizontally. You can make more pierces vertically if you wish.

12. Now move the bin and cheese to a cooler (50° to 55°F/10° to 13°C) location. Keep the lid on the box but not locked down. Turn the cheese every 3 days. Begin to wipe the rind with your fingertips or a small piece of cheesecloth if excessive molds start to grow. Eventually, the rind will start to feel sticky and turn brown or pinkish in color.

13. For extra veining, pierce the cheeses again between days 10 and 14.

14. Ripen the cheese for 6 to 8 weeks, flipping and maintaining the rind and moisture levels. Ripen the cheese for 3 to 5 weeks longer if aging in a refrigerator.

15. Enjoy, or wrap the cheese in aluminum foil and keep in the fridge, uncut, for up to 1 month.

(FORME D'AMBERT STYLE)

MAKES ONE 1- TO 2-LB/
455- TO 910-G WHEEL

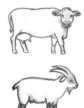

UNHOMOGENIZED
MILK, HEAVY CREAM

**CULTURE
SUGGESTIONS**

MM100 PLUS LM 57;
PENICILLIUM
ROQUEFORTI MOLD
POWDER; LIPASE

FINAL FORM

MEDIUM WHEEL

CATEGORIES

(INTERIOR)
MOLD-RIPENED,
SOFT-RIPENED,
SEMI-LACTIC,
DOUBLE-CRÈME

TIME TO COMPLETION
10
WEEKS

This cheese has a more pliable paste than the Stilton on page 140. It's a similar make process to the cheese *Forme d'Ambert*. I suggest making it as one larger wheel instead of several smaller ones in order to have more space to pierce. I've named this cheese after a bright blue mineral commonly found in my hometown of Bisbee, Arizona.

INGREDIENTS

2 gal/7.5 L whole unhomogenized milk
2 cups/480 ml heavy cream
¼ tsp prehydrated mesophilic cultures
**Pinch of prehydrated *Penicillium
  roqueforti* mold powder (about ¹⁄₁₆ tsp)**
Pinch of lipase (optional)
¼ tsp CaCl₂ diluted in ¼ cup/60 ml water
**¼ tsp liquid rennet diluted in ¼ cup/60 ml
  water**
Saturated brine (see page 221)
Salt

SPECIAL EQUIPMENT

**Medium cheese form, with follower;
medium (#60) cheesecloth to fit the form;
digital kitchen thermometer; #6 knitting
needle or equivalent for piercing**

1. Clean all surfaces and equipment before beginning. Set up a draining station by lining the cheese form with cheesecloth and placing it on a draining rack in the sink. Rinse a colander, line with cheesecloth, and place in the sink as well.

2. Pour the milk and cream into a heavy-bottomed stockpot and warm over medium heat to 90°F/32°C, stirring gently.

3. When at temperature, turn off the heat and add the prehydrated cultures and mold powder to the milk. Stir in gently.

4. Add CaCl₂ solution and stir. Add the rennet solution. Stir in for 20 seconds, stop the motion of the milk. As you add the rennet, start a timer and watch for the flocculation point (see page 218). When reached, stop the timer. Multiply the number of minutes elapsed by 5. This is how long you need to wait before you cut the curd. Goal time is 60 to 90 minutes.

5. At the timed moment, cut curd to hazelnut-size pieces, about ¾ in/2 cm. After cutting, let the curds heal for 2 minutes.

6. Begin to stir slowly, starting at the top of the vat and working your way down, gently bringing all the curds into motion. Stir continuously for 55 minutes, then pitch curds (or let them settle to the bottom of the vat) for 5 minutes.

7. Pour off the whey from the top of the vat into the colander until you see the surface of the curds, then gently move all the curds into the colander.

8. Drain the curds for 10 minutes, then move them into the prepared form. Press down onto the cheese with your fingertips, then cover the top of the cheese with cheesecloth and the follower. Place a small weight (5 lb/2.2 kg) on top. After 20 minutes, remove the weight, flip, and redress the cheese. Press for another 20 minutes. Continue pressing for 5 to 7 hours more, flipping once midway through and making sure the weight stays centered on the cheese.

9. Afterward, remove the cheese from the press and its form. Place in the brine for 5 hours at room temperature (making sure to dry salt the part of the cheese that floats above the brine surface). Flip once halfway through the brining.

10. Remove from the brine. Place the cheese on a clean aging mat on top of a draining rack. Cover with a piece of cheese-cloth. Leave at room temperature for 2 to 3 days, flipping regularly until the rind feels smooth and just slightly damp. Move the wheel and aging mat into an aging bin with the lid loosely placed on top. Set in a 50°F/10°C location. For the first week, flip daily and remove built-up moisture. After 1 week, pierce the wheel using the knitting needle. Push the needle all the way through the cheese vertically, making holes every 1½ in/4 cm. To ensure blue veining, re-pierce the cheese again after 3 weeks.

11. Continue aging the cheese, turning twice weekly for the next 8 to 12 weeks. Blue, white, and grayish colored molds will grow on the rind. Control these molds by regularly brushing or rubbing the rind using a piece of cheesecloth, a soft brush, or your fingertips. With time, the rind will grow slightly sticky and possibly pinkish in color.

12. Enjoy, or wrap in aluminum foil and store in the fridge, uncut, for up to 1 month.

MAKES THREE
6-OZ/170-G LOGS

MILK

GOAT

SUGGESTED CULTURES

FLORA DANICA;
PENICILLIUM
ROQUEFORTI MOLD
POWDER

FINAL FORM

LOGS

CATEGORIES

LACTIC-ACID,
(INTERIOR)
MOLD-RIPENED

TIME TO COMPLETION

3

WEEKS

These colorful goat-cheese logs are bright blue (or green) on the outside and bright white on the inside. This cheese has the shortest ripening time of the three blue recipes. Plan to enjoy it around 3 weeks. If you use raw milk and let the cheese age longer (5 weeks or more), it will be very picante and the cheese will turn gooey just under the rind. This recipe is different from the others because you'll form the cheese into log shapes after it has first drained in a colander or cheesecloth pouch—meaning it's a good cheese to make if you don't yet have cheese forms to play with.

INGREDIENTS

2 gal/7.5 L goat's milk
¼ tsp prehydrated mesophilic cultures
Pinch of prehydrated *Penicillium roqueforti* mold powder
2 drops CaCl₂
2 drops rennet
2 to 3 tbsp salt

SPECIAL EQUIPMENT

Fine (#90) cheesecloth; digital kitchen thermometer

1. Clean all surfaces and equipment before beginning. Set up a draining station by lining a colander with cheesecloth and placing on a draining rack in the sink.

2. Pour the milk into a stockpot and warm over medium heat to 75°F/22°C, stirring gently.

3. Pour in prehydrated cultures and mold powder and stir.

4. Add the CaCl₂ while stirring. Add the rennet and stir for 20 seconds. Stop the motion of the milk and cover the pot with a lid. Leave the pot in a vibration-free location, at room temperature, for 16 to 20 hours. (Maintain the temperature using a method explained on page 40 if needed.) After the incubation, look for a firm yogurt-like curd and some whey collecting at the edges and on the top of the curd block.

5. Using a skimmer, scoop the curds from the pot into the prepared colander. When the colander is full, gather the corners of the cheesecloth to form a pouch. Suspend the pouch (see page 220), so the whey can drain freely. Drain for 20 to 24 hours. For best results, gently shake the pouch (to open up new drainage channels) halfway through. You'll notice when you empty the bag that curds nearer to the cheesecloth are drier than the curds in the middle.

6. Afterward, shake all of the curds out of the cheesecloth and into a bowl. Using a mixer or clean hands, mix to even out the texture. Add the salt in two passes, mixing thoroughly each time.

7. When curd is homogenous and properly salted, take a third of the contents of the bowl and roll into a smooth and uniform log shape, approximately the size of a cucumber. Repeat with the rest of the curd. Set the logs on top of a clean aging mat, inside an aging bin. Allow the cheeses to drain for 1 day more at room temperature, removing excess moisture as needed, before moving the bin to a 50°F/10°C location. Keep the bin covered but not airtight. (Do not pierce this cheese as the middle is kept unveined and white.)

8. Ripen for 2 to 3 weeks, rolling or turning every several days, until a beautiful blue mold covers the surface of each log. Enjoy, or age for up to 2 weeks.

CHAPTER SIX

CHEDDAR-STYLE

Cheeses

Cheddar is truly America's cheese. It is the cheese people most frequently tell me is their favorite, the cheese I find in every fridge, the cheese that can be substituted for almost any other cheese in a recipe. It is a wonderful cheese—and quite variable in texture and flavor, depending on the recipe and the age.

Capital-C Cheddar is technically reserved for products made in the region in southern England from whence the style came and for which it was named. But the qualifications for a lowercase cheddar are this: the cheese should be cooked moderately (commonly to about 102°F/39°C) and stirred substantially, often for over an hour, in order to reach a low pH level, before being hooped. When the curds reach this pH, they get salted—not after pressing, as most other cheeses are. This salting before pressing is another signature sign of cheddar cheeses. Finally, a *true* traditional cheddar makes use of a process called, yes, "cheddaring," in which the cheesemaker cuts and stacks blocks of curd after draining. The stacking and then turning of these stacks gives the cheese time to develop more acid and also presses out more whey. After this stage, the blocks are milled into smaller chunks—becoming the "cheddar curds" so famous in the Midwest. You'll be asked to run through this lengthier traditional cheddaring process in the Traditional Cheddar recipe (page 156) only. With the other two cheddar types in this chapter, we get to take shortcuts.

MAKES ONE 4.5-LB/2-KG WHEEL

UNHOMOGENIZED

SUGGESTED
CULTURES

BUTTERMILK,
MA 4000, OR
MM100

FINAL FORM

LARGE WHEEL

CATEGORIES

COOKED, PRESSED,
FIRM, MILLED-CURD

TIME TO COMPLETION

5

WEEKS

Baby Jack is a good cheese to make if you don't yet have a pressable cheese form. You'll only need a large square of cheesecloth. This will leave you with an irregularly shaped wheel with an indent in the middle and beautiful imprints from the folds of the cheese-cloth. It is a classic shape for this style of cheese.

INGREDIENTS

4 gal/15 L unhomogenized milk

4 tbsp cultured buttermilk or ½ tsp prehydrated mesophilic cultures

¾ tsp $CaCl_2$ diluted in ¼ cup/60 ml water

¾ tsp rennet diluted in ¼ cup/60 ml water

About ¾ cup/215 g salt

Cheese wax, cream wax, or Traditional Jack Rub (page 155) for the rind treatment

SPECIAL EQUIPMENT

Large cheese form with follower (optional); medium (#60) cheesecloth; digital kitchen thermometer; press or pressing setup

1. Clean all surfaces and equipment before beginning. Set up a draining station by lining the cheese form or a colander with cheese-cloth and placing it on a draining rack in the sink.

2. Pour the milk into a heavy-bottomed stockpot and warm over medium heat to 86°F/30°C, stirring gently. Remove from the heat.

3. Add the buttermilk, and stir in with an up-and-down motion. Cover the pot and ripen for 1 hour. If necessary, gently reheat the milk to 86°F/30°C (or maintain heat using a method explained on page 40).

4. Add the $CaCl_2$ solution and stir gently. Add the rennet solution. Stir for 20 sec-onds. As you add the rennet, start a timer and watch for the flocculation point (see page 218). When reached, stop the timer. Multiply the number of minutes elapsed by 3.5. This is how long you need to wait before you cut the curd. Goal time is 35 to 40 minutes.

5. At the timed moment, cut the curd into hazelnut-size pieces, about ¾ in/2 cm. Let the curds heal for 2 minutes, then start stirring, starting at the top of the vat and working slowly downward, cutting up large curd pieces as they rise to the top.

6. When all the pieces are in motion, turn on a low heat. Warm the curds to 95°F/35°C over the course of 40 minutes, stirring gently and continuously.

CONTINUED

7. Next, increase the heat to medium and bring the curds up to 102°F/39°C over the course of just 15 minutes. Stir the entire time. Once at temperature, remove from the heat. Continue stirring for another 45 minutes. By the end of this cooking time, the curds should bounce off the back of your hand like ping-pong balls when you dip it into the pot.

8. Stop stirring and pitch the curds (see page 73) for 5 minutes, then pour off the whey while capturing the curds in the prepared colander. Return the curds to the pot.

9. Using your hands, break or mill the curd into roughly hazelnut-size pieces.

10. Add the salt in three passes, mixing it in well and pausing 2 minutes between each addition (to allow time for the salt to be absorbed). When finished, the curds should taste saltier than you think they should be. (If they don't, add more salt.)

11. Finally, moving quickly to preserve some of the heat still left in the curds, transfer the curds back to the prepared cheese form or colander with cheesecloth. Gather the ends and twist to form the cheese into a tight ball, and place under a very heavy weight (50 lb/23 kg) for 10 minutes (see Note).

12. After 10 minutes, remove the cheese from the press, open up the form or cloth, flip, redress, then press again, now at medium weight (25 to 40 lb/9 to 18 kg). Press overnight, or for 10 to 12 hours more. Afterward, set the cheese on an aging mat and draining rack, covered with a piece of cheesecloth. Allow the cheese to dry at room temperature for 2 days. Turn regularly to expedite the process.

13. When the rind feels nearly dry but still the slightest bit damp, cover with cheese wax, cream wax, or Jack rub. If using the cream wax or the rub, you must age the cheese in an aging bin; if using cheese wax, an aging bin is not necessary. Place on a wooden board inside the fridge or aging cave. Ripen at 51° to 54°F/11° to 13°C for at least 5 weeks, or up to 3 months.

NOTES

- *Only with cheddar curds do you press so heavily at first. This is because milled curds often have a hard time fusing or knitting back together after being salted.*

- *For a yellower cheddar, add ⅛ tsp of liquid annatto to the milk during step 3.*

TRADITIONAL JACK RUB

MAKES ¼ CUP/60 G

INGREDIENTS
2 tsp paprika
2 tsp cocoa powder
2 tsp salt
¼ cup/60 ml olive oil or vegetable oil

1. In a small bowl, stir together the paprika, cocoa powder, and salt. Add the oil and stir to make a paste.

2. Apply a portion of the rub onto the rind of your finished, air-dried cheese. Reapply the rub twice weekly for the first several weeks. The cheese should already be set up inside an aging bin on an aging mat at this point. As the rind dries and stabilizes, use less rub. When the rind gains a stable color and firmness, continue to turn and monitor the cheese until it is finished. The rub not only gives the cheese a richly colored exterior, but the motion of the rubbing knocks back unwanted molds. Store unused rub in a closed container in the fridge.

TRADITIONAL Cheddar

MAKES ONE 4.5-LB/2-KG WHEEL

MILK

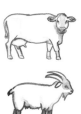

UNHOMOGENIZED

SUGGESTED CULTURES

MA 4000

FINAL FORM

LARGE WHEEL

CATEGORIES

COOKED, PRESSED, MILLED, FIRM, AGED

TIME TO COMPLETION

3

MONTHS

This recipe is more time intensive than its chapter-mate Baby Jack (page 152), but lets you practice the art of "cheddaring," a process by which you cut, stack, and flip bricks of drained curds in order to draw off more whey. For those interested in using pH measurements, this is a good cheese for trying it out. I've listed suggested pH targets as a way for you to track your cheese's acid development.

INGREDIENTS

4 gal/15 L unhomogenized milk

½ tsp prehydrated mesophilic cultures

¾ tsp CaCl$_2$ diluted in ¼ cup/60 ml water (if using pasteurized milk)

¾ tsp rennet diluted in ¼ cup/60 ml water

½ cup/120 ml salt, or more to taste

SPECIAL EQUIPMENT

Large cheese form, with follower; medium (#60) cheesecloth to fit the form; digital kitchen thermometer; cheese press or other pressing setup with capacity for 40+ lb/18+ kg; pH strips or meter for testing acidity (optional)

1. Clean all surfaces and equipment before beginning. Set up a draining station by lining the cheese form with cheesecloth and placing it on a draining rack in the sink.

2. Pour the milk into a stockpot and warm over medium heat to 86°F/30°C, stirring gently. Remove from the heat.

3. Add the prehydrated cultures and stir in using an up-and-down motion. Cover the pot and let the milk ripen for 1 hour. If necessary, reheat the milk to 86°F/30°C degrees (or maintain heat using a method explained on page 40).

4. Add the CaCl$_2$ solution and stir gently. Add the rennet solution. Stir for 20 seconds. As you add the rennet, start a timer and watch for the flocculation point (see page 218). When reached, stop the timer. Multiply the number of minutes elapsed by 3. This is how long you need to wait before you cut the curd. Goal time is 25 to 30 minutes. The pH target at renneting is 6.4.

5. At the timed moment, cut the curd into hazelnut-size pieces, about ¾ in/2 cm (see page 219). Let the curds heal for 2 minutes, then start to stir, working at the top of the vat and gradually moving toward the bottom. Cut down large curds as they rise up from the bottom.

6. When all the curds are in motion, warm them over low heat to 95°F/35°C over the course of 45 minutes, stirring the entire time. When the curds reach 95°F/35°C, turn up the heat slightly and, while stirring, bring the curds to 104°F/40°C over the course of 15 minutes.

7. Remove the pot from the heat but continue stirring for another 30 minutes. Your curds are done when 1) they make a funny squeak against your tooth when eaten; and

SQUEAKY CHEESE

This standby of Midwestern pride is simply cheddar curds that never got pressed into a wheel. From whence does this music come? For the first few hours after the nuggets form, they squeak against the tooth when chewed because the proteins are linked together in a tight matrix. (Imagine that matrix as something like rubber bands—that, if for whatever reason you, like me, have done it, you know also squeak when chewed.) It's a special window; after time and the inevitable continued fermentation, the squeak goes away, as the proteins become less elastic and deform less when bitten into. For this reason, if you love squeaky cheese, you either have to make your own—or be friendly with a cheesemaker on the day he or she is making a traditional cheddar!

2) they bounce off the back of your hand if you dip it into the pot. The pH target at draining is 5.9. Pitch the curds (see page 73) for 5 minutes, then pour the whey from the top of the pot. With a clean hand, gather the curds toward one side of the pot, pressing them together into a firmer block. Pour off extra whey.

8. Now it is time for cheddaring. Cut the curd block into two blocks and stack one on top of the other. Cover the pot and wait 15 minutes, then open up the pot again. Dump off extra whey. Take the bottom block, flip it so the top is now facing down and place it on top. Cover the pot and wait another 15 minutes. Continue flipping and rotating the blocks for 1 hour while maintaining a warm (at least 95°F/35°C) temperature in the vat. By the end, you should start to smell a slightly sour, yogurty smell from the curd.

9. Now the curd is ready to be milled. Using a clean, sharp knife, roughly chop into walnut- and hazelnut-size chunks. Make sure to work quickly to conserve heat. The pH target at milling is 5.3 to 5.5.

10. Add the salt in three passes, allow several minutes for the salt to be absorbed in between each. When finished, take a taste; the curds should taste saltier than you think they should be. Now quickly move the curds into the prepared form and place under very heavy weight (50 lb/23 kg or more) for 10 minutes (see page 224).

11. After 10 minutes, remove the cheese from the press, turn, redress, and press again at medium (25 to 40 lb/9 to 18 kg) to heavy weight for 10 to 12 hours more. Afterward, set the cheese on an aging mat and draining rack, covered with a piece of cheesecloth. Allow the cheese to dry at room temperature for 2 days. Turn regularly to expedite the process.

12. When the cheese is almost dry but still slightly moist, start a rind treatment of natural rind, bandages, cream wax, or cheese wax. (See pages 222 to 223 for more information on rind treatments. Bandage wrapping is a beautiful and traditional treatment for this cheese.)

13. Set the cheese in an aging bin (required if bandaging or cream waxing but not if using cheese wax) and in a 55°F/13°C location. Age for 3 months or up to 1 year. Pay close attention to your cheddar during the first several weeks, flipping it every day and brushing away mold. Remove built-up moisture as needed. Afterward, turn the cheese regularly until finished.

BANDAGE-WRAPPED CHEDDAR

Bandage wrapping is the most eco-friendly rind covering you can choose. You don't need to buy any special "cheese bandages." An old bedsheet, a floral blouse, or a cut-up flour sack will all work perfectly. And the fat coating you spread on top is a perfect destination for that can of bacon grease you've been saving up.

Note that a cheese that has been pressed in a form with straight sides (not curved, as with a Gouda form, for example) works best. After the cheese has been pressed and dried, apply the bandage wrappings.

INGREDIENTS

1 well-made, well-sealed wheel of Traditional Cheddar (page 156)
1 to 2 lb/455 to 910 g vegetable shortening, lard, bacon fat, coconut oil, or butter

SPECIAL EQUIPMENT

3 large pieces medium (#60) cheesecloth or medium-weave cotton fabric

1. Place two of the cheesecloth pieces, one on top of the other, on a clean work surface. Center the cheese wheel on top. Using sharp scissors, cut around the cheese to make two circles 3 in/7.5 cm larger in diameter than the cheese. (This is just like the way you would trim a pie crust, using the pan as a guide.) These circles are the top and the bottom pieces; set aside.

2. Next, from the third cheesecloth piece, cut one long rectangular strip, exactly the height of the cheese and long enough so that it reaches all the way around the wheel and overlaps by at least 1 in/2.5 cm, like a belt. Set aside.

3. In a saucepan over low heat, melt the shortening. Meanwhile, place the cheese wheel in the fridge for several minutes to make the rind extra-cool.

4. When the shortening is melted, remove the cheese from fridge. Using a pastry brush, brush the melted fat over the top and down the sides of the cheese, then quickly apply one circle of cheesecloth to the top, roughly centering it. Press the circle onto the cheese, starting from the center and moving toward the edge (this motion will help remove air bubbles). Rub into place and smooth the excess down the sides, then apply a second coat of fat to the top of the cloth.

5. Flip the cheese over and repeat this process on the bottom using the second circle of cloth.

6. Finally, turn the cheese onto its side and apply fat (covering a portion of the overhanging cloth from both the top and the bottom), then quickly belt the cheese with the last piece of cloth. Make sure the edges of the belt stay even with the edges of the cheese. Apply more fat to the outside of the belt. When finished, the cheese will be completely covered.

7. Now return the cheese to its original cheese form and place in the press, with the bandages on. Apply heavy weight (50 lb/23 kg) for another 24 hours to tightly secure the bandages in place. For an extra-secure rind covering, repeat this entire process after removing the cheese from the press—applying the second bandage directly over the first. The cheese does not need to be pressed a second time, though. Age the cheese as directed on an aging mat inside an aging bin, flipping, and brushing away molds regularly.

MAKES ONE 4½-LB/2-KG WHEEL

MILK

UNHOMOGENIZED

SUGGESTED CULTURES

MA 4000

FINAL FORM

LARGE WHEEL

CATEGORIES

COOKED, PRESSED

TIME TO COMPLETION

3

MONTHS

This cheddar is unique—for one thing, because it's stirred for much less time than the Traditional Cheddar (page 156) or Baby Jack (page 152). The majority of the time the curds are in the pot, they are simply sitting under whey, not being stirred but still developing acid. Also, this cheddar is not salted in the pot like the other versions. A long period of pressing without salt leads to a tangy sharpness and an extra-crumbly, almost creamy texture. It is eaten younger as well. Try making it with a natural rind or with raw milk for added flavor.

INGREDIENTS

4 gal/15 L unhomogenized milk
½ tsp prehydrated mesophilic cultures
¾ tsp CaCl₂ diluted in ¼ cup/60 ml water
¾ tsp rennet diluted in ¼ cup/60 ml water
Saturated brine (see page 221)
Salt

SPECIAL EQUIPMENT

Medium (#60) cheesecloth; cheese form with follower; digital kitchen thermometer; cheese press or other pressing setup

1. Clean all surfaces and equipment before beginning. Line a colander with cheesecloth and place it in the sink. Set up a draining station by lining the cheese form with cheesecloth and placing it on a draining rack in the sink.

2. Pour the milk into a heavy-bottomed stockpot and warm over medium heat to 91°F/33°C, stirring gently. Remove from the heat.

3. Add the prehydrated cultures and stir in gently. Cover the pot and let the milk

ripen for 45 minutes. If necessary, reheat to 91°F/33°C degrees (or maintain heat using a method explained on page 40).

4. Add the CaCl₂ solution and stir gently. Add the rennet solution. Stir for 20 seconds. As you add the rennet, start a timer and watch for the flocculation point (see page 218). When reached, stop the timer. Multiply the number of minutes elapsed by 2.5. This is how long you need to wait before you cut the curd. Goal time is 20 to 25 minutes.

5. At the timed moment, cut the curd into pinto bean–size pieces, about ½ in/12 mm (see page 219). Let the curds heal for 2 minutes, then start stirring at the top of the vat and gradually moving downward. Cut large curds into smaller ones as they rise to the top. Eventually all the curds will be in motion.

6. Turn on the heat to low and warm the curds to 96°F/35°C over the course of 30 minutes while stirring gently. If the temperature is rising too quickly, turn off the heat intermittently.

7. When at temperature, remove from the heat, cover the pot, and allow the curds to rest under the whey for 1 hour.

8. Pour off the whey and catch the curds in the prepared colander. Transfer the curds into their prepared form or, if pressing without a form (see page 220), gather the ends of the cloth and twist to draw out more whey.

9. Apply medium weight (about 20 lb/9 kg) to the cheese for 10 minutes, then open up the form and/or cloth, flip the cheese, redress, and return to the press.

10. Increase the weight slightly to about 30 lb/14 kg and press for 8 to 10 hours.

11. Unwrap the wheel and place in the brine for 6 to 8 hours at 65°F/18°C, being sure to salt the parts of the cheese that float above the brine and flipping at least once midway through the brining.

12. Afterward, place wheel on a drying rack, covered with a piece of cheesecloth. Air-dry for 2 days, or until the rind feels just slightly moist. Move the cheese to an aging mat inside an aging bin. Allow a natural rind to form or seal with cream wax or cheese wax (see pages 222 to 223).

13. Age at 50°F/10°C for at least 3 months, or up to 6 months. If cultivating a natural rind, turn the cheese every other day, wiping, rubbing, or brushing the rind regularly and removing built-up moisture from the bin.

RESEALING A CHEDDAR RIND

If, after pressing, cracks cover the surface of your cheddar where individual curds came together, don't fret. This is a poorly sealed rind and you have a second chance to form a good one.

Bring 1 to 2 gal/3.8 to 7.5 L of water to a boil. Take the room-temperature cheddar (no more than 2 days old and preferably less than 1 day) and swaddle loosely with cheesecloth to form a sling. Lower the wheel into the boiling water and hold (suspended in the water, not sitting on the bottom of the pot) for 3 minutes. Next, bring the wheel out of the water and place back in its cheesecloth-lined form, straightening out the cloth first then applying heavy weight (50 lb/23 kg) for 3 to 5 hours. An easier solution is to age the cracked-surface cheese in a vacuum-sealed bag.

CHAPTER SEVEN

STRETCHED-CURD

Cheeses

Now widely available are home mozzarella-making kits, which include instructions and ingredients for making a ball of mozzarella with just 1 gal/3.8 L of milk and 30 minutes of time. Sadly, the kits don't always work out (because store-bought milk is variable and the recipe is finicky), which can damper one's home-cheesemaking enthusiasm. A common refrain I hear in my mozzarella-cheesemaking classes is: "I made mozzarella once and it was great; then I tried to make it again and . . . " or "I tried to make mozzarella but everything just turned to mush." For this reason, don't start with mozzarella. Make your way there.

The name *pasta filata* tells you what the cheese is: *pasta* (Latin: dough) and *filata* (Latin: column). It translates from Italian to "spun paste" or "spun dough." When I think of *pasta filata*, I think of phyllo, or filo, dough, both for the etymological connection as well as the mental visual of layers. As we pull these cheeses into their final forms, we spin curds into thin phyllo-dough-like striations. This transformation changes the texture and form of the cheese, but it also releases moisture and fat and is where we introduce salt, changing the internal chemistry of the cheese as well as extending shelf life.

AN ACIDIC SWEET SPOT

To make mozzarella, start with fresh milk. Turn the milk into a gel then cut, heat, and stir the curds to a proper temperature. Next, drain everything. Then, depending on if you're making a direct-acid version (Quick Mozz) or a cultured version (the others), stretch the dough immediately, or within several hours of ripening.

The ripening period, like the ripening period that happens before adding rennet, gives the cultures time to break down more lactose into lactic acid. As acid builds inside the draining curd, the proteins change in nature. When the acidity reaches the perfect level, the proteins form long, elastic threads. This will only happen for a short window of time (because the cultures continue producing acid that

continues to change the nature of the proteins). If the curds haven't ripened enough, they won't stretch. If the curds are overripe, they break apart.

You can track this acidic sweet spot by monitoring pH (target pH levels are listed on the chart below). Or, if you don't have a pH meter or strips, use the Stretch Test (described below).

pH Range for Stretching Cheese

TYPE OF PASTA FILATA CHEESE	PH RANGE FOR OPTIMAL STRETCHING
Direct-Acid (Quick Mozz)	5.2 to 5.4
Cultured Dough (Scamorza, Provolone, etc.)	5.1 to 5.3

HOW TO DO A STRETCH TEST

1. Cut a french-fry-size piece of curd from the drained curd block.

2. Place the piece in a small bowl and cover well with very hot (155° to 175°F/68° to 79°C) water.

3. After 1 minute, using a spoon, take the piece out of the water and tug gently. If the curd breaks or stretches only ½ in/12 mm and then breaks, the curd needs more time to ripen. If it stretches freely, it is ready to be shaped.

LIKE OVERWORKED PASTRY

Treat your mozzarella curds as you would delicate pastry dough. The less you handle it, the more successful it will be. The more you work it, the tougher it will be. Often, I see first timers attacking their dough, packing it together tightly, then pulling it open again with as much strength as if they were working with duct tape. They keep at it, thinking the dough will "come around." Don't do this.

If your stretching temperature is correct (between 150° and 180°F/66° and 82°C), the curds, after a minute or two in hot water, should feel drapey. You fold these curds together to form a smooth, uniform disk shape. Next, bring the edges of this disk together as though you are closing a coin purse. Pinch off the edges of the "coin purse" and drop the just-sealed ball into cold water.

TIPS FOR STRETCHING

- *When making Cultured Mozzarella (page 174) and Provolone (page 176), make sure the curds are properly acidified before stretching. If they don't pass the "Stretch Test," hold longer at ripening temperatures.*

- *If the curd collapses into a ricotta-looking mess when you try and stretch it, the milk you used was ultra-pasteurized or pasteurized at too high of a temperature. Or, if your curd turns into the densest rock-like object ever, try another brand.*

- *Warm the curd to room temperature before stretching it. After stretching, drop the formed cheese immediately into cold water to help hold its shape.*

- *Don't stretch the whole recipe worth of curds at once. Stretch small, handful-size amounts.*

HOW TO STRETCH CURDS

1. Gather a large bowl filled with cold water, a small bowl of salt, and a medium bowl in which you will do the stretching. Have ready heat-resistant gloves (if you need them) and a thermometer.

2. Take the drained, ripened curd and cut into french-fry-size strips. Place a handful of strips in the stretching bowl, then cover with 1 in/2.5 cm of 155° to 175°F/68°C to 79°C water. If the water is too cold, the cheese will not stretch; if the water is too hot, you will be in pain and the cheese will fall apart.

3. Stir the strips in the water to expose all sides to the heat. Wait 1 to 2 minutes, then test to see if a strip is ready by doing a stretch test. If necessary, replace the stretching water with hotter water.

4. When ready, move the strips to one side of the bowl (using a spoon if needed), then gather them in your hand. Fold and pull until the cheese is smooth and shiny. Fold in ¼ tsp of salt per ½ cup/120 ml worth of curd. Form a ball by pressing the cheese through your thumb and forefinger, then pinching off the excess as shown in the bottom-left photo on page 167. Try not to overwork the cheese.

5. Drop immediately into the cold water.

HOW TO STORE STRETCHED-CURD CHEESES

Storing your beautiful homemade mozzarella correctly will keep its flavor bright.

FRESH MOZZARELLA

To store in water or whey: Mix 1 qt/960 ml filtered water or boiled and cooled whey with 1 tsp CaCl$_2$ and ½ tsp white vinegar. Pour into a large container. Add the mozzarella balls. Store in the fridge for up to 5 days.

To store in plastic wrap: Take the mozzarella out of the cold-water bowl. Place one ball at a time onto squares of plastic wrap. Roll up tightly and tie the ends of the plastic wrap to secure. Place the wrapped balls in a bowl in case of drips. Store in the fridge for up to 10 days.

BURRATA

To store in a container: Place the just-filled, sealed burrata directly into a small, clean storage container (skipping the cold-water bath). The cheese eventually will "melt" into the shape of the container. You can also choose, for increased moisture, to pour some salted heavy cream over the top. Store, covered, in the fridge for up to 4 days.

CULTURED MOZZARELLA AND PROVOLONE

To age with a natural rind: After brining, dry the cheese for several days on a draining mat or by creating a pouch of cheesecloth and hanging it up with string. When the rind feels dry, move the cheeses to an aging bin or, if in the shape of a scamorza, hang up directly inside an aging cave. Brush away or cut off molds from the rind before eating.

To smoke: After brining, move the cheese to aging mats placed on top of a drying rack. Dry for 1 to 2 days. When the rind feels nearly dry, place into a cold smoker. Smoke according to the instructions, or for several hours. Afterward, vacuum-seal and keep at 55°F/13°C or cooler for up to 6 months.

To vacuum-seal: When cheeses have dried, store in vacuum bags in the fridge or cave for several months to 1 year.

To store in plastic wrap: After brining, wrap the cheese tightly in plastic wrap. Store in the fridge for up to 2 weeks.

MAKES 20 OZ/560 G FRESH
MOZZARELLA

MILK

UNHOMOGENIZED

FINAL FORM

VARIABLE

CATEGORIES

FRESH UNRIPENED,
PASTA FILATA

TIME TO COMPLETION

1

DAY

This recipe makes a fresh mozzarella that is simple, milky, and soft as opposed to the other stretched-curd recipes that are firmer or more complex in their flavors. To be successful, you have to start with high-quality, very fresh, unhomogenized milk, and I highly recommend using cow's milk. Without the right milk, the cheese won't come together, won't stretch nicely, or will be too tough—not the luscious cheese you wish for. For a list of possible milk sources, visit www.cheesemaking.com and search the "Good Milk List."

Note: You won't use CaCl$_2$ in this recipe, though you will use it in the Cultured Mozzarella and Provolone recipes that follow. In ways, this recipe feels as much like a variation of Ricotta or Paneer as it does a mozzarella.

INGREDIENTS

2 gal/7.5 L unhomogenized milk

1½ cups/330 ml white vinegar or 3 tsp citric acid diluted in ¼ cup/60 ml cool water

⅛ tsp lipase powder (optional)

½ tsp rennet diluted in ¼ cup/60 ml water

SPECIAL EQUIPMENT

Digital kitchen thermometer; heat resistant gloves

1. Clean all surfaces and equipment before beginning. Set a colander in the sink. Set up an area for stretching cheeses (see page 164).

2. Pour the milk into a pot. Then, when the milk is cooler than 70°F/21°C, add the vinegar while stirring. This brings the pH value of the milk down to 5.2 to 5.4.

3. Warm the milk over medium heat to 90°F/32°C, while stirring. Remove from the heat. Sprinkle the lipase (if using) over the top and allow 1 minute for it to dissolve, then stir in.

4. Add the rennet solution. Stir for 20 seconds, then stop the motion of the milk. A curd will form in about 3 minutes.

5. After 8 minutes, cut the curd into a grid, with approximately 1 in/2.5 cm between the cuts.

6. Next, gently cut the columns horizontally by scooping the curds from the edge of the pot and moving them toward the middle. After 2 to 3 minutes, this motion will free up enough whey that all the curds will start to move. Stir gently and cut down large chunks as needed.

7. Return the pot to the heat and warm to 95°F/35°C over the course of 10 minutes, stirring the whole time.

8. Drain the pot into the colander, collecting the curds and discarding the whey. Drain for 20 minutes, flipping once midway.

9. Proceed with the stretching instructions. Eat within 2 days.

MAKES THREE 6-OZ/170-G BALLS

Burrata tastes like decadent cream with a unique feathery texture. If you've never had it, you're not alone. It can be hard to find because its moisture—as well as its sweetness and lack of acidity—make it *highly* perishable. That's one good reason to make your own.

As you make burrata, you'll find it is essentially cheese-stuffed cheese with some cream in the middle. The more cream you can manage to stuff in, the softer and gooier the burrata will be. Unfortunately, stuffing a thin sheet of cheese with runny cream isn't easy. Go slowly and remember that no matter what your final product looks like, it will all taste good. The traditional filling for burrata, called *Stracciatella*, uses up bits of curd left over from making mozzarella balls.

MILK

UNHOMOGENIZED MILK, HEAVY CREAM

FINAL FORM

BALLS

CATEGORIES

FRESH UNRIPENED, *PASTA FILATA*

INGREDIENTS

½ cup/120 ml leftover mozzarella bits

1½ cup/360 ml heavy cream (can also be sour or clotted cream, butter, or ricotta)

½ tsp salt

1 recipe Quick Mozz (page 168, for a softer curd) or Cultured Mozzarella (page 174, for a firmer, more aromatic curd)

SPECIAL EQUIPMENT

Teacup for shaping burrata; several 12-in/30-cm strips food-grade cord; heat-resistant gloves (optional)

1. Shred the mozzarella bits so they look like shredded chicken. Place the shreds in a bowl.

2. Add the cream and salt. Mush the cream and shreds together with your fingertips until they form a fine paste. Set the *Stracciatella* aside.

3. Per the stretching instructions on page 164, work approximately ½ cup/

120 ml mozzarella curd into a smooth and symmetrical ball (see page 166).

4. Flatten the ball to form a 4-in/10-cm disk. Open up the disk wide enough to drape over the top of the teacup or just cup your hand as in the photos, making sure excess cheese hangs over the edge of the teacup, like a pie crust over a pie plate. Moving quickly to conserve the warmth of the just-stretched dough, take ½ cup/120 ml of *Stracciatella* and place it in the center of the cheese in the teacup. Try to not have filling spill on the edge of the cheese bowl or it will not reseal properly.

5. Working quickly, bring the edges of the cheese together to form a pouch. Squeeze the pouch closed very tightly, pinching off the excess tab or tying closed with a strip of cord. Store as directed on page 165. The burrata will soften over the course of a day though it can be eaten immediately. Eat within 4 days.

TIME TO COMPLETION

1

DAY

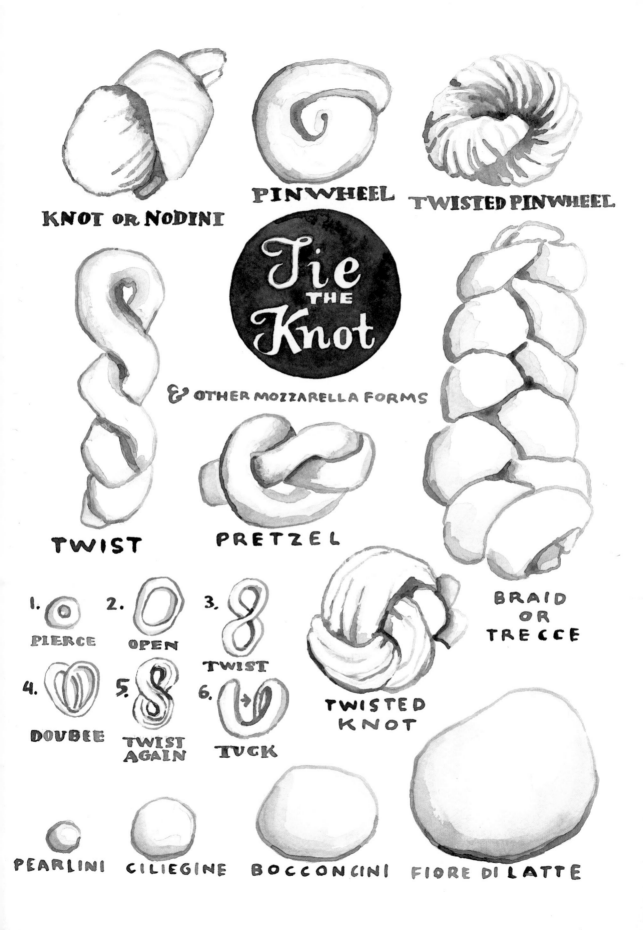

KNOT OR NODINI

PINWHEEL

TWISTED PINWHEEL

Tie the Knot

& OTHER MOZZARELLA FORMS

TWIST

PRETZEL

1. PIERCE

2. OPEN

3. TWIST

4. DOUBEE

5. TWIST AGAIN

6. TUCK

TWISTED KNOT

BRAID OR TRECCE

PEARLINI   CILIEGINE   BOCCONCINI   FIORE DI LATTE

CULTURED mozzarella

A.K.A. PIZZA CHEESE, QUESO OAXAQUEÑO, QUESO ASADERO

MAKES FOUR 6-OZ/170-G BALLS

MILK

UNHOMOGENIZED

SUGGESTED CULTURES

TA50 AND MM100; LIPASE

FINAL FORM

BALLS

CATEGORIES

PASTA FILATA

TIME TO COMPLETION

1

DAY

This slightly more involved mozzarella uses both direct acid (citric acid) as well as a mixture of cultures (both thermophilic and mesophilic), and it's my favorite of the three *pasta filata* recipes in *Kitchen Creamery*. This recipe takes several hours from start to finish (instead of just one, as with the Quick Mozz on page 168), but the flavor, texture, and shelf life are well worth it.

INGREDIENTS

2 gal/7.5 L cold (below 65°F/18°C) unhomogenized milk

⅛ tsp prehydrated mesophilic cultures

⅛ tsp prehydrated thermophilic cultures

Pinch of lipase (optional)

1¼ tsp citric acid diluted in ¼ cup/60 ml water

½ tsp CaCl$_2$ diluted in ¼ cup/60 ml water

½ tsp rennet diluted in ¼ cup/60 ml water

SPECIAL EQUIPMENT

Metal colander with legs that can fit inside a larger pot to serve as the "ripening station"; medium (#60) cheesecloth; digital kitchen thermometer; pH strips for testing ripeness (optional); heat-resistant gloves (optional)

1. Clean all surfaces and equipment before beginning. Set up an area for stretching cheeses (see page 164). Line the colander with cheesecloth and place in the sink.

2. Pour half of the milk into a large pot and warm over medium heat to 97°F/36°C, while stirring. Turn off heat.

3. Add all the mesophilic, thermophilic, and optional lipase cultures and stir in. Cover the pot and allow the milk to ripen

for 45 minutes while maintaining the temperature.

4. After the ripening period is up, in a separate pot, combine the citric-acid solution with the remaining cold milk. Stir well.

5. Next, combine the cold milk with the warmer cultured milk in a large pot. Place over low heat and bring the temperature up to 92°F/33°C, while stirring gently. When at temperature, remove from the heat.

6. Add the CaCl$_2$ solution and stir in. Add the rennet solution. Stir for 20 seconds, then stop the motion of the milk. Cover the pot and let the milk rest for 30 minutes.

7. Afterward, cut the curd into a grid of grape-size pieces, or in 1 in/2.5 cm columns (see page 219). Let the curds heal for 2 minutes, then, starting slowly and at the top of the pot, cut the columns of curd horizontally. Scoop about 1 in/2.5 cm below the curd surface, lift up a spoonful of curds and then lay them down in the center of the pot. Scoop from the edges and move the curds toward the middle. In this way, you are more lifting and moving the curds (as well as cutting them) than actually stirring them,

ADVANCED

initially. Work your way downward to the bottom of the pot, until all the columns have been broken down into smaller pieces.

8. Once all the curds are broken down, start to stir. When all of the curds in the pot are in motion, place the pot over low heat and warm slowly to 100°F/38°C over the course of 20 minutes, while stirring. Do not heat too quickly or the curds will not dry out sufficiently. Check the temperature of the pot frequently and adjust the heat.

9. When the pot reaches 100°F/38°C, turn off the heat and allow the curds to settle to the bottom. Pour the contents of the pot into the prepared colander. Drain briefly then move the curd-filled colander back into the empty cheese pot. Prop up the colander if needed to make sure the curds will drain freely and not sit in whey.

10. Cover the pot and maintain the temperature at 100°F/37°C for the next 1 to 4 hours, or until the pH reaches 5.1 to 5.3. To identify this point without a pH meter or pH strips, continue to perform "stretch tests" (see page 163). Once the curd is ripe, proceed with stretching, or wrap tightly and store the unstretched, ripened curd in the fridge for up to 24 hours before proceeding with stretching. Do not overripen or the curd will crumble when you try to stretch it.

MAKES FOUR 6-OZ/170-G BALLS
OR BRAIDS

ADVANCED

MILK

UNHOMOGENIZED

SUGGESTED CULTURES

TA 60 OR 61

FINAL FORM

BALLS

CATEGORIES

COOKED, *PASTA FILATA*, SMOKED

TIME TO COMPLETION

2

MONTHS

I learned to make this cheese while living on a ten-cow dairy in the Apennine Mountains, not far from Parma, Italy. I remember how pleasant the *caseificio*, or creamery, felt in late November when the ground outside was covered with frost and the sky was dark. We would stand at the vat, in clouds of steam, stretching the curd and feeling happy to be warm.

Provolone can be enjoyed young (*dulce*) or aged (*picante*). When younger, it is almost indistinguishable from mozzarella. Aged, it becomes spicy and distinct. You can shape your provolone into easy-to-slice logs by stuffing the pliable just-stretched dough into about 2-in-/5-cm-diameter PVC piping. Or you can form it into scamorza or caccioca-vallo shapes.

This recipe is different from Cultured Mozzarella (page 174) because the curd is cooked to a higher temperature, making it drier but better for aging. When stretching it, you'll notice it's firmer than the Quick Mozz (page 168) and similar to the Cultured Mozzarella dough.

INGREDIENTS

2 gal/7.5 L unhomogenized milk
¼ tsp prehydrated thermophilic cultures
½ tsp CaCl₂ diluted in ¼ cup/60 ml water
½ tsp rennet diluted in ¼ cup/60 ml water
Saturated brine (see page 221)

SPECIAL EQUIPMENT

Metal colander with legs that can fit inside a larger pot to serve as the "ripening station"; medium (#60) cheesecloth; digital kitchen thermometer; pH strips for testing ripeness (optional); heat-resistant gloves (optional)

1. Clean all surfaces and equipment before beginning. Set up an area for stretching cheeses (see page 164). Line the colander with cheesecloth and place it in the sink.

2. Pour the milk into a heavy-bottomed stockpot and warm over medium heat to 92°F/33°C, stirring gently. Remove from the heat.

3. Add the prehydrated cultures and stir in, then let the pot rest for 30 minutes.

4. Add the CaCl₂ solution and stir gently. Add the rennet and stir in for 20 seconds. As you add the rennet, start a timer and watch for the flocculation point (see page 218). When reached, stop the timer. Multiply the number of minutes elapsed by 3. This is how long you need to wait before you cut the curd. Goal time is 25 to 30 minutes.

5. At the timed moment, cut the curd into lentil-size pieces, ¼ to ½ in/6 to 12 mm (see page 219). Let the curds heal for 2 minutes. Start stirring at the top of the vat and slowly work your way downward, increasing in speed as more whey flushes out of the curd. Cut down large pieces that rise to the top. Once all the curds are in motion, place the pot back over low heat.

6. While stirring, bring the temperature of the curds up to 115°F/46°C over the course of 40 minutes, taking care to not raise the temperature too quickly. If needed, turn off the heat intermittently.

7. Once the pot reaches 115°F/46°C, remove from the heat and maintain this temperature for 30 minutes, stirring every several minutes to prevent the curds from clumping together, or "knitting." Afterward, let the curds settle for 10 minutes.

8. Pour off the whey from the pot, reserving about 1 gal/3.8 L, then pour the curds into the prepared colander. When all the curds are in the colander, flip the curd block so the top becomes the bottom. With the curd block in the colander, place the colander back into the pot. Pour the reserved whey into the bottom of the pot until it almost reaches the bottom of the colander— essentially suspending the curd block over a warm steam bath. Cover the pot with a lid.

9. Allow the curd block to ripen for approximately 3 hours, flipping regularly and making sure the temperature inside the pot is at least 95°F/32°C and not more than 105°F/41°C. If using pH strips or a pH meter, ripen until the pH reaches 5.1 to 5.3. If needed, turn on the heat to bump the temperature of the pot back up.

10. After 2 hours, test if the curd is ready to stretch by doing a "stretch test" (see page 163). If the curd does not stretch easily, wait another 30 minutes before trying again.

11. When the curd is ripe, proceed with stretching, forming, and salting.

12. Afterward, allow the cheeses to air-dry for up to 2 days, then age for 2 months or more on an aging mat, inside an aging bin in a 50°F/10°C area or packaged in a vacuum-sealed bag. This is also a great cheese to cold-smoke (see page 193), if desired.

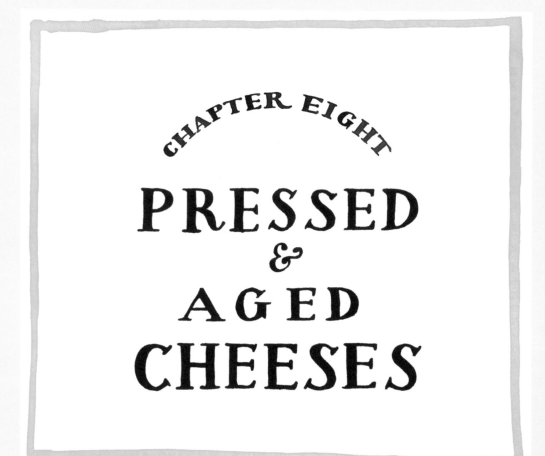

CHAPTER EIGHT

PRESSED
&
AGED
CHEESES

THE TASTE OF TIME

Finally, I thought it would be wise to include a few recipes for cheeses you can age. Indeed, you can age several of the earlier recipes, including Divino (page 106), Traditional Cheddar (page 156), and Marbler (page 118), but I'm grouping these last few recipes together as they are all considered cooked, pressed, or hard cheeses. All of them will be delicious aged out to 1 year.

Not all cheeses can be aged forever (and really, should any cheese be?). An aging cheese needs to be pointed in the right direction while still in the vat. As you cook and stir the curds in the recipes ahead, the thoroughness with which you stir is vital. Whereas with a chèvre or a feta recipe, the stirring segment is short or nonexistent, here stirring and heating drive moisture out of the curds. If you notice large clumps of curds forming (often at the bottom of the vat), stir more quickly and make sure you are reaching all of the curds in the pot.

Sometimes if my vat is deep and my stirring utensil modest, I just scrub my whole arm clean and use it to stir the curds.

(GRUYÈRE STYLE)

MAKES ONE 3- TO 4-LB/1.4- TO 1.8-KG WHEEL

This recipe is unique in terms of cooked and pressed cheeses because the renneting time is short (20 minutes), the cooking time is long (over an hour), and the curds are brought to the (reasonably high) temperature of 115°F/46°C. A shorter ripening period plus a bit of washing yields a sweeter (not acidic) cheese, dry enough to age and pliable enough to cut without crumbling, unless of course you overage it like the one in the photo here.

MILK

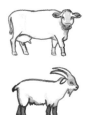

UNHOMOGENIZED

SUGGESTED CULTURES

THERMO C PLUS
PROPIONIC
BACTERIA

FINAL FORM

LARGE WHEEL

CATEGORIES

WASHED RIND,
COOKED, PRESSED,
ALPINE-STYLE,
SMEAR-RIND

TIME TO COMPLETION

5

MONTHS

INGREDIENTS

4 gal/15 L unhomogenized milk
½ tsp prehydrated thermophilic cultures
¾ tsp CaCl₂ diluted in ¼ cup/60 ml water
¾ tsp rennet diluted in ¼ cup/60 ml water
Saturated brine (see page 221)
Salt

SPECIAL EQUIPMENT

Large cheese form, with follower; medium (#60) cheesecloth to fit the form; digital kitchen thermometer; cheese press or other pressing setup

1. Clean all surfaces and equipment before beginning. Set up a draining station by lining the cheese form with cheesecloth and placing it on a draining rack in the sink.

2. Pour the milk into a heavy-bottomed stockpot and warm over medium heat to 86°F/30°C, stirring gently. Once at temperature, turn off the heat.

3. Add the prehydrated cultures, then stir in gently. Allow the pot to sit for 10 minutes.

4. Add the CaCl₂ solution and stir in. Add the rennet solution. Stir for 20 seconds, then stop the motion of the milk. As you add the rennet, start a timer and watch for

the flocculation point (see page 218). When reached, stop the timer. Multiply the number of minutes elapsed by 2. This is how long you need to wait before you cut the curd. Goal time is 20 to 25 minutes.

5. At the timed moment, cut the curd into lentil-size pieces, about ¼ in/6 mm (see page 219). Let the curds heal for 2 minutes, then start stirring at the top of the vat and work your way down, getting all the curds into motion. Start slowly but quickly increase your stirring speed.

6. Once all the curds are in motion, return the pot to the heat and, while stirring, bring to 113°F/45°C over the course of 45 minutes. Do not heat too quickly. Stir continuously to prevent the curds from matting together. Remove from the heat.

7. After waiting a moment for the curds to sink, remove 2 qt/2 L of whey and replace it with an equal amount of 135°F/57°C water. The goal temperature of the vat is 115°F/46°C. This modest washing step slows acid development, leading toward a more pliable texture in the finished cheese.

CONTINUED

8. With the heat off, stir for another 25 minutes. By this time, the curds should feel firm and rubbery. If you reach into the vat, the curds should bounce off the back of your hand like ping-pong balls. When you take a handful of curds from the pot and squeeze them tightly in your fist, they should stick together but then readily break back apart when crumbled.

9. Pitch the curds (see page 73) for 5 minutes, then, with a clean arm, reach into the pot and start to press or push the curds together to form a curd block. Press and compact the block under the whey for 5 minutes.

10. Finally, lift the curds out in large chunks and pack directly into the prepared cheese form. Filter the remaining whey to collect the last cheese bits. Add these to the form.

11. Pull tightly on the cheesecloth to remove wrinkles then cover with the follower. Press lightly (10 lb/4.5 kg) for 20 minutes, then open up the form, flip, and redress the cheese. Top with the follower and press at medium weight (about 20 lb/9 kg) for 30 minutes, then flip and redress again. Finally, press under heavy weight (25 to 30 lb/11 to 14 kg) for 14 to 16 hours, at room temperature.

12. Unwrap the cheese wheel and move it into the brine. Sprinkle the exposed cheese surface with salt. Brine for 8 hours at room temperature. Flip once, midway through.

13. Remove the cheese from the brine and set on an aging mat on top of a drying rack and cover with a piece of cheesecloth. Air-dry until the rind feels just slightly moist.

14. *For a Smear-Ripened Rind:* Start your rind off by washing gently, every other day for the first 2 weeks, with a weak (3 percent) salt solution (see page 221) or the Red-Rind Wash (page 121). You can also help the rind establish by rubbing the rind of a mature red-rinded cheese against the rind of your fresh one.

After 2 weeks, or once the rind starts to seem established (regular color, appropriate stinky smell, etc.), introduce moisture only when needed. Use your hand to rub back any molds that might crop up. Maintain the humidity (removing built up moisture with a clean paper towel and washing with more liquid if too dry) and continue to turn and rub regularly until done.

For a Cream-Waxed Rind: Use a clean 1½-in/4-cm brush to coat the entire top surface and sides of the cheese wheel with cream wax. Allow the wax to dry, then flip and apply to the other surface and sides. If desired, apply a second coat.

Set the coated cheese in an aging bin on a aging mat. Turn weekly and brush off molds if they appear. Note that a cream-waxed cheese will have less flavor intensity than the smear-rinded version.

MAKES ONE 3- TO 4-LB/1.4- TO 1.8-KG WHEEL

This is the cheese with which I learned to use an "adjustable cheese ring." This ring is just what it sounds like: a belt that is progressively tightened to shape the cheese as it drains. I learned this technique using a beautiful wooden ring that tightened with a hand-woven cord—exactly the materials you could never use in a commercial creamery here in the States.

Note that Asiago can be made as a lower-fat cheese. Substitute 1 gal/3.8 L of whole milk with skim milk. If lowering the fat, give the cheese an additional month or two to age.

INGREDIENTS

4 gal/15 L whole milk
½ tsp prehydrated thermophilic cultures
⅛ tsp lipase powder
¾ tsp CaCl₂ diluted in ¼ cup/60 ml water
¾ tsp rennet diluted in ¼ cup/60 ml water
Saturated brine (see page 221)
Salt

SPECIAL EQUIPMENT

Large cheese form, with follower; medium (#60) cheesecloth; digital kitchen thermometer; press or pressing system; olive oil or cream wax for rind

1. Clean all surfaces and equipment before beginning. Set up a draining station by lining the cheese form with cheesecloth and placing it on a draining rack in the sink.

2. Pour the milk into a heavy-bottomed stockpot and warm over medium heat to 100°F/38°C, stirring gently. Turn off the heat.

3. Add the prehydrated cultures and lipase. Stir in gently, then allow the pot to sit for 10 minutes.

4. Add the CaCl₂ solution and stir gently. Add the rennet solution. Stir for 20 seconds, then stop the motion of the milk. As you add the rennet, start a timer and watch for the flocculation point (see page 218). When reached, stop the timer. Multiply the number of minutes elapsed by 2.5. This is how long you need to wait before you cut the curd. Goal time is 25 to 30 minutes.

5. At the timed moment, cut the curd into lentil-size pieces, ¼ in/6 mm (see page 219). Let the curds heal for 2 minutes, then start stirring at the top of the vat and work your way down. Make sure all the curds are in motion before turning on the heat.

6. Turn on the heat to low and warm the curds slowly to 110°F/43°C over the course of 25 minutes. Stir continuously and make sure the temperature of the pot doesn't rise too quickly.

CONTINUED

MILK

UNHOMOGENIZED

SUGGESTED CULTURES

THERMO B; LIPASE

FINAL FORM

LARGE WHEEL

CATEGORIES

COOKED, PRESSED, ITALIAN-STYLE

TIME TO COMPLETION

3 MONTHS

7. Once the curds reach 110°F/43°C and 25 minutes have passed, start to raise the temperature more quickly—up to 118°F/48°C over the course of 15 minutes, while stirring. At 118°F/48°C, turn off the heat, cover the pot, and allow the curds to rest for 15 minutes. By this point, the curds should feel dense and bouncy. When you take a handful of curds from the pot and squeeze them tightly in your fist, they should stick together but then readily break back apart when crumbled.

8. With a clean arm, reach into the pot and press the curds together into a curd pack for 5 minutes, then lift chunks of the curds out of the vat and directly into the prepared form. Tug on the ends of the cheesecloth to smooth out wrinkles, then cover the form with the follower. If working without a form, gather the ends of the cheesecloth together and twist to form a pouch (see page 220).

9. Press at medium weight (20 lb/9 kg) for 5 minutes, then open up the form, flip, and redress the cheese. Press again for another 15 minutes, then flip and redress again. Finally, press with heavy weight (30 to 50 lb/15 to 25 kg) for 10 hours at room temperature.

10. Remove the cheese from the press and place in the brine for 6 to 8 hours at 65°F/18°C. Flip the wheel once midway through. Cover the exposed cheese with salt.

11. After brining, cure the cheese on a draining rack covered with cheesecloth for 2 days, or until the rind feels barely moist. Turn often.

12. Either apply several coats of cream wax to the cheese, dip the cheese into traditional cheese wax, vacuum-seal, or rub with olive oil daily for 1 month to form a natural rind.

13. Keep at 55°F/13°C in a humid aging cave or aging bin for a minimum of 3 months, or up to 1 year.

ONE 6-LB/2.7-G WHEEL

MILK

RAW SHEEP'S MILK

SUGGESTED CULTURES

THERMO B OR FLORA DANICA

FINAL FORM

LARGE WHEEL

CATEGORIES

COOKED, PRESSED, ITALIAN-STYLE, NATURAL RIND

TIME TO COMPLETION

4

MONTHS

I end this section with the cheese recipe that began my entire cheesemaking journey: Pecorino Toscano. I know the chances of a car-free, urban-dwelling cheesemaker finding a large volume of fresh sheep's milk are slim, so say I'm planting a seed.

I've always wished there were more sheep dairies in the United States because sheep's milk is the most beautiful milk I've ever worked with. After just a few months of aging, the cheese this milk makes is pure ambrosia. I've heard cheesemakers say that all you have to do is look at sheep's milk, and it becomes cheese. It is that destined. My hope is that one of the readers of *Kitchen Creamery* will read this and know that the fantasy you've had about buying land and getting sheep is now endorsed. I beg you to go forward and, if you ever need a hand in the milking parlor or ever have a bit of milk to spare, give me a call.

INGREDIENTS

4 gal/15 L raw sheep's milk

¼ tsp prehydrated thermophilic cultures

¾ tsp rennet diluted in ¼ cup/60 ml water

About 1½ cups/340 g salt

SPECIAL EQUIPMENT

Large cheese form with follower; medium (#60) cheesecloth; digital kitchen thermometer; cheese press or other pressing setup

1. Clean all surfaces and equipment before beginning. Set up a draining station by lining the cheese form with cheesecloth and placing it on a draining rack in the sink.

2. Pour the milk into a heavy-bottomed stockpot and warm over medium heat to 91°F/33°C, stirring gently. Turn off the heat.

3. Add the prehydrated cultures and stir in. Cover the pot and let the milk ripen for 25 minutes.

4. Add the rennet. Stir for 20 seconds. As you add the rennet, start a timer and watch for the flocculation point (see page 218). When reached, stop the timer. Multiply the number of minutes elapsed by 3. This is how long you need to wait before you cut the curd. Goal time is 20 to 25 minutes.

5. At the timed moment, cut the curd into lentil-size pieces, ¼ in/6 mm (see page 219) or larger if you plan to enjoy a moister, younger cheese. Let the curds heal for 2 minutes, then start stirring, working your way from the top of the vat downward, cutting large pieces as they rise to the top. (If you've only worked with cow's milk, you'll notice how outrageously dense sheep's milk curds are in comparison!)

6. Once all the curds are in motion, place over low heat and warm the curds to 98°F/ 37°C over the course of 30 minutes, stirring the entire time and making sure the temperature doesn't rise too quickly. Once at temperature, pitch the curds (see page 73) for 15 minutes.

7. With a clean arm, reach into the pot and press the curds together into a curd block. Press and compact in this manner for 10 minutes, then lift large chunks of curd out of the vat and into the prepared cheese form.

8. When half the curds have been hooped, stop and, using your hands and the weight of your body, press into the cheese in the form to push out more whey, then finish filling with the curds still in the pot.

9. Tug on the ends of the cheesecloth to straighten out the wrinkles, then cover with the follower. Press lightly (10 lb/4.5 kg) for 10 minutes, then open the press, flip the cheese, redress, and press again. This time, press with medium weight (20 lb/9 kg) for another 4 to 5 hours, flipping at least once.

10. Remove the cheese from the press and coat with the salt. There should be at least ¼ in/6 mm of salt caked onto all sides of the cheese. Set the salted cheese on an aging mat for 5 to 7 hours at room temperature (about 70°F/21°C), flipping once midway through.

11. Rinse off the salt with cool tap water, then cure the cheese on an aging mat (on a drying rack, covered with cheesecloth) at room temperature for 2 days, turning regularly. When the surface of the cheese is barely damp to the touch, move the cheese to an aging mat set inside an aging bin. Set in a 55°F/13°C location. Regularly turn the cheese and brush away excess surface mold. Ripen for 4 to 8 months.

CHAPTER NINE

ARTFUL AGING

As a cheese grows older, sugars, fats, and proteins inside the wheel change to a diversity of smaller, simpler molecules (amino acids, fatty acids, CO_2, and NH_3). What causes these changes are mainly enzymes—the rennet or lipase you added earlier, enzymes naturally present in the raw milk, enzymes that cultures leave behind when they die off, or enzymes infiltrating from microbial activity at the rind. With these remarkable and complex transformations comes flavor—salted caramel, beef broth, burnt toast, wet earth—and tastes for which there are not yet words.

You've gotten to the last and maybe most important step in the cheese's journey: affinage. The most important thing to remember now is that this wheel is alive! It's breathing and changing and the moisture and temperature you keep it at will affect it profoundly. From here on out, I'll refer to the environment you will keep your cheese in as a "cave." Some cheese styles are more sensitive to the conditions of their cave than others—vacuum-sealed cheeses and cheeses covered with cheese wax or cream wax are less impacted by the world around them than a soft-ripened cheese like the Truffle Brie on page 133. Step by step, you'll figure out a system and cave that works best for you.

AGING BASICS

Here are some simple guidelines to aging your cheese.

- Aim for an aging process that is slow and steady versus quick and fluctuating.

- Lower aging temperatures reduce the likelihood of developing off-flavors.

- A higher temperature aging environment is sometimes used—for example, to produce the eyes in Swiss-style cheeses like Rising Moon (page 111).

- Too low a temperature means a cheese ages too slowly. This is problematic if the cheese is losing moisture over time. Additionally, a cheese (or rather, its aging bin) takes up valuable cave space.

- If the humidity in the aging environment is too low, the cheese may crack; if the humidity is too high, molds, yeasts, and bacteria (whether desirable or undesirable) grow too aggressively.

WHICH STYLES TO AGE

You can generally age any cheese that has a stable form, such as a wheel, square, or pyramid, and a well-sealed skin. This means you cannot age a tub of fresh chèvre or a bunch of mozzarella balls in water. A cheese whose rind didn't seal correctly shouldn't be aged. An unclosed rind means inlets for unwanted microorganisms to flourish. You want these on the outside of the cheese (where you can brush, wipe, or rub them off) or not at all. The only way to age a cheese with a poorly sealed rind is in a vacuum-sealed bag.

CHOOSING THE RIGHT WHEEL SIZE

Of the ageable cheeses, and especially those not using a wax or a vacuum-seal, larger wheels age more effectively. A larger wheel has less surface area to volume. This means, in the end, you won't have a wheel that is nearly all rind with no innards. And if you want to play with a cheese trier (see page 34), you'll need a wheel that's large enough to do so (more than 2 lb/910 g).

To make a larger wheel, you need more milk, which means you need a large pot. Earlier recipes in this book require only 1 to 2 gal/3.8 to 7.5 L of milk, so initially you can get by using an average big pasta pot. Later, nearly all the recipes take 4 gal/15 L of milk. Although you can cut a recipe in half, I encourage you to step up to the larger-sized vat if you want to play with the art of affinage.

RIND TREATMENTS

We've talked about which recipes you can age and the ideal wheel size. Now, let's go over ways to work with the rind. There is an enormous difference in the amount of tending that each different rind treatment requires. Cheese wax and vacuum-sealing (and, to a slightly lesser degree, cream wax) are the easiest ways to treat a rind. Bloomy-rinds, smeared-rinds, washed-rinds, and natural rinds take much more work. However, you'll be paid back in the flavors these processes can create.

Figuring out what rind treatments work for you is part of your job as "head cheesemaker." To achieve the cheese you are hoping for, you may not need the influences of a rind. The majority of cheddars produced in the United States today are aged in vacuum-sealed bags. On the other hand, if you want the mushroomy notes of a Camembert or the boldness of a smear-rinded Alpine cheese, waxing or vacuum-sealing are not an option. The uniqueness of these cheeses are a direct result of what's happening on the rind.

Just as when you chose which recipe to make, which milk to work with, which cultures to buy, and which forms to use, here again, you have a significant decision to make. A cheese's rind treatment is the most significant impact you can have on your cheese post vat.

Rind Treatments

	DIFFICULTY	BENEFITS	DRAWBACKS
Bloomy (primarily *P. Candidum* or *Geotrichum*)	Medium	Unique, aesthetically pleasing white and colored rinds ranging in textures, flavor, and aroma	Mainly suitable for soft-ripened, higher moisture cheeses; can be prone to bitter tones and over-ripening; needs well-controlled aging cave
Cheese Wax (e.g. Divino)	Easy	Classic rind aesthetic for some cheese styles; good moisture control; different colors make for easy identification; reusable	Synthetic ingredient; molds can still grow beneath; can be messy to apply; expensive; not easy to substitute with paraffin or beeswax
Cloth-Bandaging (e.g. Cheddar)	Advanced	Nice aesthetic; plastic-free; excellent flavor potential	Prone to cheese mites; more work and supplies; proper aging humidity needed
Cream Wax (e.g. Rising Moon)	Medium	Minimal moisture loss; beautiful cleaner-looking rind; easy to tend; easy to apply; available with Natamycin mold inhibitor	Synthetic ingredient; eaters may not know to remove the skin; cheese still needs to be aged in proper humidity; needs to be turned and brushed
Herb-Rubbed, Leaf-Wrapped, Bark-Bound (e.g. Harbison)	Advanced	Unique presentation; potential for unique flavor characteristics	Hard to find; inconsistent material inputs; labor-intensive assembly; shortened shelf-life because of exposure to more organic matter
Natural Rind (e.g. Pecorino)	Advanced	Greatest potential for "locally grown" flavor because natural rinds showcase native flora; beautiful rind aesthetic	Labor intensive; can be difficult to control molds and mites; few remedies for take-over by unwanted molds; needs well-controlled aging cave
Oil-Rubbed (e.g. Asiago)	Medium	Natural ingredient; forms classic "Parmesan-like" rind	Labor intensive; can be difficult to control molds; needs well-controlled aging cave
Smoked	Medium	Imparts subtle to bold smoke flavors; flavors can be unique to the wood burned; adds pleasing caramel tone to the rind	Requires setup for cold smoking; requires an additional sealant to prevent excessive moisture loss after smoking (cream wax, cheese wax, vacuum-seal)
Vacuum-Sealed (e.g. Cheddar and Jack)	Easy	The simplest "affinage" treatment possible; with care, bags can be re-used	Inhibits unique, regional flavor contributions from the rind; requires appropriate bags and sealer; often leaves telltale wrinkles on cheese (looks less artisanal); seen as an industrial practice
Washed or Smear-ripened (e.g. Gruyère)	Advanced	Potential for robust flavors and pink to orangish colors; leads to classic, soft-ripened or Alpine cheese styles; older wheels can help inoculate younger wheels	Smelly and labor intensive; once certain yeasts and *Coryneform* bacteria establish in your aging environment, they are liable to invade other cheeses

bandaged

smeared

wax

bloomy

cream wax

brined

herb rolled

natural rind

leaf wrapped

oiled

vacuum bag

Leaves and Wraps

CHERRY

EDIBLE FERN

BAMBOO

CORN HUSK

WILD OR DOMESTIC GRAPE

SAGE

WRAPPING CHEESE IN LEAVES, BARK, OR BANDAGES HOLDS IN MOISTURE, KEEPS OUT CONTAMINANTS, GIVES STRUCTURE, AND IMPARTS UNIQUE FLAVORS. HARVEST LEAVES WHEN YOUNG AND TENDER.

NETTLE

HOJA SANTA

LOTUS

CABBAGE

FIR BARK

SPRUCE

BANANA

CHESTNUT

SASSAFRAS

FIG

LARD

BANDAGES

LEMON GRASS

COLD-SMOKING

Many smoked cheeses on the market today never see a wisp of smoke. Smoking cheeses, as opposed to adding smoke flavoring, is labor intensive and a commitment of time—which is why it isn't the commercial standard. But using real wood to produce a smoky flavor will be worth it. Smoking helps a cheese seal at the rind, locking in some moisture and discouraging mold growth. This is a bonus for a cheese you plan on aging.

I've only smoked whole cheese wheels freshly out of the brine. However, while doing research for this book, I came across the idea of taking an aged wheel, such as cheddar, removing its cheese wax, cutting it up, and smoking the pieces individually. This method will take less time because, by cutting the cheese, you increase the amount of surface area.

STEPS FOR COLD-SMOKING CHEESE

1. Choose a smoking method (for example a commercial smoker or a meat smoker with homemade "cold smoke" accompaniment).

2. Gather or purchase wood chips; good woods for this process include apple, cherry, mesquite, maple, and pear. The chips should be roughly the size of a pencil. Presoaking is not needed in cheesemaking, as chips won't be heated enough to warrant this cooling-off step.

3. Light your fire or start your heating element. Get your chips smoking a good hour ahead of adding the cheese. When a steady smoke has formed, set the cheese inside the smoking box, on a perforated rack, as far away from the heat as possible.

4. Maintain the smoke by keeping the coals or other fuel fed and by adding more wood chips as needed. Flip the cheese and check the temperature every 15 to 20 minutes (especially on your first run with a new setup). The temperature of the cheese should not go above 80°F/27°C or the cheese will start "oiling off," or leaching precious butterfat.

5. Smoke the cheese for any length of time, taking into account the density of the smoke, the volume of the cheese and how much smokey flavor you want. Plan 2 to 3 hours for full-smoke flavor or 40 to 50 minutes for lighter flavor on a medium wheel.

6. Remove the cheese from the smoker and cool. When cool, cover with wax, cream wax, vacuum-seal or enjoy right away.

THE CAVE

The "cave"—by which I mean a converted fridge, wine cooler, or perfect root cellar—is as fundamental to the cheese's aging process as the vat is to the cheesemaking—you can't do without it for many cheese styles. Fresh cheeses, feta, and vacuum-sealed cheeses are the only exceptions.

INSIDE OR OUT?

Should you age your cheeses inside a fridge or out? The answer depends on whether you have a space outside the fridge that is consistently cool (less than 60°F/16°C) but not too cold (above 37°F/3°C). You don't want your cheeses to freeze. You can remedy too-low humidity by keeping cheeses in aging bins but a consistently cool location is crucial for cheese affinage.

While the temperature of a regular fridge won't stop a cheese from ripening, it does slow the process down. A cheese aged at 52°F/11°C (an ideal temperature for a cave) might ripen in 4 months, but that same cheese aged in the fridge (37°F/3°C) needs an additional chunk of time to reach the same flavor potential. Another downside of using your fridge to age your cheeses is that your fridge will soon (hopefully) be taken over by projects. There'll be no room for the eggs!

If you're "lucky" enough to have a frigid house or, better, a root cellar, basement, or shed, you might be able to age cheeses there. Before leaving cheeses in any of these spots, make sure the temperature isn't spiking at midday or plummeting at night. And make sure the area is inaccessible to hungry rodents. Nothing's more delightful to a mouse than stumbling upon a shed filled with *artisan* cheese!

You can easily turn a fridge into a cheese cave using an analog thermostat, which brings the fridge's running temperature up. The ideal temperature for aging cheese is warmer than your refrigerator (which runs about 37°F/3°C) and cooler than most ambient temperatures (about 70°F/21°C). An analog thermostat shuts the fridge off when it goes below the set temperature, keeping it warmer and just where your cheeses should be.

There are also wine fridges, which already run at the correct temperature. Below are the pros and cons of all plugged-in caving options. Depending on your space limitations, price point, and how active you plan on being in maintaining the cave's environment, there's an aging solution for you.

CAVE SETTINGS

As a general rule, cheeses age best near 85 to 90 percent relative humidity and between 45° and 55°F/7° and 13°C. There are few cheeses (for example,

Cheese Cave Options

	PROS	CONS	ADVICE
Dorm fridge	Easy to find; inexpensive; takes up minimal space	Small capacity limits air flow; solid plastic shelving limits air flow; freezer unit (if included) does not work with analog thermostat and will cause perpetual moisture build-up	Highly likely you can find an abandoned, perfectly good dorm fridge near college campuses each year when school lets out. Do a drive-by or check with the campus's facilities management.
Kitchen fridge	Cheese stays in your line of sight, so is less likely to be neglected; no additional purchase	Aging temperature is very cold, which means cheeses ripen slowly; aging bins take up space; lack of space may discourage more cheesemaking	Ideal for the home cheesemaker who makes cheese only periodically; works well with waxed and vacuum-sealed wheels, which don't require aging bins.
A second kitchen refrigerator (versus the main fridge in your kitchen) fitted with analog thermostat	Used fridges are easily found, an extra one provides space to run many cheese projects at once; an analog thermostat is easily assembled and fit to the fridge	Freezer component is wasted space; requires purchase of thermostat; additional full-size fridge may be too large for apartments or smaller homes; energy usage increases	Find an inexpensive used fridge online. Choose "freezer on the bottom" models and anything manufactured after 1993 for increased energy efficiency. Wire racks are preferable to glass shelving for air flow.
Upright freezer	Most efficient use of space because no unused compartment; works with analog thermostat; may have moveable shelving	Requires purchase of an analog thermostat; harder to come across used upright freezers	Higher resale value because less common (if you find the setup doesn't work for you).
Root cellar, wine cellar, bulkhead	Potential for aging many wheels at once; easier to use wooden aging boards; good oxygen circulating potential	May require construction; keeping up the humidity may be a constant battle; requires forfeit of space; will attract rodents	Choose a location that stays at an even and cool temperature; stabilize temperature by framing area with insulation.
Wine cooler	Storage temperature is ideal, roughly 55°F/13°C; cooler is appropriately sized for apartments and smaller homes	Shelving is ideal for wine bottles, not cheese wheels so you may have to tinker with the shelving design; humidity may have to be increased	Because wine coolers are small, open the door daily to increase air circulation and add a water dish with a rag wick to increase humidity.

blues and *Propionic*-culture cheeses) that go outside this range or need temperature shifts during the aging process. The chart below shows the ideal aging conditions by cheese style.

ANALOG THERMOSTATS

To convert a regular fridge to a cave, you'll need to change the fridge's baseline temperature using an analog thermostat. This device shuts off the fridge's cooling element once the fridge is cold enough (55°F/13°C or whatever you set the alternative temperature to) by regulating the electric current coming from the wall outlet. To install an analog thermostat:

1. Place the temperature probe of the thermostat inside the refrigerator, in a position that allows the door to close. Use duct tape to secure in place.

2. Place the temperature adjustment box of the analog thermostat near the fridge, in an accessible place. (I hang mine from a hook right next to the door handle.) Set the thermostat to the desired temperature, or 55°F/13°C for a starting point.

3. Plug the power cord of the fridge directly into the analog thermostat.

4. Plug the thermostat into the wall outlet.

5. After 1 day, check the temperature of the fridge against a second thermometer to confirm the analog thermostat is accurate.

HUMIDITY HELP

Working to achieve the right humidity can be a challenge, especially if your aging cheeses are not waxed and if they aren't in aging bins. I am always struggling to keep up the humidity in my converted-fridge cave. On the other hand, I also struggle to make sure the cheeses are dry enough. Moisture often collects at the top of the aging bin then drips down from the lid onto the surface of the cheese. If I don't catch it in time, these extra moisture droplets cause the top of the cheese to rot.

Temperature and Humidity Chart for Cheese Aging

CHEESE TYPE	RECIPE EXAMPLES	IDEAL HUMIDITY	IDEAL TEMPERATURE OR RANGE
Bloomy-rinds	Camembert, Truffle Brie, Valençay	95 to 97% RH	45° to 52°F/7° to 11°C for ripening; when ripe move to 37°F/3°C
Blues	Bisbee Blue, Stilton, Blue Capricorn	90% RH	50° to 55°F/10° to 13°C for the first 2 months, then move to cooler temperature of 42° to 45°F/5°to 7°C for the last months of aging
Brined	Feta	NA	55° to 60°F/13° to 15°C
Caerphilly and bandaged cheddar	Bandage-Wrapped and Caerphilly	90 to 95% RH	52°F/11°C
Cheddars	Stirred Curd with Vacuum Seal	NA	51° to 54°F/11° to 13°C
Cheese with *Propionic* secondary cultures	Zeller, Jarlsberg with Cream Wax Rind	85% RH	First three weeks: 50°F/10°C Next three weeks: 72°F/22°C Last several months: 55°F/13°C
Hard and pressed	Mountain Top	85% RH	50° to 55°F/10° to 13°C
Leaf-wrapped	Aged Chèvre	90% RH	55°F/13°C
Semifirm	Gouda, Cultured Mozzarella	85 to 90% RH	50° to 55°F/10° to 13°C
Washed- and smeared-rinds	Zeller, Marbler	95% RH for the first month, then 85 to 90% afterward	53° to 56°F/12° to 13°C

One way to improve humidity is to place a bucket or glass of water inside the aging cave with a cloth tucked in. Half the cloth sits in the bucket and half hangs over the edge. This cloth serves as a wick, drawing water up from the bucket and evaporating it into the air. Change out the water in the bucket as well as the cloth regularly as it is the perfect place for molds to grow.

If you are maintaining proper humidity, your cheeses will neither crack nor turn to mush (the two worst-case scenarios). There will, naturally, be a certain amount of moisture lost from the cheeses if they are natural-rinded or even cream-waxed (meaning they will shrink with time). Vacuum-sealing and cheese-waxing hold most of the moisture in. To see how much moisture your cheese loses throughout the aging process, weigh your wheels at the beginning of aging and again when they are finished.

BREATHING CHEESES

The hardest part about keeping the right humidity in your cave is that there also needs to be enough airflow. These two requirements work against each other, unfortunately. Lots of airflow leads to drier air. Slow or stagnant air often means humid air.

Luckily, the cheeses are working on your behalf. Cheeses are breathing and releasing moisture all the time, just like you and me. Subsequently, the more cheeses you have in the fridge, the more humidity there will be. This doesn't mean you can rely on the cheese alone—outside of an aging bin, most cheeses will crack. But having a fridge full of cheeses is going to be easier than having a large fridge holding just one lonely cheese. As you fill your cave, remember that more cheese means there needs to be more air. Cheeses will suffocate if crowded. Try and fill your cave to 60 percent capacity (by volume) with cheese. The other 40 percent should be air space.

Proper airflow, proper humidity, and proper temperature all work together in the ripening process. The cheese takes in oxygen and releases CO_2 and other gases created through the breakdown of fats and proteins. Limiting the availability of oxygen or allowing the gases the cheeses are releasing

(ammonia, for example) to build up can inhibit or redirect a proper aging process. Before you feel overwhelmed, just remember to breathe and to let your cheeses breathe.

CAVING TIPS

- *Place your cave in the coolest part of your home or property, such as the north side of your garage. This will cause the fridge to turn on less often, saving energy.*

- *Visit your cave regularly, not only to flip cheeses but also simply to open the door and let air in.*

- *Place your cave where you can get to it easily (which hopefully isn't too far from the north side of the garage). Place the cave somewhere you'll walk past daily or figure out a reason why you'll have to visit on a regular basis (keep your cell phone charger nearby, perhaps). Forgotten cheeses are dead cheeses.*

- *It is okay to have a mixture of binned and unbinned cheeses in your cave. As long as the humidity is working for the cheese style, anything goes.*

- *Waxed and vacuum-sealed cheeses are the most forgiving rind treatments if you're uncertain about your cave setting. These treatments are a good way to maximize on shelf space since wheels can be stacked and/or do not need to be placed in aging bins (unlike other treatments).*

RIND SCIENCE

Cheese rinds can be grouped into two distinct categories: living rinds and sealed rinds. Living rinds mean any rind that's actively colonized by microorganisms. These microscopic friends, some species of which you introduced back at the vat in the form of freeze-dried inoculants, are busy growing and multiplying, digesting some aspect of the rind (could be a part of the cheese itself or could be another species of microbe they are chewing up) as they bring the cheese to a state of ripeness. Sealed rinds are a much simpler rind situation. These

Managing Cave Challenges

CHALLENGE	SIGNS OF PROBLEM	HOW TO DEAL WITH IT
Mites	Dust piles appear along shelves and at base of fridge; cheese surfaces appear pocked	Turn cheese more often; create a "bug barrier" on your cave by stopping all production, cleaning, and then vacating the fridge for 2 weeks; use a vacuum cleaner with a clean faucet head to clean cheese surfaces regularly
Too-high humidity	Puffy, excessive mold growth on mold-ripened and natural-rinded cheeses; cat hair, or "Poil de Chat," mold shows up	Open the fridge for daily "breaths of air"; open the lids to the cheese boxes and offer them time to breathe and dry out a bit as well
Too-little air flow	Smells like ammonia when you open the cave door	Open the fridge for daily "breaths of air"; open the lids to the cheese boxes and offer them time to breathe and dry out a bit as well; lower the ripening temperature by a degree or two
Too-low humidity	Natural-rind cheeses show cracks; bloomy-rinded and blue cheeses aren't developing proper molds; wheels sound hollow when tapped	Open the door *less* often; add a second water pan with wick; tuck clean, sodden paper towels around the inner edges of aging bins; lay a clean plastic shower curtain over all the shelves inside the fridge so less moisture is lost each time you open the door
Unwanted molds	Black, gray, white, blue, yellow, pink, and other unwanted molds growing on cheeses and other cave surfaces	Regularly clean all cave surfaces; decrease the humidity by opening the cave door daily; spray the boards and surfaces with a wash such as Red-Rind Wash (page 121) to proactively inoculate with the microorganisms you *do* want; create a "bug barrier" by stopping production and cleaning out cave for a period of time

cheeses are covered in either cheese wax, cream wax, or a vacuum-sealed bag, limiting oxygen and preventing a natural rind from forming.

Because what's happening on a living rind is so exciting yet also so complex, it's worth taking a moment to discuss some of the science in a bit more depth. The discussions of mold successions, growth inhibitors, and cheese mites pertain only to the living—not the waxed or vacuum-sealed—rind types.

MOLD SUCCESSIONS

What you see growing on a cheese initially will not be the final state of the rind. Rinds are living, evolving, complex communities that are interacting with the environment around them and in a regular state of change. On a microscopic level, the millions of microorganisms living on a rind are like a demographic chart on fast forward: populations are surging ahead, plateauing, dying back, conquering, and being conquered. Rinds are dynamic!

Trust in the ongoing evolution of the cheese rind. It is very much part of the magic of cheesemaking. If you want to learn more, follow the research of Ben Wolfe and Rachel Dutton, cheese rind microbiologists working currently to key out the vast array of microbes found on the rinds of American farmstead cheeses. Know that, at the home scale and arguably at the commercial scale too, one cannot perfectly control the succession of species that will occur. One species often preps the environment for a later species by changing the pH or nutrient availability. An earlier mold or bacteria might be pushing back another population—and inadvertently holding space for later species to take root.

It is important to keep things clean (now that you know "clean" for a cheese includes having molds present) and meet the cheese's needs for humidity, temperature, and airflow to the best of your ability. This is your job as cheese affineur!

GROWTH INHIBITORS

Aging a cheese is a careful art. If the cheese starts to go in the wrong direction—because of uneven moisture or too-high temperatures or contaminated milk—it can be tough or even impossible to pull it back into line. This doesn't mean the minute your cheese project looks funny you beeline for the compost pile. It is to say there's a reason a beautifully aged wheel can be quite expensive.

If you like to roll on the safe side, consider some of the methods professional cheesemakers use to trim away uncertainty and steer cheeses in the right direction. A first step is to use pasteurized milk to control a number of variables. Another is to be meticulous in how you keep your cheesemaking space and aging cave—many cheesemakers don't allow any outside visitors into their creameries for fear of introducing new or unwanted microbes into the environment.

Another option for achieving a more controlled cheese is to use growth inhibitors. Some of these additives can be natural in that they are biologically based or as common as table salt. Others might be considered more synthetic. These options are effective at keeping flavors and surface growth on track, but they also change the nature of your craft. If your reason for making cheese in the first place is to eat it "the old-fashioned way," then ignore the chart on the facing page without fret. I put together the table less to encourage you to use additives and more to give you information about how cheeses are made in a more commercial setting. Better to know how things *are really made* than to stay in the dark.

CHEESE MITES

The longer a non-waxed, non-vacuum-sealed cheese sits around, the more time it has to entertain visitors, a.k.a. cheese mites (Latin names: *Tyrophagus casei* and *Acarus siro*). Nearly every cheesemaker experiences these microscopic pests at some point. Luckily, tending your cheeses regularly is an easy way to keep mites under control. Mites get to your cheese in the first place because they feast on other foods, including grains, honeycomb, and smoked meats. These things are their vehicles into your home or cheesemaking space.

Mites may not be feasting on the cheese alone. They may be eating proteinaceous yeasts and other microbes growing on the rind—making them a parasite of a parasite of your homemade cheese treasure. How dare all of them! As the mites eat, they open up the rind, making air channels where more mold can grow. In this way, little crevices become big crevices and that unblemished, pencil-thin rind you'd wished for becomes a thick layer of loss.

Mites reliably show up for me anytime I have a natural-rinded, well-aged, somewhat neglected cheese. I know how it happens; the wheels are looking good and smelling right so I start to think they can take care of themselves. Then I realize mites have arrived because I see fresh piles of dust in the cave. When I brush the dust away, more shows up only a day or two later. If you're looking to avoid the mite situation altogether, wax-dip, cream-wax, or vacuum-seal your cheeses. But really, a regular vacuuming with a vacuum cleaner or simply regular turning and tending will keep the mites at bay.

JUDGING RIPENESS

Following are guidelines for when to stop aging and start eating your cheeses. As you will soon see, it isn't an exact science but one perfected by repeating the same recipe over and over again.

Making the Cut

Judging when a wheel is ready to cut is a skill that will take time to perfect. Start with aging the cheese for the prescribed time noted in the recipe. As you open a wheel, have your make sheet (see page 232) nearby. Note as much as you can about the cheese's appearance, smell, taste, and texture.

If you find yourself remarking on a cheese's blandness, that cheese likely could have used more time. In general, time adds flavor. If you find yourself commenting on a cheese being too firm and chalky (specifically with soft-ripened styles), this means it might be underripe. On the other hand, if the guts of your Camembert run off the table, if you can't get an axe through the Asiago, and if your blue cheese

Additives for Controlling Unwanted Growth

ADDITIVE	DESCRIPTION	INFLUENCE	NOTES
AfiLact	A naturally occurring enzyme mix used to hold back unwanted microbial growth and, in particular, some strains of Clostridia.	The active ingredient in AfiLact is lysozyme, an enzyme found in human tears and saliva whose function is to attack foreign bacteria.	AfiLact is produced from egg whites. It is an allergen, so proper labeling is required.
Hold Bac	Strains of *Lactobacillus rhamnosus* and *Propionicbacterium freuden-reichii* subsp. *shermanii* added to the milk to inhibit unwanted yeast, mold, and bacterial contaminants.	May decrease undesired flavors, acidity development, or textures. Effectiveness is influenced by extent of possible contamination (how long milk has been exposed and how large the unwanted populations are) and by correct handling (storage temperature, exposure to humidity, etc.) of Hold Bac.	A natural and organic option (generally speaking and in terms of organic certification) for controlling a cheese's outcome. Will not produce eyes because of non-ideal conditions.
Natamycin	A naturally occurring fungicide used to control spoilage molds in a variety of foods, including fresh and aged cheeses. Natamycin can be added to the initial milk, the brine, the brine wash, or the cream wax.	Cleaner rinds because of inhibiting effect on surface blue and white molds. Natamycin will help hold the space for the red rind bacteria (*Coryneform*) to get established (if making washed or smeared rind). Do not use if intending to grow a bloomy-rind, blue, or natural-rinded cheese.	Neutral flavor impact, used for decades throughout the food industry, commonly used in cottage cheese, sour cream, and yogurt.
Potassium sorbate	A chemical salt added to cheese milk to inhibit yeast and mold growth. Used in numerous food, beverage, and personal care products.	Decreases or stops unwanted microbial growth leading to off flavors or textures, in turn increasing shelf life.	Though used in quantities with "no known adverse health affects," potassium sorbate is a chemical additive. Do your homework and figure out if it is something you want to use.
Salt	Increased salt may slow growth of unwanted microorganisms, though not all. Use a dry salt rub on the exterior of the cheese when turning.	May help inhibit unwanted growth on the rind by dehydrating and making the rind less inhospitable.	May lead to an overly salted cheese. Also, there are a number of "salt loving" microbes.
Sodium nitrate	Food preservative found in nearly all cured meats. Helps preserve color as well as hold back bacterial growth. Sodium nitrate naturally occurs, in modest amounts, in fruits and vegetables.	Decreases or stops unwanted microbial growth leading to off flavors or textures, in turn increasing shelf life.	Though a widely used meat preservative, sodium nitrate is controversial and receives plenty of media attention. Do your homework and figure out if it is something you want to use.

PERFORATED CHEESE KNIFE

CHEESE PLANE

—SOFT CHEESE KNIFE

Cheese Cutting TOOLS

SQUARE CHEESE KNIFE

PARMESAN KNIFE

CURVED DOUBLE HANDLED KNIFE

CHEESE SLICER

GRATER

ROQUEFORTAISE

CHEESE WIRE

CHEESE TRIER

MANUAL MILL

WIRE CHEESE CUTTER

GIROLLE OR CHEESE SCRAPER

reeks with so much ammonia that your nasal passage hurts, you've overaged things.

There are many successful ends to a cheese if the cheesemaker keeps an open mind. Your first recipe may be a little dry. Your next may be overripened. You might forget to flip the next one and weird molds might take over after that. Whatever the case, with each recipe, you will learn an immense amount, all of it valuable—even more valuable if you write it down and review your notes before making the next batch. Making cheese and making mistakes is the way to learn cheesemaking. That is why there aren't online degree programs on this subject. The experience has to be tactile, sensory rich, repetitive. And it will be.

CONTINUING TO AGE CUT CHEESES

You have the option of continuing to age wedges of semi-pressed, hard-pressed, and firm-pasted blue cheeses after the wheel has been cut. With all other cheese styles, including bloomy-rinds, soft blues, washed-rinds, and any other soft-ripened cheese, an opened wheel is a finished wheel. To reseal appropriate cheeses, either rewax the exposed portion or vacuum-seal the cheese.

To reseal with wax. Cut the wheel open and evaluate. For pieces you wish to continue aging, dip the just-cut surfaces into the wax, making sure the new wax wraps about 1 in/2.5 cm up around the rind or previous waxing. Apply a second coat. This seals the inner paste but lets the exterior rind continue to breathe and develop.

To reseal with vacuum bags. This is a fantastic option for opening and resealing cheeses and it's as easy as it sounds: Cut open a cheese; taste it; chop it up into as many pieces as you wish; reseal. If you want to taste-test the same wheel at various points of development (2 months, 4 months, 6 months), chop it up after brining and package in separate vacuum bags. Just be sure to secure those labels or you might not remember which is which.

CHAPTER TEN

PAMPERING *your* PIECES

You're at the very last leg of the cheesemaking journey now; getting the cheese into your mouth or the mouths of others. You've made the wheel. You've aged the wheel. You've cut the wheel. But don't rest just yet. Treating your pieces of cheese with respect—by wrapping and storing them correctly—means they'll shine when it's their turn on the dinner plate.

STORING CHEESE

Because home cheesemakers work with smaller amounts of milk, we usually don't have to worry about what to do with a whole Parmesan wheel's worth of cut cheese. Many of the recipes in *Kitchen Creamery* are sized so that you'll only have about 2 lb/910 g of cheese to give away or store. Using the right wrapping paper to store your cut cheeses will preserve flavor and extend shelf life. Remember that storing cheeses in the fridge (a very American thing to do), as opposed to on the counter, will also extend the shelf life.

In the chart below, I give you the best options for storing cheeses after cutting. For where to find the brand-name, style-specific wrapping papers, see Resources (page 234).

PAPERS FOR WRAPPING

Cheese paper comes in two main styles: those that mimic the conditions ideal for a bloomy-rind cheese and those that mimic conditions for a washed-rind. Somewhere between the two sits the wrapping conditions for blue cheese. Any of these papers will work fine for wrapping a firm, aged cheese. If you plan on buying paper and want to buy just one style, choose Crystal, Expecto, or Formaticum brands (see chart, following). They will give you an elegant presentation and superior cheese care.

FREEZING CHEESE

Every time a farmers' market customer asks me, "How long does this cheese keep?" I want to say, "Why wait?" My feeling on food is we should try and

Approximate Shelf Life for Cut Cheese

CHEESE STYLE (WITH EXAMPLES)	APPROXIMATE SHELF LIFE AFTER CUTTING	METHOD OF STORAGE
Direct-acid (Burrata, Mascarpone, Quick Mozz)	1 to 3 days	**For Burrata and Ricotta:** Store in airtight container. **For Quick Mozz:** Store in water for up to 3 days, or remove from water and wrap tightly in plastic wrap.
Soft-ripened (Camembert)	7 days	**Best wrapping:** Crystal or Formaticum brands of cheese paper. **Alternative:** Wrap in wax paper, then wrap in plastic wrap or place in an airtight container.
Washed-rind (Tilsiter)	1 to 2 weeks	**Best wrapping:** Expecto cheese paper **Alternative:** Wrap loosely in wax paper, then wrap in plastic wrap or store in an airtight container.
Blue (Stilton)	2 weeks	**Best wrapping:** Alu-Extrusion cheese paper, which is also ideal for wrapping blue cheeses during their aging process. **Alternative:** Wrap in wax paper or foil, then plastic wrap.
Smoked (Provolone)	2 to 3 months	Vacuum-seal
Semihard (Gouda, Cultured Mozz)	2 to 3 months	Vacuum-seal
Hard (Asiago)	3 to 4 months	Vacuum-seal

eat it when it's fresh instead of saving it as long as we can. Cheeses are almost always sold when fully mature and don't need to be aged any longer. Admittedly, if I didn't live in California with its year-round abundance and wasn't a home cheesemaker with often too much cheese on my hands, I might not think this way. I would use my freezer much more.

I freeze cheese for one reason only: to make mac-n-cheese. In my freezer lives a bin that often has a nice mix of hunks and rinds. Who knows why these scraps ended up in the bin—probably just a moment when there was too much cheese and more arrived—but when the time comes, I'll throw them in the food processor until I have cheese crumbles. I melt these crumbles with nonfrozen cheese and end up with one luscious cheese sauce.

RULES OF FREEZING CHEESE

If you have to freeze cheese and want to use it in any way other than a boiled-down cheese sauce, take this advice:

Wrap cheeses well. A layer of plastic wrap, followed by a layer of foil, then a seal-top baggie or bin— that's three layers of protection—works best.

Thaw cheeses slowly. Move the cheese to the fridge and thaw over the course of 2 days rather than in the microwave rapidly.

Freeze higher-fat cheeses. Double- or triple-crème cheeses freeze more successfully than cheeses with regular amounts of milk fat.

Select denser cheeses over airy cheeses. A tub of whipped chèvre won't freeze as nicely as a densely packed one. The surface is where ice crystals form.

Limit freezer time. The less time a cheese is in the freezer, the better. Plan on freezing a cheese no longer than 2 months.

Cook cheese into casseroles. After you thaw a cheese, it will likely have a different, slightly mealier texture. Don't use it in a sandwich but rather bake it into potatoes au gratin, cheese enchiladas, or good ol' lasagna.

SHIPPING CHEESE

When your cheese cave is full and the holidays are near, you might be thinking about shipping cheese treasures far and wide. Because you've poured so much energy into your cheeses, take precautions when shipping. Call the recipient ahead of time and tell him or her to be on the lookout. I once tried to surprise someone with a cheese shipment and the package sat so long in the post office that the box started leaking! Oops. The chart on the facing page gives timelines and suggestions for how to ship most successfully.

CHEESE EVALUATION

When you step onto the public cheese stage, to make heart-shaped cheeses for your best friend's wedding or, if you are extra zealous, to enter the local festival's cheese contest, your cheese is going to become public. Maybe the public arena is as simple as you presenting a cheese board at a dinner party or bringing a tray of samples to the office. When this happens, hooray! It's a rite of passage for the home cheesemaker to start being known as "that person who makes cheese." You will learn an imense amount from the feedback others offer, sometimes too freely.

Know that eaters will evaluate your cheeses through the lens they know: a comparison of your cheese to commercial versions (another reason to give your cheeses unique names—keeps the eater's mind open just a moment longer). When a cheese is formally judged in contests, there are specific characteristics of the cheese a judge will look at. Knowing these may help you to evaluate the cheeses for yourself.

RIND

A rind should be consistently colored and not overly patchy, though natural rinds are given more leeway for patchiness. A rind should not be overly thick, which would mean the cave was too dry (for pressed cheeses) or that you didn't flip and pat the cheeses regularly enough (for bloomy-rinds). The rinds on bloomy-rinds should not be separated from the

How to Ship Cheeses

CHEESE CATEGORY	HOW TO SHIP	SHIPPING SPEED
Fresh unripened	Vacuum-seal fresh cheese to prevent leakage. Double-bag tub containers. Bundle all cheeses with bubble wrap, then pack into an insulated shipping box with ice packs. Chèvre may be frozen prior to sending.	Overnight with ice ($$$)
Soft ripened	Create physical support for the cheese (such as a fitted wooden basket or smaller cardboard box), then pack the baskets or boxes tightly into an insulated shipping box. Add ice packs and more insulation.	Next-day shipping with ice ($$)
Semifirm to firm—waxed or vacuum-sealed	Firm to semifirm cheeses ship well, especially waxed or vacuum-sealed versions with which you don't have to worry about airflow. Swaddle cheese in packing paper then pack tightly into a shipping box, making sure the cheese will not shift during transport.	2-day shipping ($$), ice in warm weather
Semifirm to firm—natural, oiled, or smeared rind	Firm to semifirm cheeses ship well, although natural, cloth-bandaged, oiled, or smear-rinded cheeses must be wrapped in cheese paper first, then bundled in porous paper such as newsprint. For oil-rinded cheese, it's okay to vacuum-seal. Pack cheese tightly into a shipping box, making sure the cheese will not shift during transport.	2-day shipping ($$), ice in warm weather

cheese (this is called "slip skin"). Rinds should also have even firmness. Soft spots on firm cheese rinds are a sign of uneven moisture or a problem in the cave environment.

INTERIOR

Aim for a cheese that is consistently colored and bright. The paste can be slightly open, very open, or have no openings at all (see page 103 and illustration on page 113); whatever it is, it should be consistent throughout the wheel. For pressed, aged cheeses, if the paste crumbles when cut, this might mean the cheese developed too much acid before it got salted. Or it might just mean the cheese is quite aged. A degree of pliability is always good (except for lactic-acid coagulated cheeses and many blues).

RIPENESS

Hopefully you hit the nail on the head and crack the wheel at peak ripeness. Overripe cheeses will reek of ammonia and be off in flavor. Overripe cheeses may also be too runny, too pungent, or too dried-out. Underripe cheeses may lack flavor, be too firm, be too hard, or lack a proper finished rind.

AROMA AND TASTE

The cheese should smell pleasant on the inside (even if the rind smells overly robust). Smells and tastes can span the gamet, are subjective, and will vary, but should be pleasing. The cheese should also not be over- or under-salted.

PRESENTING YOUR MASTERPIECE

Your cheese will be special, not only because you gathered the milk, stirred the vat, pressed the wheel, made the brine, and so on but also because you'll present the cheese with dignity. Here is how to help your cheese stand in all its glory:

CLEAN UP THE RIND

When a natural-rind cheese comes out of the aging cave, it can look a little rough. Clean with a dry brush to remove the outer layer of the rind. Brushing will improve the appearance of the wheel and also balance the ratio of internal to external flavors. For firm and pressed cheese wheels with excessive mold growth, wash gently under cold water, then dry before cutting. For blue, bloomy-, and washed-rind cheeses, don't be shy about trimming away unsightly parts before serving. You understand these imperfections, but eaters will be less tolerant.

CHOOSE A NAME

Naming your cheese can be as simple or complicated as you want it to be. You can call a cheese by the name of the recipe ("Camembert"). You can doctor it up with an adjective or two ("Oscar's Asiago"). As you produce more and more cheeses, you might select a naming scheme; maybe music terms, local street names, or members of your family.

SERVE AT ROOM TEMPERATURE

You already know this but it can't hurt to be reminded: Serve cheese at room temperature. Take the cheese out of the fridge an hour ahead of time (or don't even put them in the fridge in the first place). The warmer temperature allows you to smell and taste the cheese's deeper complexities.

ENCOURAGE YOUR EATERS

Make your cheese easy to eat. If setting up a cheese board, garnish with foods that bring the cheese to life. Apricot jam is a personal favorite. Try dried and fresh fruits; candied, toasted, or smoked nuts; assorted pickles; or cured meats. For very soft cheeses, use a shallow bowl so the cheese's inner "fondue" can be enjoyed, rather than running toward the floor. For firm cheeses, precut a slice or two to encourage eaters. If wrapping cheeses to give as gifts, embellish the package with a personalized cheese sticker.

LIVING CHEESE

I should spare you this story but there's value in hearing the truths of cheesemaking. I was in college, trying to impress a dinner date. We were making pizza, and, of course, I had to go to the basement to "pick out a cheese." (Yes, now I realize how ridiculous I must have sounded.)

An hour passed with the two of us chopping vegetables, talking. Then it came time for me to hack open the cheese wheel. Before doing so, I noted how nice the rind looked and imagined how flavorful the cheese was going to be. However, I did notice a soft, slightly grayish area as I was starting to cut. I ignored it.

The kitchen was filled with twilight, that special time of day after the sun has set, before the lights come on. My knife pushed the cheese wheel open into two halves and I was just about to start shredding a portion of it when, something caught my eye. Something was moving. I kept chatting. He kept cutting the peppers he was working on. Did the cheese just move? Was I going crazy? The light in the kitchen faded a bit more.

Suddenly, I realized the cheese had maggots. Their soft bodies waved to me, so happy for the breath of fresh air. I was horrified. I looked at the unfinished pizza, then at my date (who, by a stroke of luck, wasn't looking at me).

He turned to rinse parsley or something and without thinking I raced to the back hallway and chucked both halves of the cheese out an open window to an empty lot below. I then grabbed something else—anything—from the fridge and furiously started to cut. The pizza went into the oven without hesitation and I poured another glass of wine. Perhaps he was being kind when he didn't ask about the pizza's bright orange, cheddar—this cheese I'd supposedly made myself. Perhaps he didn't want to know any more.

Note: Casu marzu, a traditional sheep's-milk cheese from Sardinia, is famous for containing living larvae from a fly (*Piophilia casei*). Once one of my students told me about his Italian grandfather, who was a huge fan of this rare delicacy. We both shook our heads in disbelief!

IN CLOSING

I've immersed myself in cheese for over a decade now and what surprises me is that my interest isn't waning. Unlike the bags of roving wool, the half-finished patchwork under the bed, the carving tools now rusted, the long dead sourdough in the fridge, the dusty hives, and the sewing machine that hasn't seen sunlight for an eon, cheese stands alone. It keeps catching my imagination.

Part of what's kept me hooked is the generous spirit I find within cheesemaking communities. I remember sitting in on a meeting of the Maine Cheese Guild one summer when I was apprenticing with Appleton Creamery, an award-winning cheesemaker in the state. Twelve cheesemakers sat at a picnic bench. On top of the bench, everyone (nearly all professionals) had brought their latest efforts to be evaluated by others. Instead of seeing each other as competitors, these cheesemakers offered one another empathy and encouragement. They'd spent enough hours at the vat and enough years peddling cheese to people who balked at the price to know that they were in this together. The thing about cheese is no one has conquered the medium—not even the big guys. It is a mystery we all humbly chip away at. Together we stand.

Another reason I can't get over the craft is that nurturing cheese feels akin to parenting (another craft I'm elbow deep in). With both topics, advice abounds. Many have "been there" and, in hindsight, know a perfect path through. Yet the advice contradicts: One cheesemaker says to never use whey to build the brine. The next says it's a best-kept secret. One cheesemaker swears by adding a specific culture. The next doesn't even know what culture the first is talking about. This mismatch, this confusion, this lack of absolute expertise delights me. It means you *have to figure out your own recipe* in the end.

Children, like cheese, are greatly affected by the inputs of their parents, but the equation is more complex. You can fuss over a child, send him to an expensive school, and it can all flop. Or, conversely, a kid can be raised on benign neglect and turn out wonderfully. Cheese is similar. Sometimes it's the cheese you give a little space that becomes something marvelous. Other times, a cheese simply needs to be held, literally. (And for beginning cheesemakers, I recommend some form of helicopter parenting).

It's an adventure to work with living things, to be part of projects that extend beyond oneself. I love that one day, when a wheel is ripe, a story is told. I'll be part of that story but so will the cows, the pasture, the farmer, the grass, and the eater, whom I might not ever know. I hope I open each wheel at the right time too—not prematurely when it lacks flavor and not too late when the funk has set in. I hope that as each morsel of goodness meets the mouth, it tastes as big as the story captured within.

GLOSSARY

ACIDITY: As the cultures digest lactose in the milk, they create lactic acid. This acidity 1) helps proteins link to form a gel; 2) creates a food less prone to spoilage; and 3) affects the moisture level, texture, and aging of the cheese.

AFFINAGE: The art of aging cheeses.

AFFINEUR: A professional whose job is to select cheeses for long-term aging as well as to guide the cheeses through to maturity.

AGING MATS: Synthetic or natural-fiber mats used to age cheese. Mats increase air circulation as well as prop the cheese up, away from whey that may be collecting underneath.

AMINO ACID CRYSTALS: The "crunchies," best known in Parmesan, aged cheddar, and aged Gouda cheeses, form when Tyrosine, an amino acid that makes up the majority of the casein protein, crystallizes under correct conditions. In some cheeses, the crystals may be calcium lactate.

AMMONIA PRODUCTION: A by-product of the breakdown of proteins.

ANNATTO: Seeds from the subtropical tree *Bixa Orellana*, which are used to create yellow to orange hues in butter and cheese. Annatto is most often used in liquid extract form.

ASH: Incinerated vegetation used to make distinct black lines in the middle of a cheese's paste or on its exterior. In addition to visual contrast, ash may discourage unwanted microorganisms by affecting surface acidity.

BANDAGING: A rind treatment for aging cheeses, mainly cheddar, using cheesecloth and fat to form a protective barrier for the cheese.

BLUE MOLD: The secondary or ripening cultures *Penicillum roqueforti* or *Penicillum glaucum* used in styles such as Roquefort or Stilton.

BODY: A term describing the density, pliability, and homogeneity of yogurt and cultured dairy products, though possibly also cheese. Words such as *thin*, *medium*, *heavy*, or *very heavy* are common qualifiers.

BREVIBACTERIUM LINENS: Secondary or ripening cultures added to the vat or applied to a cheese rind to produce a robust, stinky flavor and pink to orangish colors. These bacteria are categorized by their broader phylogenic name of *Coryneform*.

BUTTER MUSLIN: A substitute for fine-weave (#90) cheesecloth.

BUTTERFAT: The fatty portion of milk, a.k.a. milk fat. Amount of butterfat depends on the type of product (light cream versus heavy cream) as well as the commercial brand. If buying milk and cream directly from a farm, the breed of animal, stage in lactation, climate, and diet all affect butterfat levels.

CALCIUM CHLORIDE (CaCl$_2$): An ingredient, originally derived from limestone, added to the milk prior to renneting. CaCl$_2$ helps correct the damaging effects that pasteurization has had on the casein protein.

CASEIN: The primary protein in the cheesemaking process, the one that reacts to rennet.

CAVE: Slang term for the area (usually a fridge or wine fridge) in which cheeses are ripened.

CHEDDARING: A special step in the production of cheddar-style cheese whereby curd blocks are cut, stacked, then flipped in order to draw out more moisture, causing the curds to knit more tightly together and to allow time for more acid to develop. Blocks are then milled into small pieces, mixed with salt, put into forms, and pressed.

CHEESE: Any fermented milk product from which a portion of the water has been removed.

CHEESE PAPER: Paper engineered to meet the needs of ripening and finished cheeses.

CHEESE WAX: A synthetic wax with a low melting point and high flexibility used to coat cheeses; and in particular, Dutch-styles and cheddars. I advise against using paraffin or bee's wax because it is too brittle. Cheese wax's low melting point ensures butterfat does not leach out when cheeses are dipped.

CHURN: 1) v. To agitate cream to cause butterfat globules to stick together; 2) n. A container used to churn cream.

CHYMOSIN: The primary enzyme found in rennet.

CLEAN BREAK: A way of testing the doneness of renneted milk by inserting a knife or fingers into the curd then pulling upward. The way in which the curd splits indicates if more time is needed.

COAGULANT: Also called *rennet*. A broader term to describe the animal-, plant-, bacterial- or fungal-based enzymes that causes the casein proteins in milk to link together and form a gel.

COAGULATE: When a substance changes from a liquid to a solid material, as when milk becomes a gel (or yogurt).

CORYNEFORM: The name of a bacterial genus that includes *Brevibacterium linens* (*b.linens*) and *Arthrobacter* species, known for producing pungent, often pink, orange, or red rinds.

CREAM WAX: Also called "Clear Coat," this water-based polymer is used to coat cheese, preventing moisture loss and slowing down mold growth during aging.

CULTURED BUTTER: Butter made from fermented cream, technically the opposite of sweet cream butter, though the term *sweet cream* is often misused.

CULTURED DAIRY PRODUCT: Any milk or cream that has been fermented but not drained.

CURD: The coagulated milk solids, which separate from the whey in the cheesemaking process. Curd forms when the casein proteins link together, trapping butterfat, lactose, and other solids.

CURD BLOCK: The amalgamation of curds, and mainly those that occur at the bottom of the vat during pre-pressing and before draining.

CURD KNIFE: A cutting tool with a long blade that allows the cheesemaker to cut the gel at the bottom of the vat without damaging the curds at the top. A non-offset cake spatula works well.

CURING: The process of letting just pressed, just salted cheese dry at a temperature slightly warmer than the final aging temperature. Curing usually lasts 1 to 3 days.

DENATURE: The way in which milk proteins are changed through pasteurization. Denatured milk proteins often are less desirable for the cheesemaker but can be improved through using $CaCl_2$.

DIACETYL: A flavor compound created during the milk fermentation process. Diacetyl is the flavor we perceive as "butter." *Lactococcus lactis* ssp *diacetylactis* and *Leuconostoc cremoris* are two strains of bacteria that act on the milk to produce diacetyl.

DRAINING: The separation of the curds from the whey.

DRYING: The brief period after brining or salting and before aging when a cheese dries, often at warmer temperatures. This period helps seal the rind and to prevent excessive early mold growth. Also known as *curing*.

EMULSION: The suspension of one substance within another, usually a fat within water, so that the substance appears mixed. Milk is an emulsion.

ENZYME: A substance, produced by a living organism, that creates a biological reaction. Chymosin and pepsin (which make up rennet) and lipase are the main enzymes of cheesemaking.

EQUILIBRIUM: The movement of molecules—in cheesemaking it's often the sugars and minerals—from greater to lesser concentration, causing the medium to become equilibrated.

EYE FORMATION: The openings in a cheese that result from gas production by the various cultures, the most common being *Propionibacterium shermanii*, used in Swiss-style cheeses.

FLAVOR COMPOUNDS: Chemical compounds that we perceive as flavor through a combination of smell and taste (and often texture as well). Diacetyl is one example.

FOLLOWER: The cover to a cheese form, which fits tightly on top so that when the cheese gets pressed, curd cannot mush up and out and pressure is evenly distributed.

GEOTRICHUM CANDIDUM: A rapidly growing fungus or yeast used in numerous cheese styles. It is a secondary or ripening culture known to cultivate the rind in as little as several hours. It is also known as "buttermilk mold."

GRAM SCALE: A small scale used for weighing very small and lightweight items, such as cheese cultures.

HAND-MILLED: Using your hands to break up or squeeze curds into smaller bits.

HARP: The grid-like tool used to cut the just-set milk into curd pieces. Harps may have vertical, horizontal, or grid lines.

HOMOGENIZATION: The breaking down of butterfat globules into smaller particles that then stay in suspension and do not separate out from the milk to form a cream line.

HOOPING: Moving curds out of the vat and into the cheese form for pressing. Cheese forms were once opened-bottomed hoops, which is where the term originates.

INTERIOR RIPENING: The transformation of a cheese from fresh to aged takes place within the core of a cheese, namely through the use of blue molds.

KADOVA: A brand name for a particular cheese form made from heavy plastic with a removable mesh liner and a tightly fitting follower. Produces Gouda-shaped wheels.

KNITTING: The process of curds connecting to each other to form a unified shape or wheel. Knitting is more positive than "matting" (which is essentially the same process but happening too early on in the vat).

LACTIC ACID: The acid produced when cultures ferment lactose. The amount of lactic acid present in the vat is an indicator of how a recipe is progressing.

LACTOBACILLUS: A genus of bacteria, which are part of the lactic acid group. *Lactobacilli* convert sugars into lactic acid. Members of this genus assist in the fermentation of many foods beyond cheese, including sauerkraut, kimchi, wine, beer, hard cider, silage, and more. Of over a hundred species within the genus, cheesemakers are most interested in *L. delbrueckii* subsp. *delbrueckii, L. delbrueckii* subsp. *bulgaricus, L. delbrueckii* subsp. *lactis, L. acidolphilus,* and *L. helveticus.*

LACTOCOCCUS: A genus of bacteria in the lactic acid group. *Lactococci* are homofermentors, meaning they produce only one type of acid during fermentation. Of the *Lactococcus* genus, cheesemakers are mainly interested in *Lactococcus lactis* and, within that species, two subspecies: *L. lactis* subsp. *lactis* and *L. lactic* subsp. *cremoris.*

LIPASE: An important enzyme used in many Italian-style cheeses to produce signature "picante," flavors. Lipase is added to the milk along with the cultures prior to renneting.

LIPOLYSIS: The breakdown of butterfat (through hydrolysis) to release fatty acids (flavor).

MATTING: The premature joining of curds in the vat as a result of rapid temperature increase and/or stirring too slowly.

MESOPHILIC: Cultures that thrive near 90°F/32°C, a cooler range than needed by thermophilic cultures.

MOLD: A confusing term that can either mean the form in which a cheese drains or the microorganisms, such as *Penicillum candidum,* used to ripen a cheese. In this book, I use the term *form* instead of *mold* when talking about the object cheese drains in.

MOTHER CULTURE: When cultures are grown into a yogurt-like gel before being added to the vat (as opposed to being added directly to the vat in freeze-dried form), the primary "seeding" gel is called "the mother."

NEEDLING: *See* piercing.

NSLAB OR NON-STARTER LACTIC ACID BACTERIA: A group of bacteria used to culture cheese whose primary function is not to produce acid so much as it is to produce enzymes that assist in the ripening process. NSLABs are often part of culture mixes and are abundant in raw milk.

PASTE: The inner part of the cheese, not the rind.

PENICILLIUM CANDIDUM: A secondary culture, a fungus, that produces the white "crust" of Brie. For professional cheesemakers, different subspecies of *P. candidum* exist and can be chosen based on desired height of the fuzz, density of the fuzz, and for specific fat and protein digesting abilities. The result of *P. candidum* digesting cheese is a fondue-like texture.

PENICILLIUM GLAUCUM: A secondary culture, a fungus, used in blue cheeses. Less common than *Penicillium roqueforti.*

PENICILLIUM ROQUEFORTI: A secondary culture, a fungus, used to create distinct "blue" flavor, color and texture in cheeses.

pH: A scale, running from 1 (highly acidic) to 14 (highly basic). pH measurements may be taken from the milk, the vat of curds and whey, or the final cheese to help the cheesemaker determine how a recipe is progressing. Milk is near neutral but slightly acidic (about 6.7).

PICANTE: A flavor term describing a peppery, spicy component found in cheeses, many of which are Italian-style. Often the effect of the enzyme lipase.

PIERCING: The process of pushing a skewer into a blue cheese during the first few days and then weeks of ripening. The piercing creates channels of oxygen where the molds will bloom. Also called *needling.*

PITCHING: Allowing the curds to settle to the bottom of the vat prior to draining.

PREHYDRATING: The process of placing DVI or "Direct Vat Inoculant" cultures (also known as freeze-dried cultures) into warm milk for 1 to 2 hours prior to adding them to the vat. This waking up period helps the cultures develop acid more quickly and effectively. Prehydrating is less important for secondary cultures and not necessary when using liquid cultured buttermilk.

PREPARED FORM: A term I use to describe a cleaned cheese form lined with a cleaned cheesecloth (or a mesh liner) placed in an area where the cheese can be pressed and whey can drain freely.

PRE-PRESSING: The gathering of curds into a curd block by pressing under the whey, prior to draining, while still in the vat.

PRESSING: Applying varying degrees of weight to a freshly hooped cheese wheel to encourage the curds to knit together, a rind to form, and more whey to be pushed out.

PROBIOTICS: An overused term identifying fermented dairy products containing healthful microorganisms. These microorganisms are active in the food product as well as in the human gut and produce enzymes and digestive benefits. All freshly fermented dairy products are arguably probiotic.

PROPIONIBACTERIUM SHERMANII: A secondary culture, a bacteria, that is used to form typical "Swiss cheese" flavor as well as the signature eyeholes.

PROTEOLYSIS: The digestion of cheese proteins by cellular enzymes called proteases or by intermolecular digestion.

RED RIND: A generic term I use to describe a pungent, robust rind resulting from a diversity of microorganisms and, most important, *Coryneform* bacteria.

RENNET: A generic name for coagulant that may come from animal, plant, fungal, or bacterial origins.

RIPE: When the chemical breakdown of fats, proteins, and sugars in a cheese reach a state of balance and complexity in both flavor and texture.

RIPEN: The fermentation of milk or cream.

RIPENING CULTURES: Also known as "secondary cultures," these are bacteria, yeasts or molds that are added to the milk or applied to the rind to produce specific flavors or textures. They are the opposite of primary cultures whose purpose is to produce lactic acid early on.

SCALDING: During a washing process, replacing removed whey with warm water to cause the temperature of the vat to rise and the curds to form a skin.

SECONDARY CULTURES: *See* Ripening Cultures.

SPECIES SUCCESSION: The process by which communities of organisms, especially those on a cheese rind, change over time. In cheesemaking, species succession occurs on natural-rind, bloomy-rind, smear-rind, and washed-rind cheeses.

STRAINING: Separating curds from whey using cheesecloth or form.

SWISS-STYLE CHEESE: An informal cheese category describing cheeses that are cooked to high (about 110°F/43°C) temperatures, have a sweet and nutty flavor, a pliable elastic texture, and use the secondary culture *Propionibacterium shermanii* to form eyes.

TERROIR: The idea that food cultivated in a particular bioregion exhibits flavors specific to that region. This uniqueness is a result of the complex microbial communities that reside there.

THERMOPHILIC: Cultures that thrive near 110°F/43°C, a warmer temperature range than needed by mesophilic cultures. Often used in firm, cooked-, and Italian-style cheeses.

TRIER: A T-shaped metal tool with a curved blade used to remove cores from a cheese wheel for testing and monitoring development.

VAT: A large vessel in which cheese is made. The word is more appropriately applied to larger vessels but I use it to include the reader in cheesemaker's lingo. Synonymous with "pot."

WASHED RIND: The process of aging a cheese through regularly washing it with water, beer, spirits, or a mold-and/or herb-infused tea. Washing encourages the growth of *Coryneform* bacteria.

WASHING: Removing whey from the vat and replacing it with water. Washing lowers the calcium and lactose content in the cheese and leads to a milder, more pliable product.

WEEPING: When Swiss-style cheeses have moisture collect in the eyes caused by proteins breaking down during the ripening process. Can be a positive sign of maturity.

WHEY: The watery part of milk, counterpart to milk solids. Whey is mainly water but also contains some casein, albumin, and lacto albumin proteins as well as butterfat, lactose, and minerals.

TROUBLESHOOTING

CULTURED MILK & CREAM

My yogurt never set up—it just stayed liquid. What happened?

Either the cultures you used were no longer active or the incubation temperature wasn't consistent (likely too cold). Try another batch but, this time, start with a new container of yogurt and use a thermometer to confirm that the incubator stays near 105°F/40°C.

My yogurt set up but wasn't smooth—it has an almost chunky texture and is very sour. There was lots of yellow whey on top. I didn't like it.

When this happens, it means the incubation temperature was too hot.

My yogurt came out very, very stringy or ropey. It wasn't appealing. What went wrong?

This ropey texture can be fixed by simply changing the type of cultures or brand of yogurt you are using. Also, it might occur when using powdered milk to form a thicker body. Try the recipe again with new cultures and without powdered milk.

Can I use kefir in place of buttermilk in any of the cheese recipes?

No. Though they are made through similar processes, kefir contains yeasts, which you don't want. The bacteria (present in both), you do.

DIRECT-ACID CHEESES

My whey ricotta never clumped together and only bits formed at the bottom of the vat.

Too much time passed between finishing your batch of cheese and starting the whey ricotta recipe. Next time, start the ricotta right away. Also, be sure to stop stirring soon after adding the acid to allow the proteins to clump.

My first round of whole milk ricotta turned out tough and stringy. The second round was different and much better. Why?

There are several types of proteins in milk and they precipitate out (when you add acid) at different rates. Your first round on the whole milk ricotta yields a cheese higher in the casein protein. Your second round, one richer in albumin and lacto-albumin proteins. In a sense, the first round is like making a regular batch of cheese and the second round is more similar to making whey ricotta with the leftovers.

When can I add flavorings to the ricotta?

The best time to season your ricotta is after it's been drained for at least 6 hours in the fridge. Transfer to a medium bowl and gently fold in flavorings of choice. Some ideas include chopped dried cranberries; powdered sugar, mini chocolate chips, and almond extract; chopped basil and roasted garlic.

BEGINNING CHEESES

When I start to stir my curds, the pieces fall apart into tiny bits. What's wrong?

This is a sign that the milk you are using has been over-pasteurized. Switch brands and look for one that is more local, possibly also organic.

My pot cheese tastes bad after just a week.

Most of the recipes in chapter 2 are meant to be eaten right away and not saved or ripened. That is especially true for *queso fresco*, pot cheese, mascarpone, and ricotta. All of these cheeses are very sweet (meaning little acid) with very high moisture—exactly the kind of food that doesn't last.

Can I make ricotta with the leftover whey from any cheese recipe?

Not really. You can make whey ricotta from any whey leftover from rennet-set cheeses.

WASHED-CURD CHEESES

My Rising Moon doesn't have much flavor.

Try reducing the amount of whey you remove by 2 to 3 cups/480 to 720 ml. Sometimes cheeses get over-washed, which depletes flavor. More likely, though, your cheese needs more time to age. If the flavor isn't where you'd like it to be, add 2 to 3 months more. You can reseal this cheese, after cutting, in a vacuum-seal bag.

The Divino tastes bitter.

Bitterness is a pitfall for home cheesemaking. Try another rennet (different type or new bottle). Try resealing the cheese and tasting again after another several months. Or try a different culture mix by calling the culture company and finding an alternative.

WASHED-RIND CHEESES

I'm not seeing red on the rind.

The mixture of microorganisms that create a red, stinky rind often arrive after the rind has been cultivated by other species. Give your rind time. Wash the rind regularly using the Red-Rind Wash (page 121) or Herb Wash (page 125). Make sure the aging temperature is correct.

Should I be scraping off the blue and white spots?

Other species will grow on your rind, especially before the *Coryneform* community establishes. Catch these other visitors early on and rub, brush, or wash them gently away. Don't let them establish for a week before trying to scrape them off.

My rind looks more pink than red.

There is a range of colors, from light peach to deep red, that qualify as appropriate for a red or washed-rind cheese. The color depends on the collection of organisms present and how they are responding to the rind's moisture, acidity, and salt levels. It makes me think of how hydrangeas turn pink or blue depending on the acidity of the soil they're growing in.

There is red but it isn't covering the rind, just sections.

Patchiness results from imbalanced moisture either inside or outside of the cheese. Do your best to rotate the cheese regularly and to maintain a constant environment. Cut your curds as evenly as possible on your next batch. Also, as the red rind starts to grow in one area, it likely spreads to other sections, given you are washing and rotating.

My cheese is not gooey on the inside.

Washed-rind cheeses are loved not only for their stink but also for their shiny, smooth insides. If the paste of your cheese is too firm, it may be that the cheese got too dry in the vat. Try cutting your curds ¼ in/6 mm larger than before. Also, increase the humidity of your cave as maybe the cheese is simply drying out.

BLOOMY-RIND CHEESES

What if the white mold only grows in patches?

Uneven mold growth can be due to uneven moisture during ripening. Be sure to flip your cheese regularly so the top and the bottom have equal exposure. If the aging bin is too dry, increase moisture by adding a damp towel to the corner of the bin, making sure it doesn't touch the cheese. Try dipping the patchy cheese in a bath of water and *Penicillium candidum* spores. Or eat it as it is!

My Camembert is not getting soft. It's been rubbery for two months.

Given that you've been aging the cheese at proper temperature and humidity, the culprit is the cultures. They were not active enough for the cheese to develop. Your best bet is to eat the cheese in this less-than-soft stage and then try the recipe again with fresh cultures. A Camembert should bloom and soften within 4 to 6 weeks if aged at 50°F/10°C and at 90% RH. Another possibility is that you had slow acid development, which leads to too much calcium being retained in the final curd. Slightly increase the dosage of cultures on the next batch.

There is a strong bitter flavor.

Bitterness is a potential problem of bloomy-rind cheeses. Try to 1) use the freshest milk and the freshest cultures possible, 2) use pasteurized instead of raw milk, 3) use *Geotrichum candidum* or switch to a different strain of *Penicillium candidum* if possible, and 4) try a different type of rennet. Make sure you are aging the cheese under the proper conditions. Sometimes the bitter flavor will go away with a longer aging time (though sometimes it only intensifies).

The rind of my cheeses seems to be slipping away from the cheese itself.

Slip skin. This unwanted feature of a bloomy-rind happens when the moisture in the aging environment is too high, causing the surface ripening molds to move too quickly and digest the paste nearest the rind out of proportion with the rest of the cheese. Bring the humidity of the aging bin down simply by removing the lid from the bin for 5 minutes daily.

BLUE CHEESES

My cheese has been aging for two weeks and I'm not seeing any blue molds.

It may take several weeks to see blue mold growth on your rind, depending on what the aging conditions are. It is also possible that molds are growing on the inside even though you never saw them on the surface. You won't know until you've opened up the wheel but don't do that until you are ready. Follow through with the proper aging time.

I forgot to pierce my cheese at the right time. Can I pierce it late?

It is ideal to pierce early on because it gives the blue molds an "upper hand" on the battlefields within and on the rind. But also keep things in perspective; some blues are never even pierced. Try an experiment to see how a recipe turns out without any piercing. You might be surprised.

There are white and gray molds growing over the blue molds on the surface. Is this okay?

If you've had a hearty first bloom of blue on the cheese rind, you're pointed in a good direction. Subsequent colonization by other rind microorganisms will have flavor impact but the blue flavor will dominate. Continue to flip and brush or smear the cheese wheel regularly.

I smell a lot of ammonia.

Ammonia is a natural by-product of the breakdown of proteins (proteolysis), a key process for ripening cheeses. Make sure to open the aging bin regularly to give your cheese a breath of fresh air—try 5 minutes each day. Also, try lowering the aging-room temperature and/or humidity by several degrees. Before eating the cheese, allow it to sit out, uncovered, for an hour. Most of the ammonia should dissipate.

The inside of the cheese has hardly any veining.

Your cheese may simply be too dense, pressed too hard, or so moist that the tunnels you created when you pierced the cheese collapsed. To dry your cheese out a bit, try stirring 5 to 10 minutes longer when the curds are in the vat. When making the Stilton, try draining the curds longer in the colander (for 5 hours more), then break the curds into larger chunk sizes. Try not to overmix when folding in the salt.

CHEDDAR CHEESES

What if the curds never came together and sealed into one complete form?

The salt you added in the pot caused each curd to tighten up. You want that tightening to happen when the curds are in the press and still slightly warm, not when the curds are still separated and cooling off in the pot. Work quickly when hooping the cheese. Alternatively, curds may have accidentally cooked to too high of a temperature. Lower the final cooking temperature by several degrees and cut back on the stirring time by several minutes.

My cheddar wheel was full of holes and cracks when I opened it up. Why?

Unwanted holes often occur with harder, cooked and pressed cheeses. These holes are due to unwanted bacteria or improper pressing. Improve the sanitation on your next batch. Remember that the cleaner and fresher your milk, the less likely you'll have extra eye holes and fissures. To improve mechanical openings, get the cheese into a press as soon as possible, flip soon afterward (within the first 10 minutes), and press under heavy weights (50 lb/23 kg) for at least 8 to 10 hours to create a more sealed body.

My cheddar is really crumbly. If I try to cut a slice, it falls apart. Why?

The curds developed too much acid in the vat. Fix this by shortening the pre-rennet ripening time by 15 minutes or your stirring time by 15 minutes. Alternatively, try stirring in 2 tbsp of salt 30 minutes before starting to drain. Age for a shorter period of time.

STRETCHED-CURD CHEESES

My curds won't stretch.

If your curds won't stretch, and you've given it many, many hours (on the order of ten!) to ripen, the cultures you used may not be strong enough or even active at all. Repeat the recipe with freshly purchased cultures. Also, try switching the brand of milk.

The mozzarella I made is too tough.

Making sure the mozzarella has reached the correct acidity will make the stretching process easier, which means you'll work the dough less, which means your finished cheese will be softer. Other ways to improve the softness of your mozzarella include initially cutting the curds to a larger size (greater than ½ in/12 mm thick) as well as adding 1 qt/960 ml of warm water to the vat as you are stirring the curds, prior to draining and ripening.

The leftover whey looks almost like milk.

The clearer your whey is, the more proteins you've "caught." Very milky whey means you lost some potential cheese. This may be due to cutting the curd too early, using milk that is over-pasteurized or rough treatment of the curds (stir very slowly at first).

My Quick Mozz was great the first day but now it is slimy.

Quick Mozz needs to be eaten, not aged. If you are looking for a cheese that lasts longer and gets better in terms of flavor and texture, go with the Cultured Mozzarella (page 174) or Provolone (page 176).

PRESSED AND AGED CHEESES

The rind is colorful with mold. How do I know if it's safe to eat?

Mold rinds, from my experience, may make your cheese taste odd but they aren't going to make you sick. It is very hard to identify the precise microorganisms you may have growing and would require sending a sample to a laboratory. If you want to play it safe, you can always trim the rind away before eating.

My cheese has eye holes even though I thought it was going to be a cheese with no eyes. What happened?

I have this problem often. Eye holes (if you weren't planning on them) and excessive eye holes (if you wanted just a few) could be a sign of contamination or maybe just gas-producing native bacteria in the milk. Too many eyes can be prevented by bringing down the temperature of the aging environment, changing the type of cultures you're using, working with pasteurized milk, or pre-pressing the curds more thoroughly when they are still under the whey.

My Asiago tastes too peppery. How can I tone it down?

The spiciness in the Asiago comes from the lipase you added. Lipase breaks down the fat globules and forms flavor compounds that taste spicy. Tone this down by choosing a milder lipase (calf lipase is the mildest, followed by young lamb, then kid lipase). Or decrease the amount of lipase you are using by half. Try aging the cheese for a shorter amount of time.

APPENDICES

CHEESEMAKING PROCESSES

WHEN TO CUT THE CURD USING THE CLEAN BREAK METHOD

In the beginning cheeses of chapter 2, you're instructed to cut the curd after renneting according to a specific amount of time, usually about 30 minutes. This is a reliable enough method when you're just learning to make cheese or if you're making a very simple, fresh cheese that won't be aged. As your cheesemaking skills advance or you start to make more involved cheeses, you can use the Flocculation Method at right.

1. After renneting the milk and waiting for the alloted time, uncover the pot. Look for a faintly yogurty aroma. This is one way to know things are working.

2. With a clean hand, slowly insert several of your fingers into the curd at a 45-degree angle, up to the second knuckle. Slowly push these fingers toward the surface of the curd and watch how the curd splits open. If it splits into one or two clean fissures, the curd is ready to cut. If the curd opens up loosely, looking more like undercooked egg white, allow the milk to set for another 10 minutes. If the curd is so tough it simply bends as you gently press upward, you've waited too long or used too much rennet.

3. If the milk does not show a clean break after an additional 30 minutes, there's likely a problem with your milk or rennet. Start again with new ingredients.

WHEN TO CUT THE CURD USING THE FLOCCULATION METHOD

As you advance in your cheesemaking skills, a more accurate method for determining when to cut the curd is necessary. This method uses the flocculation point—the moment after adding rennet to the milk, when the milk becomes a perceivable gel. Here's how to calculate that moment and then use it to determine when to cut the curd:

1. Add rennet to the milk, stir it in thoroughly, stop the motion of the milk, and then immediately start a timer. Let's say it is 10:00 a.m.

2. At the same time that you start the timer, set a bottle cap (upside down) or a Styrofoam bowl (right-side up) on the surface of the milk. It should float.

3. Use your finger to tap the cap or bowl. It should glide across the milk's surface. Keep tapping until it stops moving easily and seems to bounce backward toward your finger; at that moment, stop the timer. This is the flocculation point. Let's say the time is now 10:10 a.m.

4. Take the number of minutes that passed (in our example 10 minutes, and in most cases somewhere between 4 and 15 minutes) and multiple by the numerical factor given in the recipe. Some cheeses have high flocculation factors (you'll multiply the minutes by 5 or 6). Others have low factors (1.5 or 2). The higher the factor, the more moisture retained in the final cheese. For example, you'll cut an Asiago cheese at three times the flocculation point because it is a drier cheese, whereas you'll cut Brie at six times the flocculation point.

Multiplication Factors If Using Flocculation Point

CHEESE STYLE	MULTIPLY BY	WHY
Firm, cooked cheeses	2 to 2.5	An earlier cut will mean a looser protein web. A looser web releases water more readily and creates a drier cheese.
Cheddars, washed curd, cultured mozzarellas	3 to 3.5	These intermediate cheeses retain more water than the firmer cooked cheeses.
Feta, blues	4	Also intermediate cheeses, but those with a higher moisture content than cheddar and washed-curd styles.
Bloomy-rinds, some blues	5 to 6	These styles have the highest water content of the renneted cheeses. The protein web traps a lot of the water.

HOW TO CUT SQUARE CURDS FROM A CYLINDRICAL POT

You've probably been wondering how on Earth you can cut a cylindrical pot of milk into identical cubes using only a cake spatula. This is the goal—uniform curd pieces release water at the same rate—but it isn't entirely possible. In commercial creameries, retangular vats of renneted milk can be cut into perfect squares using cheese harps. In your kitchen creamery, you'll just do a close approximation. Here are two methods for this inexact art.

THE GRID METHOD

Start with the vertical cuts. Position a long knife such as a curd knife (12 in/30.5 cm) or cake knife (10 to 15 in/ 25 to 38 cm) at either the left or the right edge of the pot. Make a series of straight cuts all the way to the bottom of the pot, and equal distance apart—the distance between the cuts will be specified in the recipe (e.g., hazelnut-size curds or ¾-in/2-cm curds). Next, rotate the pot 90 degrees and make cuts perpendicular to the first. You will end up with a grid. Next, use your skimmer to make rough horizontal cuts from the top to the bottom of the pot.

CUT the CURD

VERTICALLY WITH CURD KNIFE   **HORIZONTALLY** WITH SKIMMER

THE ANGLE METHOD

Because the Grid Method (above) requires a final set of horizontal cuts that is technically impossible (starting awkwardly and getting harder as you work toward the bottom of the pot), try a second method that fudges the challenge a different way. Instead of making an initial grid, start by cutting into the curd at a 45 degree angle. Work your way from one side of the pot to the other and make the distance between the cuts as specified in the recipe (e.g., hazelnut-size curds or ¾-in/2-cm curds). After cutting in one direction, rotate the pot 90 degrees and repeat. Cut the curd in all four directions (north, south, east, west). This will land you with a bunch of trapezoids but they will be nearly uniform trapezoids, which is what matters.

HOW TO PRE-PRESS CURDS UNDER THE WHEY

Pressing curds under the whey before draining, also known as pre-pressing, helps the curds to knit together prior to being exposed to air and when they are still very warm. The result of pre-pressing is a denser, less-open paste in the finished cheese.

1. After you've finished cooking and stirring the curds, pitch the curds, allowing them to sink to the bottom of the vat for 5 minutes.

2. With a clean arm, reach to the bottom of the vat. With your hand or a clean cheese form, slowly gather and press the curds together. Press for the amount of time specified in the recipe.

3. Afterward, pour off a portion of the whey and then move chunks of curd directly into the final form for pressing.

HOW TO FILL FORMS WITH LACTIC-ACID OR VERY SOFT SET CURD

Lactic-acid curds, such as you'll create when making Chèvre (page 82), Fromage Blanc & Quark (page 84), Gosling (page 134), and Blue Capricorn (page 148) are tender, more so than curds formed through a rennet set. One rarely stirs lactic-acid set curds. Instead, gently scoop the curd directly into the draining forms.

1. Use a skimmer or wide spoon to gather a scoop about 1 in/2.5 cm deep from the top of the vat, then lay this scoop gently into the bottom of the form (as opposed to dropping, dumping, or pumping it in). The more gently you treat the curd, the higher the yield (as fewer bits break off to be lost in the draining whey).

2. Fill the first form until it is brimming (looks like an ice-cream cone) before moving on to the next form. Do not be tempted to return to the first form to "top it off" until you've finished filling the other forms. Whey will rapidly drain off, making the curd that has been in a form longer appear to be less full. This is not the case—it is just more compacted.

3. If needed, after time has passed, return to the first form and refill all the forms again. Wait until the curds have drained at least 1 in/2.5 cm before attempting a first flip.

HOW TO DO A FIRST FLIP WITH SOFT CURDS

An early flip with soft curd cheeses (Camembert, Chevre in forms, Buttercup) ensures the top and the bottom of the cheese are symmetrical and well-sealed. This is important biologically—so the cheese drains evenly and so there aren't gaps and fissures on the cheese's rind. Do a first flip as early as possible—flipping the first form as soon as you can after filling the last form of the fleet. When I make higher-fat soft-curd cheese (Buttercup), the curds take a very long time to drain, and it's hours before I can do the first flip. With other cheeses, I can manage the first flip within the first 5 to 10 minutes.

TO FLIP A SMALLER CHEESE

1. Hold the curd-filled form in one hand, then invert it into the palm of the other hand.

2. Remove the form and set it down.

3. Move the free-standing cheese from one palm onto the other, flipping as you do so.

4. Quickly replace the form over the cheese in your hand, then invert and set on the aging mat. The cheese will slide down the form, with what was once the bottom now as the top.

TO FLIP A LARGER (SOFT CURD) CHEESE

Larger cheeses with very soft curds (mainly the Brie on page 133) are best made in bottomless forms. Using a second aging mat, cover the top of the form you're about to flip. Use your hand to hold it in place. Carefully slide the fingers of your other hand underneath the mat beneath the cheese. Invert. In this way, soft curds never lose the support of the sidewalls.

HOW TO FLIP AND REDRESS A CHEESE

For a cheese to drain properly and be symmetrical on the top and the bottom, you'll need to flip it at least once while it is pressing. When you flip the cheese, you'll need to remove the cheese from the press, take off the follower, take off the cheesecloth, invert the cheese, and return it to the press. This process is called flipping and redressing.

1. After the cheese has pressed for an initial period of time (about 5 minutes), remove the weights and the follower. Peel off the cheesecloth. Take the cheese wheel out.

2. Flip so the top of the cheese becomes the bottom, then place again in the cheesecloth. Place in the form. Tug on the cheesecloth to tighten. Replace the follower and reapply weights.

HOW TO FIGURE OUT THE AMOUNT OF WEIGHT TO USE

I press cheeses by thinking in general terms: "unpressed," "lightly pressed," "medium pressed," or "hard pressed." It isn't scientific but it's worked. Each of these categories is a ballpark range because I use barbells that come in 10-lb/4.5-kg increments. Here are some pressing guidelines.

- In general, begin pressing with lighter weights and then increase in amount. For firmer cheeses, you can start off with medium pressure. Cheddars are the only cheeses where you'll start off with a heavy pressing.

- Consider the volume of cheese you are working with—the more cheese, the more weight you need to apply.

- Cheese pressing can be as light as 5 lb/2.2 kg and as much as 50 lb/23 kg, but does not need to go beyond this range.

HOW TO PRESS A CHEESE WITHOUT USING A FORM

You don't have to have a pressable form with follower to make a pressable, ageable cheese. You can simply use a piece of cheesecloth!

1. Clean a large (no less than 24-in/61-cm) square of fine (#60 or #90) cheesecloth by boiling it in water for 3 minutes.

2. Spread the cheesecloth over a colander, then place colander in the sink.

3. Transfer the curds out of the vat and into the colander.

4. Let the curds drain for 1 minute, then gather the corners of the cheesecloth and twist them together to wring out more whey. While twisting, quickly turn the twist into a knot, securing it as close to the cheese as possible. Alternatively, you can secure the twist with twine.

5. Place the cheese on a plate or board, setting the knot portion of the cheesecloth in the center of the

wheel (to form that characteristic indent you can see on page 153). Place a second board on top of the cheese, then put weights on top of the board. Make sure the weights stay centered over the cheese.

6. Flip and redress the wheel twice during the pressing to ensure the wheel is complete and folds of the cheesecloth aren't lost inside.

SALTING YOUR CHEESES

At the first creamery I worked at, we only dry salted the cheeses. At the next creamery, we only brined. The benefit of dry salting is it saves time (you don't have to prepare and maintain a brine). On the other hand, dry salting wastes salt because you can't save what doesn't get absorbed; and managed brine can last decades. The choice is really yours for which method to use.

TO DRY SALT A CHEESE

1. Remove the cheese from its form. Weigh the cheese then calculate 2 percent of the cheese's weight. (If the cheese weighs 2 lb/960 g, use 0.7 oz/20 g of salt). Weigh out the correct amount of salt.

2. Rub half the measured salt over the top and sides of the cheese. Some salt will fall away. Set the wheel on a draining rack and allow the salt to soak in for an hour. Afterward, flip and apply the second portion of the salt to the other side of the cheese.

TO MAKE A BRINE

1. Bring 1 gal/3.7 L of water to a boil, cool to 75°F/24°C or a similar temperature, then transfer to a plastic or glass container (not metal).

2. Add the salt to the water according to the desired brine strength (see chart at right). Stir until the salt has dissolved (unless you're making saturated brine in which case add salt to the point of saturation—until no more salt can dissolve). Be sure to add salt at the same temperature every time you make a batch to ensure the salt content stays consistent from batch to batch (water absorbs more salt at higher temperatures).

3. Cool the brine in the fridge until it reaches between 55° and 60°F/13° and 15°C. Make sure your cheese is also at the same temperature as the brine when you combine the two. If the brine is too warm, it causes the cheese to release butterfat at the rind. This creates a shield against incoming salt, thwarting your efforts. Keep the cheese in the brine for the prescribed amount of time.

Salt: Water Ratios for Brine

	WATER (AT ABOUT 75°F/24°C)	SALT BY WEIGHT	% SATURATION
Washing brine	1 gal/3.8 L	0.25 lb/113 g	3%
Light Brine	1 gal/3.8 L	0.40 lb/181 g	5%
Medium	1 gal/3.8 L	0.75 lb/340 g	8%
Medium-Heavy	1 gal/3.8 L	1.5 lb/680 g	15%
Saturated	1 gal/3.8 L	2.5 lb/1.1 kg	22%

HOW TO FIGURE OUT DURATION OF BRINING

I learned this equation for figuring out how long to brine a cheese from cheesemaking master Peter Dixon. It is based on using heavy (>20% salt saturation) brine.

(height in inches) x (weight in pounds) = (number of hours to brine)

For example, if your cheese is 2.5 in/6.4 cm high and weighs 8 lb/3.6 kg, plan to brine your cheese for 20 hours at 55°F/13°C. Remember, if the aging area is cooler than this, your cheese will need to brine for longer and vise versa if the room is warmer. Also, remember other factors affect the brining process; if the brine tank if overflowing with other cheeses, if the cheese is soft- or firm-pressed, if the cheese has a higher or lower fat content, and if the cheese rind got oily while in the press (due to high temperatures).

HOW TO MAINTAIN BRINE OVER TIME

To maintain your brine from batch to batch, start with a saturated brine. Brine the first round of cheeses. When finished, remove the cheeses and filter the brine by pouring through layers of fine (#90) cheesecloth. Discard the sediments. Return the brine to a clean, closed container and store in the fridge.

For quality control, before brining your next recipe, you might choose to pasteurize the brine by heating it to 180°F/82°C and adding more salt to bring it back to the correct concentration. An instrument called a salometer reads how much salt is in a solution by measuring its density. Remember to always cool the brine before submerging new cheeses.

HOW TO USE A HYDROMETER TO JUDGE BRINE STRENGTH

If you are a home brewer or have a saltwater fish tank, you already have a device to measure the strength of your brine. A hydrometer measures the density of a fluid. For home brewers, that means the sugar content. For cheesemakers, that same device can measure a brine's salt content. I learned this from the Beverage People in Santa Rosa. To translate the hydrometer's specific gravity readings into brine strength, use the following chart.

BRINE STRENGTH	HYDROMETER READINGS IN SPECIFIC GRAVITY
Light	1.057 to 1.074
Medium	1.088 to 1.110
Heavy	1.148 to 1.169

HOW TO DRY OR CURE A WHEEL PRIOR TO AGING

When a cheese comes out of the brine, it needs to dry before going into an aging bin or cave. There are several reasons for this. First, a curing period gives the cheese a few days at a warmer temperature (I dry my wheels on the countertop, which is a little too warm but works), allowing the salt to dissipate and more acid to be produced. Next, a curing period keeps the cheese in your line of sight during the first few critical days. This is the time period when you should watch for bloating or cracking (possibly signs of contamination) and when the cheese needs to be turned and whey removed. Finally, curing helps seal and establish the rind, an essential step for a wheel that's going to roll down the long, winding road of *affinage*.

TO DRY OR CURE YOUR CHEESE

1. Remove the cheese from the brine. Pat dry with a clean towel.

2. Set the cheese on a clean aging mat, which sits on top of a drying rack.

3. Cover the cheese with cheesecloth to keep away flies and dust.

4. Flip the cheese twice daily until the rind feels just barely damp.

5. If your climate is exceedingly humid, set the aging rack in front of a desk fan set on the lowest speed. This air movement will dry the cheese in less time.

HOW TO PREVENT CHEESE FROM STICKING TO CHEESECLOTH

In recipes where the end temperature of the vat is higher than 110°F/43°C, the curds get hooped when they are still relatively warm. There are benefits to warm curds, such as they knit together nicely to form a perfect rind. But there is one potential drawback. If the curd is warm and heavy pressure is applied right away, the pressure will push the cheese through the pores of the cheesecloth. This cheese will reconnect on the outside of the cloth and essentially encapsulate the cloth.

To prevent this, place your cheesecloth, or the mesh liner, in the whey of the vat for a minute before hooping the curds. This will bring the cloth to a temperature and acidity closer to that of the cheese. Another trick is to apply pressure gradually, starting with a light pressure and, over the course of an hour, moving to heavy pressure. Last, cheese is unlikely to stick if you flip and redress the wheel regularly, especially in the first 30 minutes.

HOW TO ASH A CHEESE

Covering a rind with vegetable ash makes for a beautiful aesthetic. There are a number of ways to apply the ash but this is what works best for me.

1. Gather disposable gloves, several sheets of newspaper, and an empty saltshaker.

2. Fill the saltshaker with vegetable ash.

3. Close the windows and turn off any fans. Cover the countertop with the newspaper.

4. Select a cured or curing cheese when the rind is no longer wet. There should be little to no mold growth yet in the case of bloomy-rinds.

5. With one hand, hold the cheese (assuming it is small enough). With the other hand, shake the ash three to four times onto one surface, then rotate the cheese and apply to the other side. You may also apply ash internally to a cheese, while hooping, as you'll do with the Marbler.

6. Set the ashed cheese on top of a mat, inside a bin. Cover and proceed with aging.

HOW TO USE CREAM WAX

Applying cream wax feels like painting your cheese with white glue. Oddly, cream wax even smells like glue. Remember that you can purchase cream wax either with or without Natamycin, a mold-inhibitor. It should be stored in a dry, dark, cool place and never subjected to freezing temperatures.

1. Cure the wheel thoroughly.

2. When the cheese is dry, paint the cream wax over the cheese's top and sides. Allow this to dry (for several hours to a day) then flip the cheese and repeat on the bottom, making sure to overlap at the sides. If the room is humid, be careful when flipping the cheese. Cream wax will easily peel off and leave you with spots that need to be retouched.

3. Apply two or three coats of cream wax in total. Set on an aging mat and proceed with aging according to the recipe.

HOW TO USE CHEESE WAX

Waxing works for semi- to firm-pressed cheeses. Waxing will not work for soft, unpressed, or mold-ripened cheeses such as *queso fresco* or Buttercup. It is also not appropriate for cheeses that need their rinds to develop proper flavor (such as the Marbler).

1. Remove the cheese from the press. Trim cheese with a pairing knife to make the wheel smooth and symmetrical. If an area is distinctly rough or knobby, it will be coated in wax but then, ultimately, that wax may not easily separate from this area. Smooth surfaces work best.

2. Cure the cheese until it is dry. Do not dry cheese so long that it starts to crack.

3. Place at least 5 lb/2.3 kg of plain or colored cheese wax into a designated pot. You will not reuse this pot for any other purpose once you've put cheese wax inside. Be sure the pot is wide enough that, if dipping, the wheel can fit. There are options other than a slow-cooker for melting the wax (a doubled-up disposable aluminum baking tray placed directly on the stovetop), but I find a second-hand slow-cooker is easy to find and easy to use.

4. Allow the wax approximately 2 hours to melt, depending on the size of the chunk. Melt at the lowest temperature setting, also, to preserve the quality of the wax. Too hot of a temperature will destabilize the wax. While melting the wax, place your cheese in the fridge to cool.

5. Place newspaper or foil underneath the area where you'll be working. Wax drips are hard to clean.

6. Remove the cheese from the fridge and, while holding on tightly to one half of the wheel (as though it's a big cookie you're about to dip), dip half the cheese into the wax pot, then pull immediately back out.

7. Hold the dipped cheese in midair for 30 seconds to allow the wax to harden, then rotate and hold on to the just-dipped section. Dip the other half in. Continue rotating and dipping as though you were dipping a clock: first cover the clock face from 12 to 6 p.m., then rotate and cover from 6 to 12 p.m., then rotate and cover from 9 to 3 p.m. and so on. Make sure the seams overlap. Touch up as needed using a cotton swab or a brush.

- *Alternative Option: Apply the wax using a clean 2-in/5-cm natural-fiber brush. Paint multiple layers onto the wheel until the cheese is completely covered. This method creates a rougher rind and will use up more wax but also gets the job done.*

- *Note: You may discover molds growing beneath the wax on the surface of the cheese when you open up the wheel months later. If this happens, use stricter sanitation. Or precoat the rind with cream wax containing Natamycin. Allow the cream wax to dry for 2 to 3 days before applying the cheese-wax coat.*

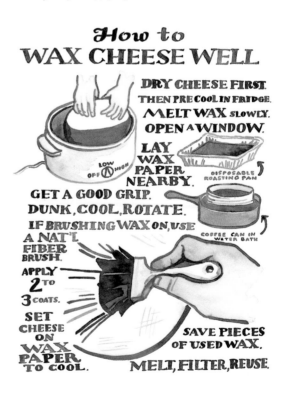

How to **WAX CHEESE WELL**

DRY CHEESE FIRST.
THEN PRE COOL IN FRIDGE.
MELT WAX SLOWLY.
OPEN A WINDOW.
LAY WAX PAPER NEARBY.
LOW OFF HIGH
DISPOSABLE ROASTING PAN
GET A GOOD GRIP.
DUNK, COOL, ROTATE.
IF BRUSHING WAX ON, USE
COFFEE CAN IN WATER BATH
A NAT'L FIBER BRUSH.
APPLY **2** TO **3** COATS.
SET CHEESE ON WAX PAPER TO COOL.
SAVE PIECES OF USED WAX.
MELT, FILTER, REUSE.

FORMS AND PRESSES

CHEESE FORMS

HOW TO CHOOSE THE CORRECT CHEESE FORM

Though I make general recommendations on which size and style of form to use for each pertinent recipe, the truth is that you'll likely make most cheeses in the same form! I have three Kadova molds and use them to make almost everything—from Bisbee Blue to Rising Moon to Marbler to Mountain Top. By admitting this, what I'm really doing is lobbying for you to buy one nice cheese form to start with. Once you land an easy-to-use form that fits with your pressing setup (if you're pressing), you won't change a thing. All of your cheeses will begin to look identical in shape. But that's less important than the fact that they'll be properly shaped, properly drained, and properly pressed. Of course, you may want a variety of shapes in your cave; read on for the most common options.

CHEESE FORM TERMS

Bottomless: An open tube or square shape. Ideal for cheeses that need to be flipped before they are drained enough to be very sturdy (meaning cheeses that are liable to spill apart when taken out of the form). An open bottom allows you to place an aging mat on the opposite side and simply invert instead of removing the cheese from the form.

Disposable: Made from lightweight, less-durable plastic; though with care, can be reused. Not for pressed cheeses. Usually used for ricotta or very soft cheeses, which may be sold with the cheeses in them.

Follower: The lid to the cheese form, necessary in order to apply pressure evenly onto the cheese and perfectly fitting so that cheese is not squeezed out in the gap where the form and the follower meet.

Kadova: A three-part form including a base, a mesh liner (which replaces the cheesecloth called for in most recipes), and a follower. Easy to use, relatively easy to clean and made with replaceable parts.

Microperforated: A newer cheese form option with pinpoint-size holes and an imprinted cheesecloth design. These forms make perfectly sealed rinds with no wrinkles or imperfection. They can be difficult to clean.

Here's how to choose the correct form:

- Identify if the cheese needs to be pressed. If not, you have many more choices, because you won't need a follower or lid to the form.

- Identify if the form's volume is in proportion to the volume of milk used. Remember, the cheese yields will be between roughly 12 and 17 percent for fresh cheeses and between 8 and 14 percent for aged cheeses.

- Cheeses, such as the Asiago or the Zeller, cook in the vat and become drier and smaller before the curds are hooped, so they won't take up as much space in the form, initially, as opposed to, say, the Camembert.

- Remember that forms for cooked, pressed cheeses will need to be lined with cheesecloth when pressed to help wick the moisture out of the cheese. Cheesecloth is not necessary if the form includes a mesh liner or is microperforated.

- Cheeses that are not cooked or stirred and won't be pressed (such as the Camembert) need taller forms. This is because the curds release most of their whey over many hours, not in the vat. These cheeses start out bulkier and shrink more.

CHEESE PRESSES

Pressing cheeses using heavy objects from the house (instead of buying a cheese press) is innovative and low cost but also risky. I have two favorite "pressing" horror stories. The first is a student who used a tall stack of books to press his Gouda then, for kicks, added a glass bottle of whisky to the top of the stack. The stack didn't topple but when I saw the picture, I gasped. The second story is of a cheesemaker who set up a makeshift press in his kitchen sink. After dinner, his boyfriend, not knowing why there were water-filled jugs in the sink, proceeded to wash the spaghetti plates right over the cheese that had taken all day to make.

OFF THE WALL (DUTCH-STYLE) PRESS

The Dutch-Style or Off-the-Wall press is a smart, inexpensive style, which you can construct or purchase at minimal cost. This system uses a long lever arm fastened to a wall or stand. Off of the arm comes another downward facing arm, which pushes against the follower on the cheese form. To the end of the main arm, the cheesemaker attaches any amount of weight. These presses are often made of wood treated with natural sealant.

THE CAR-JACK PRESS

One of my favorite cheese-pressing ideas comes from cheesemaker Kathy Biss in the west Highlands of Scotland. Kathy's idea is to use a car jack to press cheese. In order for this system to work, there needs to be a low "ceiling" for the jack to work against. Don't even think of pressing your cheeses under the car. Perhaps there is a low cabinet or the underside of a very heavy table. Have a jack reserved for cheese pressing alone. No one wants car grease in his Caerphilly.

BARBELL WEIGHTS

Though I always meant to do the research and buy a nice stainless-steel press, I ended up mastering a setup using gym weights. Barbell weights are helpful because you'll know the exact weight you are using. They are easy to come by and easy to adjust. What they do need, though, I've learned, is support so that as the cheese compresses, the weights don't topple over. My handy husband put together a frame using little more than a drill and some 2×4 scraps.

WOODEN AGING BOARDS

Wooden planks make wonderful platters for your aging cheese wheels, replacing the "aging mat" mentioned in many recipes. These planks will most likely need to be placed inside an aging bin, which keeps the humidity up if you are aging in a converted fridge. The humidity conditions of a walk-in aging cave or root cellar may be different. Planks should be made of unplaned, non-cracked wood. If using planed wood, you must place a mat between the board and the cheese to prevent the cheese from sticking to the board and to make sure the cheese gets enough oxygen underneath.

If you are aging cheeses using aging bins and aging mats, you won't need aging boards. However, if you have a well-humidified cave, you may be able to abandon the plastic bins and mats and simply set your cheeses on top of wooden boards. The type of boards you use is less important if cheeses are wax-dipped, cream-waxed, or vacuum-sealed and more important if the cheeses are smear-, bloomy-, or natural-rinded. The boards play a meaningful role in mold and flavor development and are discussed more thoroughly in the next section.

WOOD TO USE

Wooden aging boards should be sturdy enough to stand up to the rigor of regular washings. They should also provide the right amount of moisture and oxygen exchange. These woods will all work well: ash, beech, birch, cedar, cypress, fir, maple, pine. These following woods may stain your cheese or release compounds that slow or stop the development of the cheese's rind: mahogany, oak, redwood, teak, walnut.

Note that you don't have to age your cheese on wooden boards, however. You can place them on an aging mat directly on the bottom of an aging bin. The bin will serve as the support, and the mat will encourage a balance of oxygen and moisture.

HOW TO CLEAN AGING BOARDS

Between batches of cheese or on a regular calendar schedule, scrub the boards with only water and a gentle scrub brush. Do not use soaps or detergents, which may deteriorate the wood. To dry the boards, leave in direct, bright sunlight for several days. This will not only dry the wood but will help control yeasts and molds by exposing the wood to UV light.

CULTURES

Because this book is directed at beginners, I've tried to keep the culture requirements as simple as possible. There's already enough to intimidate a new cheesemaker—forms, presses, milk sources, affinage! And cultures are probably the most daunting of all. There are many, many cultures to choose from; in addition, neither the naming system nor the dosage are overly obvious. Finally, how a culture works might not be revealed until months down the road—if you remembered to take good notes and if you could ever really isolate cultures as the sole reason for a cheese's outcome.

I suggest you use buttermilk for most of your initial recipes. After that, I offer specific examples of freeze-dried cultures to try. All of the cultures in the ingredients lists come from major culture manufacturer Danisco. You'll be able to source these from the companies listed on page 234. Artisangeek.com and Fromagex are good places to look if you want to find cultures made by producers beyond Danisco and Chris Hansen, another global culture company.

That said, let's go a little further into the world of cheese cultures; how they're categorized, what temperatures different strains like to hang out at, and what ways different strains affect your cheesemaking. Be brave and let's go!

MESOPHILIC VS. THERMOPHILIC

A really basic way to organize cultures is by the terms *mesophilic* and *thermophilic*. This is a simplification but it works for the beginner. Mesophilic cultures love a middle temperature range and thermophilic cultures love a higher temperature. The terms *mesophilic* and *thermophilic* refer mainly to primary cultures whose main purpose is to produce lactic acid and not secondary cultures, which we'll talk about next.

As a rule of thumb, if the recipe calls for heating and cooking the curds above 104°F/40°C, you are working primarily with thermophilic culture strains.

PRIMARY VS. SECONDARY

Another way to sort cultures is by what they do in the vat or in the cheese. Cultures can be more important initially, by creating lactic acid (primary culture) or be more important later on, by breaking down fat, proteins, and sugars into specific flavor compounds (secondary cultures). Secondary cultures—also called ripening cultures—can be bacteria, molds, or yeasts; whereas primary cultures are usually only bacteria. You'll use secondary cultures for several recipes in this book—to make the bloomy-rinds, blues, Swiss-style, and washed-rind cheeses—but you'll use primary cultures in almost all of the recipes (the exceptions being the direct-acid cheeses of Paneer, Mascarpone, and Quick Mozz).

Secondary cultures do stuff to the milk and the cheese other than produce acid. They give a cheese distinction—perhaps a unique flavor or aesthetic direction, perhaps eyes, a pinkish rind, or a furry white coat. Though they actually may produce some acid, they cannot be used in place of primary cultures. They are always used in conjunction with primary cultures. Also, know that it is common to use several secondary cultures at once. For example, when you

Comparing Mesophilic to Thermophilic Cultures

	MESOPHILIC	THERMOPHILIC
ACTIVITY RANGE	65° to 104°F/18° to 40°C	90° to 140°F/32° to 60°C
PEAK ACTIVITY POINT	90°F/32°C	110°F/43°C
EXAMPLES OF CHEESES MADE USING CULTURES FROM EACH CATEGORY	Chèvre, cottage cheese, soft cheese, Brie, Havarti, feta, sour cream	Gruyere, Swiss-style cheese, Asiago, Alpine types, mozzarella, provolone, Parmesan
EXAMPLES OF COMMERCIAL CULTURE MIXES	MM100, MA11, BMSC, Aroma B, Flora Danica	TA50, TA60, Thermo C
THE BEGINNING CHEESEMAKER'S ALTERNATIVE	Cultured buttermilk, cultured sour cream	Plain yogurt

make the Gosling, you'll use both *Penicillium candidum* (secondary culture) and *Geotrichum candidum* (another secondary culture).

In the table below, I've bolded essential secondary cultures you will need to make the cheeses in this book. The non-bolded ones are optional and are for more advanced tinkering, when you are ready.

SORTING BACTERIA CULTURES BY FUNCTION

Another way to sort cultures is to think about how a culture strain does its work. Some cultures make lots of acid right away, then die off. This type of culture would work well with a cheese that is completed in a short amount of time, such as a cheddar. It wouldn't work for a Swiss-style cheese in which the final flavor and texture depend on minimal acid levels at draining. Here,

the cheesemaker chooses a culture that produces acid slowly and over a longer period of time.

Other times, cheesemakers add bacterial cultures to the milk only to produce unique enzymes. These enzymes turn fats and proteins into wonderful flavors. Cultures that do this are known as NSLABS or non-starter lactic-acid bacteria. The term *non-starter* means these bacteria do not form that starting wave of acid that helps to initially acidify the milk into curds.

Different strains or subspecies have different acid-producing qualities or different enzymatic contributions to the cheese. You don't need to understand the intricacies of bacteriology but only to know that, invisibly right before your eyes, each microorganism you add to your vat is contributing in a unique way. These microorganisms are only one factor that determines the end product but they are an important one.

Examples of Secondary Cultures

CULTURE	TYPE	USAGE	CHEESE EXAMPLES	EXAMPLE OF PRODUCT NAME
B. linens	Bacteria	One of the most well-known red-rind forming bacteria. Only used on washed- and smear-rinds.	Zeller (via the Red Rind Wash)	B. Linens or Coryneform
Candida	Yeast	Used in addition to other ripening cultures, Candida adds aroma and flavor to washed-, smear-, bloomy-, and natural-rinded cheeses. It often "sets the stage" for other desired species.	Brie, Marbler, Camembert	CUM
Geotrichum candidum	Mold	For rapid surface mold growth. Often used with *Penicillium candidum* but also sometimes alone. Will occur naturally on numerous cheese styles.	Bloomy-rinds, washed-rinds	Geo 2, Geo 13
Kluyveromyces	Yeast	Used to complement bloomy- and washed-rind cheeses, also can be added to blue cheeses to complement mold growth, and in washed-curd cheeses such as a Gouda.	Marbler, Gouda, Bisbee Blue	KL 71
Leuconostoc medenteroides **subsp. *cremoris***	Bacteria	Used with a primary culture such as MM100, produces CO_2 gas and additional butter flavor. Great for sheep's milk.	Blues, Gouda, Havarti, Pecorino	LM
Penicillium candidum	Mold	For surface mold growth. Nearly always used in conjunction with *Geotrichum candidum*.	Brie, Camembert	PC VS, PC ABL, PC Neige
Penicillium roqueforti	Mold	Blue cheese molds can be found in different colors (green, light blue, dark blue) that have different flavors and "blue flavor" intensities.	Blue cheeses	PV
Propionic Bacteria	Bacteria	Causes gas production inside the wheel, creating signature "Swiss" eye holes.	Jarlsberg, Mountain Top	Propionibacteria or PS1

CULTURE BLENDS

You'll rarely work with just one strain, meso, or thermophilic culture. More likely, you will work with a blend containing strains that are active across a range of temperatures and at a range of rates. This can be a helpful buffer as your vat isn't likely to be at the exact temperature throughout the entire cheesemaking process.

CORRECT CULTURE DOSAGES

Although in this book I offer simplified cultures amounts—often ⅛ tsp or "a pinch"—that have been tested for success within the bounds of interpretation and standard home kitchen tools, there is a more accurate way to figure out the dosage rate when using freeze-dried cultures. On the label of every packet of freeze-dried cultures are two pieces of information: the weight of the contents of the package and the number of doses within, often listed as a DCU—which stands for Danisco (the manufacturer) Culture Inoculant. A DCU is how much to use per 26-gal/100-L batch of milk.

Figuring out how much culture to use for a 2-gal/7.5-L home batch will take a little work. You'll need a gram scale and will have to do some quick math. Take the weight of the packet (for example 39 g) and the doses per packet (for example 10 DCU). Divide the weight of the packet by how many servings are inside to find out how much one DCU weighs (in this case 39 divided by 10 equals 3.9 grams). Then figure out how your vat compares to the standard 100-L vat by doing simple algebra: 100 multiplied by 3.9 multiplied by 2 equals .078 grams or 78 mg of culture. Phew!

With this equation, you can calculate how much culture to use when scaling up and scaling down the size of recipes (given you have that gram scale). However, if you are only eye-balling it (as I often do), you're probably overadding your cultures, especially when making smaller batches (it's hard to see ¹⁄₁₆ of a teaspoon!). Use a tiny bit less culture than you think you should when scaling down.

Examples of Culture Blends

COMMERCIAL NAME	CHEESE EXAMPLES	KEY CHARACTERISTICS
Kazu	Aged Tomme	Acid production with additional complex "sweeter" aged notes
MA4000 series	Cheddars	Excellent for lactic-acid production, moderate gas production
MT1	Feta	Mix offers both acid production and good flavor development
RA Series	Cheddar, feta, chèvre	Rapid acidification

Attributes of Key Bacterial Cultures

GENUS	GENERAL CATEGORY	TEMPERATURE RANGE	OPTIMUM GROWTH	CHARACTERISTICS
Lactococcus	Mesophilic	68° to 102°F/20° to 39°C	78° to 92°F/26° to 33°C	Primary acid production for cheeses not cooked to higher temperatures
Leuconostoc	Mesophilic	64° to 86°F/18° to 30°C	70° to 78°F/21° to 26°C	Produces gas that causes eyes to form, butter flavor (diacetyl)
Lactobacillus NSLABs	Mesophilic	68° to 108°F/20° to 42°C	85° to 100°F/29° to 38°C	Highly strain dependent for flavor and aroma production
Streptococcus Thermophilus	Thermophilic	70° to 120°F/21° to 49°C	102° to 110°F/39° to 43°C	Rapid or slow acid producer (depending on strain)
Lactobacillus acidifiers	Thermophilic	90° to 125°F/32° to 52°C	100° to 115°F/38° to 46°C	Survives high temperatures and continues producing acid as temperature drops

BUTTERFAT CHART

The percentage of butterfat in store-bought milk or cream is rarely labeled and often falls within a standardized range. It's one of the imperfect parts of the home cheesemaking process because it is helpful for you to know the amount of butterfat in your milk or cream when making a recipe. Luckily, the range is narrow so you can't ever be too far off.

HOW TO MIX YOUR OWN UNHOMOGENIZED MILK

If you don't live in an area of the country that sells cream line—unhomogenized—milk, don't fret. You may be able to make your own. For this process to work, you need to confirm that the heavy cream you'll be using is unhomogenized and that the milk is not ultra-pasteurized. Much of the heavy cream in the United States is homogenized and often milk is heated above regulation temperatures, even though it is still simply labeled as "pasteurized." You may have to test run a cheese recipe or call the milk distributor to see if your cream and milk are good to go.

1. Pour 1 gal/3.8 L non-fat milk into a pot.

2. Add 1¾ cups/415 ml heavy cream (36% butterfat) to bring the butterfat level up to roughly 3.6%.

	Butterfat Range	Best Uses
Skim Milk and Non-Fat	0 to 0.5%	Quark
2% Milk and Semi-Skimmed	0.5 to 2%	Swiss-style cheese such as Jarlsberg (but only by mixing unhomogenized whole milk with skim to form a partial skim)
Whole Milk	3.6 to 4%	All recipes
Half-and-Half	12% fat (range 10.5 to 18%)	Cream cheese, whole milk ricotta
Light Cream	20% fat (range 18 to 30%)	Cream cheese, whole milk ricotta
Whipping Cream	30%	Sour cream, butter, mascarpone
Heavy Cream and Manufacturing Cream	36 to 40%	Sour cream, butter, mascarpone

SANITATION

NON-CHEMICAL AND CHEMICAL SANITIZERS

STEAM

I'm listing my favorite sanitizer first: Steam. Any metal tools you'll be using that fit into your milk vat can be cleaned beforehand with a steam bath. Add your equipment to your vat, then add water until it reaches 1 in/2.5 cm up the side. Cover the pot, bring it to a boil, and boil for 5 minutes. Afterward, carefully remove all the tools using tongs and set out on a clean (preferably) white towel near where you'll be making cheese. You can also just use the dishwasher. For towels and cheesecloth, I run them through the washing machine then through the dryer.

HEAT

Home canners confirm that heat is also an effective way to sterilize surfaces. When I first met my husband, he prepped jars for jam by placing them in the oven, then baking the whole deal for 10 minutes at 300°F/149°C.

BLEACH

The most commonly used sanitizer for home cheesemaking is bleach, hands down. The upshot of this option is that bleach is inexpensive, readily available, and isn't too difficult to work with. I've used bleach for much of my cheesemaking career, so much so that I have a bit of an association between the smell of bleach and cheesemaking altogether.

The drawback of bleach is that it isn't good for the environment. Bleach, if put into repeat or long-term contact with your (expensive) stainless-steel equipment, can also cause pitting. Its fumes can be noxious if inhaled at high concentrations over extended periods of time.

STARSAN

Starsan is a product coming to us from the brewing world. It is an acid sanitizer that needs only a minute of contact time with your equipment to be effective. It is promoted as not having to be rinsed away (if used at the proper concentration of 0.2 oz/5.6 g per 1 gal/3.8 L of water) as well as not leaving off-flavors behind. I would still rinse everything just in case.

IODOPHOR

Iodophor, a version of iodine, is another easy-to-use sanitizer option. Use at a concentration of ½ tbsp per 2.5 gal/1.5 ml per 1.9 L of water. I often prepare a large 5-gal/19-L bucket of Iodophor to have on hand during a cheesemake day. I dunk items in for 3 minutes, rinse, then place on a clean towel to drain before using.

LET THE GOOD GUYS LIVE

Now that you've cleaned every surface and scrutinized every microbe, I want to remind you why we're here in the first place: to encourage the growth of microorganisms. If you are too aggressive with a cleaning regimen, or if you aren't thorough enough in rinsing away soaps and sanitizers, you'll be working against yourself.

I remember a cheesemaker I worked with in Italy being downright nervous about the sanitizer he was made to use by the local Department of Health. He would make sure that each time cheese forms came out of the sanitizer bath that I stood with the hose and doused each individual form with water *for one entire minute*. That's a lot of water. But the point stayed with me. We are shepherding biological communities. A slight alteration may stop them from flourishing or may change the community design.

Microorganisms are found everywhere from under fingernails to the depths of the ocean floor to nooks well inside the Earth's mantel. They are everywhere in a greater way than I can really even understand. They were the first forms of life to exist on Earth, which alone should incite a bit of humility.

SAMPLE MAKE SHEET FOR HOME CHEESEMAKING

NAME OF CHEESE

RECIPE SOURCE   DATE MADE

BATCH NUMBER

MILK PURCHASED AT   EXPIRATION DATE

BRAND

NUMBER OF GALLONS/LITERS USED

ADDED CREAM

TYPE OF MILK: COW / GOAT / SHEEP / WHOLE / NON-FAT / 2% / HOMOGENIZED / RAW

	TIME / TEMPERATURE / PH	OTHER INFO
Fill vat with milk		
Add prehydrated cultures	tsp/ g tsp/ g	Type: Type:
Allow cultures to incubate	Minutes:	
Add CaCL₂ **Add Annatto**	tsp/ ml tsp/ ml	
Add Rennet	tsp/ ml	Type:
Allow rennet to set	Minutes: Flocculation Factor:	
Cut curd	Time: pH:	Lentils / beans / hazelnuts / grapes / ladled into forms
Stir / heat / wash curds		
Stir / heat / wash curds		
Stir / heat / wash curds		
Allow curds to settle	Minutes:	Prepress under whey: Y / N
Drain off whey		
Salt (if appropriate)		
Hoop curds		# of forms:
Press	Weight:	Duration:
Brine or dry salt		Duration: Brine Saturation:

AGING INFORMATION

LOCATION

TEMPERATURE   HUMIDITY

RIND TREATMENT(S)

DATE	ACTION (Flip, Oil, New Wax Coat, Brushing, etc.)	NOTES (changes in smell, coloring, cracking, etc.)

RESOURCES

When all your pasta pots are in use, all your sweater bins repurposed, the medicine dropper missing, and half your fridge given over to cheese projects, it's time to expand your collection of cheesemaking supplies and probably set up that cave. You'll find nearly everything you need at each of the companies listed here. See what works best for your location and specific cheesemaking needs.

CHEESEMAKING SUPPLY COMPANIES

ARTISAN GEEK: A source for hard-to-find specialty items, such as spruce-bark straps and thistle rennet. artisangeek.com

THE BEVERAGE PEOPLE: With a broad understanding of all fermentation processes, the Beverage People spearheaded one of the first home cheesemaking clubs in the country, called "Wheyward Bound." Inexpensive shipping and excellent customer service. www.thebeveragepeople.com

CAPRINE SUPPLY: Wide selection of equipment for milk handling and dairy farm management with a focus on goats. Look here to find stainless-steel milk cans, buckets, small-scale cream separators, and more. www.caprinesupply.com

THE CHEESE MAKER: Supplier of Chris Hansen–brand cultures (another culture line different from those cultures suggested in this book) to the home-scale cheesemaker. Excellent customer service and free shipping. www.thecheesemaker.com

CULTURES FOR HEALTH: A company focused on home fermentation, also a unique online source for Kefir grains and Scandinavian yogurt cultures. www.culturesforhealth.com

DAIRY CONNECTION: Caters to both large-scale commercial producers as well as home-scale efforts. Ideal for the committed cheesemaker (who can buy ten-dose culture packets vs. single-use ones). www.dairyconnection.com

FROMAGEX: Serves Canada and the United States with a unique selection of cultures (wide variety of ripening cultures), interesting forms, tools, ripening papers, and more. www.fromagex.com

GLENGARRY CHEESEMAKING: Run by a sage of the cheesemaking movement, Margaret Morris, Glengarry offers a selection of ingredients, tools, and even consulting services for new creamery layout and design. www.glengarrycheesemaking.on.ca

HOEGGER'S: Offers products related to goat husbandry, homesteading crafts, and especially cheese and dairy processing. Their website links to blogs and other fun community connections. www.hoeggerfarmyard.com

MOORLANDS CHEESEMAKERS LTD: A thorough selection of tools and ingredients needed for the home cheesemaker. Also, check for info on cheesemaking classes in the United Kingdom. www.cheesemaking.co.uk

NEW ENGLAND CHEESEMAKING: Focused on home- and farmstead-scale cheese operations, Ricki Carroll, the "Cheese Queen," started this hub of cheese activity (which includes classes) in 1984. Website includes helpful articles, blogs, and Q & A. www.cheesemaking.com

CLASSES AND CERTIFICATIONS

IN THE UNITED STATES

- Find classes through a cheese guild or cooperative extension.

- Take a class at The Cheese School of San Francisco— the only independent school in the United States devoted strictly to the topic of cheese.

- Take a class at a nearby creamery.

- Look for classes offered through college and university dairy programs. Examples include College of Marin's Artisan Cheesemaking Program, Basic Cheesemaker's License Program at University of Wisconsin, Cheesemaking Short Course at Cal Poly in San Luis Obispo, and short courses at the Washington State University Creamery.

IN THE UNITED KINGDOM

AB CHEESEMAKING, CHESHIRE: Well-known site for trainings and consultations. www.abcheesemaking.co.uk

ABBEY HOME FARM, CIRENCESTER: Multiple courses on topics of cooking and sustainable living. www.theorganicfarmshop.co.uk/courses/cheese-making

CHEESE SCHOOL, BRISTOL: Join Fiona and Jess for a cheesemaking and cheese tasting extravaganza. www.cheeseschool.co.uk

CUTTING THE CURD, DORSET: A homesteading enthusiast who teaches classes on making soft and fresh cheeses. www.cuttingthecurd.co.uk

HARTINGTONS, DERBYSHIRE: A cooking school with cheesemaking courses held in a converted saw mill. www.hartingtons.com

HIGH WEALD DAIRY, WEST SUSSEX: Enjoy a cheesemaking course amid award-winning cheesemakers known for their cow's, goat's and sheep's cheeses. www.highwealddairy.co.uk

RIVER COTTAGE, DEVON: A cooking school linked with an online community, several canteens, and a television show all in a breathtaking location. www.rivercottage.net

SCHOOL OF ARTISAN FOOD, NOTTINGHAMSHIRE: An excellent resource for the beginner through the advanced cheesemaker. www.schoolofartisanfood.org

WEST HIGHLAND DAIRY, SCOTLAND: Author and cheesemaker Kathy Biss offers cheesemaking courses on her dairy farm. www.westhighlanddairy.co.uk

IN AUSTRALIA

ARTISAN CHEESEMAKING ACADEMY OF AUSTRALIA, MULTIPLE CAMPUS LOCATIONS: The country's only teaching academy dedicated to the craft of cheesemaking: www.tafesa.edu.au/ artisan-cheese-making-academy-australia

CHEESE LINKS, VICTORIA: Offering hands-on classes for beginners as well as selling cheesemaking equipment and supplies. www.cheeselinks.com.au

CHEESEMAKING AUSTRALIA, QUEENSLAND: Half-day, two-day, or private cheesemaking courses offered. www.cheesemaking.com.au

IN CANADA

THE CHEESEMAKING WORKSHOP, WHISTLER, BC: Learn a variety of fun, easy cheese recipes firsthand at this workshop in British Columbia. www.thecheesemakingworkshop.com

GLENGARRY CHEESEMAKING SUPPLY: Run by cheese guru Margaret Morris, Glengarry offers resources for both the hobbyist and the professional cheesemaker. www.glengarrycheesemaking.on.ca/workshops.htm

UNIVERSITY OF BRITISH COLUMBIA FARM: Homesteading classes on topics such as bread making, brewing, and home cheesemaking. Sign up for their mailing list to stay in the loop. www.ubcfarm.ubc.ca

UNIVERSITY OF GUELPH: Has an annual five-day cheesemaking intensive. Additionally, their website is a fantastic resource. www.uoguelph.ca/foodscience/ cheese-making-technology

IN IRELAND

BALLYMALOE COOKERY SCHOOL, CORK: Situated on a 100-acre organic farm, this school offers a range of classes on topics, including butter-, yogurt-, and cheesemaking: www.cookingisfun.ie

KEEP LEARNING

- Find or start a cheesemaking club in your area.
- Join a cheese guild as an enthusiast or hobby member.
- Enter or initiate an amateur cheesemaking contest as part of a community event or county fair.
- Cheese Forum—join this incredible online community of home and professional cheesemakers sharing wisdom, recipes, and more. Nothing comes close to the quantity of information shared on this site. www.cheeseforum.org/forum/

KEEP BEING INSPIRED

BLOGS

CHEESE NOTES: Blogger Matt Spiegler will keep you in the loop, entertained, and hungry for more and more of his awesome cheese photos. www.cheesenotes.com

CURD NERD: Join the Curd Nerd on her excellent adventures in home cheesemaking. Follow her by email to get fresh updates on a range of cheesemaking ideas. www.curd-nerd.com

HEINENNELLIE: An inspiring documentation of a home cheesemaker turned professional. He sets up an aging cave under a sidewalk in Brooklyn, New York. www.heinennellie.blogspot.com

LITTLE GREEN CHEESE: Enjoy this blog by a sustainable-living expert in Australia giving detailed instructions and video tutorials on cheesemaking. www.littlegreencheese.com

MADAME FROMAGE: A beautifully composed weekly and sometimes daily essay on all things cheese. www.madamefromageblog.com

MILK'S LEAP: Enjoy the adventures of home cheese-maker Caitlin Harvey (who also kindly tested recipes for this book). www.milksleap.wordpress.com

HELPFUL SITES

FANKHAUSER'S CHEESE PAGE: A great stop for recipes, explanations, and tips. www.biology.clc.uc.edu/fankhauser/cheese/cheese.html

SMALL DAIRY: Dairy queen Vicki Dunaway created her site to help small-scale dairies and cheesemakers share info. Look here to find used dairy equipment, apprenticeships, and more. www.smalldairy.com

KEEP READING

The Art of Fermentation, Sandor Katz: A nice way to round out your understanding of fermentation. Katz will quickly become your hero, if he isn't already.

Mastering Artisan Cheesemaking, Gianaclis Caldwell: The very best book for cheesemakers ready to tackle advanced cheesemaking concepts.

MAKE FRIENDS WITH THE MONGER

Last, because cheesemaking leaves you with a product that must be eaten or shared (and sometimes, in short order), cheese can lead to friendships. As you spread the cheese, why not befriend a cheesemonger? They are busy people, but if you lean against the display cases in the quietest hours of a Tuesday afternoon, you'll find their brains brimming with knowledge. A cheesemonger's experience fits perfectly with what you are learning at the vat. Bring your mongers questions, listen to their answers, and then buy a hearty chunk of something to inspire you and to keep their (often independent) shops in business.

REFERENCES

BOOKS

Amrein-Boyes, Debra. 2009. *200 Easy Homemade Cheese Recipes*. Robert Rose Publishing. Ontario, Canada.

Biss, Kathy. 1988. *Practical Cheesemaking*. The Crowood Press. Wiltshire, England.

Fox, P.F., Guinee, T.P., Cogan, T.M., McSweeney, P.L.H. 2000. *Fundamentals of Cheese Science*. Aspen Publishers, Inc. Gaithersburg, MD.

Hill, Arthur. 1995. *Chemistry of Structure-Function Relationships in Cheese*. Plenum Press. New York, NY.

Kosokowsky, F., Mistry, V. 1997. *Cheese and Fermented Milk Foods*. New England Cheesemaking Supply Company. Ashfield, MA.

McCalman, M., Gibbons, D. 2005. *Cheese: A Connoisseur's Guide to the World's Best*. Crown Publishing. New York, NY.

Valenze, Deborah. 2011. *Milk: A Local and Global History*. Yale University Press. New Haven, CT.

Wong, N., Jenness, R., Keeney, M., Marth, E. 1988. *Fundamentals of Dairy Chemistry*. Van Nostrand Reinhold Co. New York, NY.

WEBSITES, PAPERS, AND LECTURES

Chenry, P. "Ways to Clean Fresh Herbs." (online forum comment) www.cheeseforum.org/forum/index.php/topic,11582.0/topicseen.html (July, 2013).

———."When Proteins Bind with Direct Acid." (online forum comment) www.cheeseforum.org/forum/index.php/topic,11568.0/topicseen.html (July, 2013).

Dixon, Peter. "Advanced Cheesemaking and Affinage." (class lecture) College of Marin, Novato, CA. (February 15, 2013).

Dunaway, Vicki. *Cream Line: A New Voice for Little Dairies*. (paper) Self-published. Willis, VA. (2001–2009).

Hill, Arthur. "Structural Elements of Milk," Figure 8.1, after Walstra and Jenness, 1984, *Dairy Chemistry and Physics* (section in book), Wiley and Sons, NY, (2009) University of Guelph, Food Science. www.uoguelph.ca/foodscience/cheese-making-technology/list-figures (August 2012).

Lammert, Amy. "Milk Types." (class lecture) College of Marin, Novato, CA. (March 28, 2012).

Potter, Dave. "Cheese Chemistry." (class lecture) College of Marin, Novato, CA. (October 7, 2011).

Rosenberg, Moshe. "Cheese Defects." (class lecture) College of Marin, Novato, CA. (September 26, 2011).

Wolfe, Benjamin. "Cheese Rind Microbiology." (class lecture) College of Marin, Novato, CA. (January 11, 2013).

"The Science of Artisan Cheese"—Videos of presentations. Cheesenotes.com/post/39488071028/science-of-artisan-cheese-videos (September 2012).

- Larcher, I., Kehler, M. "Quality & Control (in Artisan Cheesemaking)."

- Montel, Marie-Christine. "Raw Milk Microbial Biodiversity & Its Influences."

- Paxson, Heather. "Risk Perception & Categorization: Artisanship in the 21st Century."

INDEX

ACKNOWLEDGMENTS

Thank you to Mark and Pattie Federico (who love kitchens and creameries more than anyone I know), Claudio and Maddalena Cavazzoni, Tina and Luciano Rucci, Ana and Gil Cox, Pascale Quiviger, Caitlin Hunter, Sue Connley, Amy Gallo, Vicki Woollard, Sarah Leibel, Marian Thorpe, Ginnie Dunleavy, Barbara Simon, Eric Marton, Emma Mack, Justin Fried, Flavio Casoy, Caitlin Harvey, Juliette Rogers, Dana Berg, Sacha Laurin, Rod Kass, the Kapitulnik Family, the Suby Family, the Budner Family, Chris Lee, Ken Olander, Maria Iorillo, Rachel Betesh, Oliva Trajera, Ruth Hernandez, John Taverna, Doniga Markegard, Robert Aguilera, Ronald Pozo, Roberto Paiz, Rachel and Peter Dixon, Matt and Kate Jennings, Anne Saxelby, Cathy Goldstein, Anthea Stolz, Pav Cherny, Juliana Uruburu, the Cheese School of San Francisco, 18 Reasons, FARMcurious, the Cheese Board Collective, Little City Gardens, the Greenhorns, the California Artisan Cheese Guild, and the League of Urban Cheesemakers. Thank you to everyone in my family. Thank you to Amy Treadwell for having the idea.

ABOUT THE CHAPTER HEADINGS AND ILLUSTRATIONS

The chapter headings and illustrations in this book were done by me, at the kitchen table while the cheese drained quietly. I used a mix of Prussian Blue and Burnt Sienna watercolors, some calligraphy ink and one dog-eared copy of Albert Cavanagh's 1946 book *Lettering and Alphabets*. You can see that my calligraphy, like my cheese, is a work in progress.